AF556087

Women Reinventing Development

The Odisha Experience

Women Reinventing Development

The Odisha Experience

Edited by
Asha Hans
Amrita Patel
Bidyut Mohanty
Swarnamayee Tripathy

Women Reinventing Development: The Odisha Experience
Edited by Asha Hans, Amrita Patel, Bidyut Mohanty and Swarnamayee Tripathy

First Published 2020

ISBN 978-93-5002-671-7

Published by
AAKAR BOOKS
28 E Pocket IV, Mayur Vihar Phase I
Delhi 110 091 India
aakarbooks@gmail.com

In Association with
Development Research Institute
Gabeshana Chakra
Bhubaneswar, Odisha

Laser Typeset at
Arpit Printographers, Delhi

Printed at
D.K. Fine Art Press, Delhi

Dedicated to the
Memory of
Amrita Patel

(17.04.1965 – 27.01.2020)

Contents

IV. On the Margins

Foreword

Women are indeed reinventing development, the discourse, the policy and the practice all over the world. The Odisha story presented in this volume largely captures some crucial dimensions of that trend. Expanding inequalities and environmental degradation continue to accompany economic growth under neo-liberal reforms, and their effects on day-to-day lives of common people look most evident seen from the perspective of women.

As these papers by scholars who bring in years of empirical work on concrete issues show, there is a big gap between the principles proclaimed as the policy objectives and the actual situation on the ground. From the United Nations' Sustainable Development Goals down to the countries, provinces and districts, even panchayats, this hiatus between the agreed values and actual practice continues to stare at us. Constitutional provisions, laws and policies and institutional safeguards continue to multiply. But vast magnitude of gender disparity in employment, increasing incidence of sexual violence and meagre share in political power have persisted. Women's labour, especially in the domestic sphere and care-economy, remain undervalued, even unrecognized. The cultural milieu remained predominantly patriarchal despite the traditions of goddess-worship. The Odisha experience particularly illustrates this because, its leaders cutting across political parties had eloquently committed themselves to gender equality and women's empowerment in the recent years more than other States of India. The authors of this volume investigate this process and ask why the women's movement did not achieve the goals set by them in specific sectors.

The contributors have effectively argued that there is a solid trend of women redefining policy priorities, institutional reforms and methods of implementation, thus reinventing development to make it equitable, just and sustainable. They were doing this through social movements and campaigns of many kinds at local, national and global levels in addition to literary initiatives. Feminist research has done a great service by bringing out the reality of deprivation and marginalization of women in general as well as through multiple conditions of oppression. But despite all this, as the authors have put it, the women have remained 'invisible' in policy process and implementation. As a result, the development outcomes were not only unjust and often oppressive for women but for all disadvantaged groups—dalits, adivasis, agricultural labour, small farmers and poor as a whole. Even if token mention of targets as women, SC and ST is made, it was hardly a structural basis of policy.

This book helps in refocussing attention on economic, political and social dimensions of women and development. Focussing on concrete areas of health, education, employment, migration and political role of women in decision-making institutions, the authors suggest that only when women or any oppressed groups gained substantially on these fronts, would it have greater dignity and power in society.

One area which had a structural effect on social well-being in general and women's life in particular, was health on which demographers, economists and policy experts including women's groups have made serious contributions. The falling sex ratio in the recent decades, especially the alarming trend of falling proportion of the girl child in the age group of 0-6 years has been a source of great concern. Odisha was among the better performers in the past, but has fallen into this disturbing trend. We get some insights on why some districts did better than others. None of the common sense assumptions may hold good as the reasons were a mix of economic and cultural processes. Many new policy measures had been launched during the last decade to address this, but the reality shows otherwise. Same was true of education, especially school education, despite the enforcement of the Right to Education Act. Performance of the policy in case of the marginalized groups was very unsatisfactory despite some positive reports in a few areas. Malnutrition and low rate of school education were related to poverty.

Despite the much publicized growth successes and building of smart cities in the past decade or so, high magnitude of poverty has remained a major aspect of the state of Odisha. The contributors to this volume have focused on two significant dimensions of the discourse on poverty. One is the what is called the 'feminisation of poverty' as women both in number and in depth suffer the major burden of poverty, which gets a wider meaning linking gender, caste, ethnicity and class, in this volume. The other is the related issue of migration, especially distress migration. This analysis is enriched further by insights from different regions as the phenomenon of regional diversity in Odisha is conspicuous and regions in western and southern Odisha which have experienced acute poverty.

There was an increasing consensus around the world that women's empowerment involved both representation of women in decision-making bodies at all levels, as well as equal access to productive assets accompanied by cultural transformation. This volume takes up the experience of women's representation at the panchayat level institutions to stress that it indicated considerable possibilities in spite of many negative challenges. The prolonged battle to secure statutory representation of women in state legislatures and Parliament shows the prevailing strength of patriarchy in India. It only proves that until women emerge as a powerful political force working together with other struggling groups, their capacity to put in action the new paradigm of development will remain limited. No amount of delivery of welfare services to alleviate distress conditions at a particular time will be adequate.

I congratulate the authors and hope that the message of Women Reinventing Development will spread widely to benefit all oppressed sections of society.

January 2020

Manoranjan Mohanty
Chairperson
Development Research Institute
Bhubaneswar

Introduction

Women in the State of Odisha have played an important role in development, however they remain mostly invisible in policy and research. The anthology, *Women Reinventing Development: The Odisha Experience,* attempts to undertake a journey of the States' rich historical tradition to its present stage of development to locate women's spaces in this process. The absence of analytical work on women's role in the development of the State is being increasingly felt. This volume, we hope, will fill to some extent, the intellectual and lack of activism gap in feminist literature.

The eleven papers in this book, shed light on the fundamental changes in women's experience from a historical context to present day locations. Through the essays use of narrative as a gauge to assess the relevance, utility and potential of development for achieving gender justice in the State has been analysed.

Roles, Identities and Agency

Feminist approaches are analyzing the problems confronting women in the State. While gender provides the conceptual tool for mapping differential experiences of social realities, it also uncovers the oppressions and power relations. An indepth knowledge on the ideologies of patriarchy and subordination and the challenges women are grappling with is an important focus to be dealt with. We hope to see the roles and identities of women from a historical sense.

The articulation of women's rights and quest for equality

and justice comes from movements. We hope that this section will provide an articulation of grassroots women's movement and their struggles through their own voices.

The question of multiple authorship and gendered narratives may not have resonance in the era of the digital novel that blurs the notion of authorship and narrative boundaries; and yet a close look at literary examples in this domain is likely to throw up surprising insights regarding the 'woman' question in the colonial era. This is the major focus of the paper 'Multiple Authorship and the Gendered Narrative: *Basanti* and the Woman Question in Odisha' by Sachidananda Mohanty. This paper looks closely at the Odia novel *Basanti* that was first published by New Students Store, Cuttack, in 1931. Several issues, both ideological and societal appear to be at the heart of the novel including social reforms, religious conflicts, the need for inter-faith dialogue, and problems like the system of dowry in marriage, caste-hierarchies and the rural-urban divide. Above all, *Basanti* revolves around the larger question of female education and the need for female emancipation.

The paper 'Women's Movement for Land and Livelihood: A Case Study of Odisha' by Smita Mishra Panda and Annapurna Devi Pandey focuses on the strong resistance by indigenous rural women against the hegemonic state and its neo-liberalist policies. The two authors have examined two resistance movements of tribal women; one for land rights and another to get their traditional livelihood practices back to their locality which has been used by mega companies centreing on the imposition of state and corporate power. Despite several laws/Acts that allow autonomy to protect indigenous lands and natural habitat, they have been systematically violated by the state in the name of 'eminent domain' and benefit for the larger good of the society. It has caused terrible devastations to the natural habitats long occupied by indegenous people. The nature and forms of resistance, manifested through grassroots activism has created opposition, and practices that clearly seek to delegitimize the present state interventions.

Women strenuously argue for their right to self-determination to reclaim their lands and livelihood, which is location-based knowledge(s) and experience. The presence of such an alternative provides a strong foundation to the identity of indigenous women and their sustained activism.

Gendered Discriminations

Feminists have been concerned with identifying and analyzing gender based discriminations. The foremost of this starts before birth and in this aim for survival, the girl child loses out as is depicted by the child sex ratio imbalance. Despite enormous international financial aid for reproductive health, maternal mortality ratio remains one of the highest in the country as does the issue of child marriage, which though declining, is still a challenge in the current era.

The issue of Odisha's declining Child Sex Ratio (CSR) has been taken up by Bijaylaxmi in her paper in which she traces this deficit in the ratio of girls and boys to the heinous practice of sex-selective abortion, intense son-preference and daughter aversion. Her paper 'Gender Discrimination and the Role of the State: A Case Study of Sex Selective Abortion in Odisha', draws from secondary as well as primary data sources and presents the use of mixed methods including quantitative and qualitative methods. According to her the state in Odisha has been seen to be actively engaged with confronting the practice of sex selective abortion. The state has also been seen to be compelled by civil society initiatives both at the local and national levels to address gender discrimination and gender concerns within its policies and programmes. Simultaneously, she provides evidence to refute the well-established theories about sex-selective abortion being an upper class, upper caste, northern patriarchal-belt phenomenon.

The subject of gender discrimination has also been taken up in the paper on 'Correlates of Health Care Among Women and Children in Odisha: Understanding Barriers in Access' by Sanghamitra Acharya, Mala Mukherjee and Golak Patro who endeavour to understand the situation and experience of women when health care services are accessed. Often the inaccessibility of the services for varied reasons is likely to be associated with pregnancy loss, pre-natal and infant death; and maternal deaths. It analyses the trends and patterns which evolve due to the social location of women; and provide an in-depth account of the local-setting and contextualise it within the literature on health care access, infant, child and maternal mortality. The enquiry is focussed on understanding the factors attributing to the differential experiences of women belonging to different social groups who access health care. It examines the relevance of social background in influencing the access to services and the consequent outcome. The paper proposes that gender issue needs to be analysed from socio-demographic and economic specificities, which will be the pathway to follow for attaining the SDGs.

With a view to identifying and analyzing gender discriminations that are prevalent in Indian society even today, the paper by Monica Das takes up the issue of child marriage in the paper. Since this impacts the development process through its adverse effects on the socio-economic parameters, the paper analyzes the basis of the Annual Health Survey Data (part of 2011 Census data) of the Empowered Action Group states including Odisha. Attempt has been made to add a fresh dimension to the issue, a literature interface with the socio-economic phenomenon of 'unde-rage marriage'. This is to bring out the fact that patriarchy is an endemic historical and cultural practice that assumes male domination as the norm and the female as subordinate.

Development and Equality

The book reflects on the current patterns of development and the underlying problems of growing inequality. The current situation, a result of aggressive capitalism pursued in the last few decades raises questions from a feminist view point on development models being pursued in the State. The ongoing crisis is not only financial in nature but environmental. Food security remains a problem and linked to climate change and women's actions on the ground need to be considered in concert with other concerns such as access to food and water. Agriculture, common property for subsistence and ownership issues are being raised and linked to environment protection.

Poverty alleviation has been a big industry in the State which need to be questioned as well as gender equality issues within this large development agenda. The article 'Poverty and Food Security in Rural Odisha: The Gender Dimension' by Deepak K Mishra examines poverty and food security scenario in rural Odisha. Here the author argues that notwithstanding the impressive decline in the percentage of people below the poverty line in the recent past, a significant aspect of poverty in Odisha—its spatial and social concentration—has remained unaltered. Poverty is disproportionately concentrated in the interior districts and amongst the marginalized social groups. Although it is not possible to adequately analyze gender disparity in poverty and food insecurity on the basis of the available secondary data, by using insights from field surveys in the tribal region, the study is able to explore the gender dimension of food insecurity in rural Odisha. The paper provides insights into the underlying mechanisms that generate and sustain chronic poverty and food insecurity among the marginalized groups, including women.

The theme of education of disadvantaged persons is high on the agenda of India and Odisha because it is related to a much wider phenomena: growing deprivation and social exclusion. While the situation is dire, the paradox is that increase in poverty and exclusion goes hand in hand with economic growth. It is in this backdrop that 'inclusive education' is being proposed so as to ensure that all members of society become part of the 'mainstream'. In a multi-lingual, multi-cultural, multi-ethnic society like India, 'mainstream' is a misnomer. To find appropriate ways of responding to 'difference' is a reality and a challenge which is only being tinkered with on the margins. It would not be inappropriate to mention that education itself is becoming 'endangered' in attempting to make 'one size fit all'. The paper by Supriya

Pattanayak attempts to trace the education trajectory in the State of Odisha while focusing, through both primary and secondary data, the gender dimension of residential schools and what they have done to tribal cultures and languages.

In the paper on 'Regional Disparity and Women in Local Government', Bidyut Mohanty and Sibabrata Das examine the available evidence to give a broader scenario of regional imbalances in development in the state and document some rays of hope with women in panchayats backed by women's collectives taking lead role in monitoring MGNREGA, food security and health issues and adopting locally suitable holistic development models. For fashioning and sustaining a gender equal society it is essential that decision-making power in women's hands is ensured, although at the Panchayat level the State has shown a marked improvement.

On the Margins

The State's constitutional promise of equality remains at the periphery as many groups are on the margins of development such as the dalits, migrant women and workers in the unorganized sector.

The paper by Manasi Mohanty discusses the growth and organizational structure of the 'SEAM' named skill training centres and analyzes its relationships with the process of female migration from Odisha to the KINFRA International Apparel Park of Kerala. In an era when women constitute more than 60 per cent of the workforce in the garment and apparel industries in the country, the skill training centres of Odisha placed the trained women in the southern states of India. Both the source and destination locations have been studied for understanding the Odia female migrant workers.

Dalits in Odisha, as elsewhere in India, have been victims of caste oppression for centuries. Predominantly rural and illiterate, they have become one of society's most exploited peripheral groups. Raj Kumar in his paper 'Caste Narratives: Odia Dalit Women in Literature and Society' has found that over the years, they have been living in sub-human conditions and suffering economic exploitation and cultural subjugation. Though education might significantly improve their standards, both socially as well as economically, Odia Dalits have never been able to get its benefits on a large scale due to typical structural problems in the state. The primary aim of this paper is to locate existential conditions of Dalit women in Odisha. What is their social condition? What are their perceptions about the idea of development? How far they have got benefits from various developmental projects that the Indian nation-state has initiated over the years? These and many other questions are looked into while discussing the idea of development discourse in the context of Dalit women in Odisha. The author has used reports from the field as well as critical sources to develop his arguments.

The Indian labour market is characterized by predominance of informal employment and within it, the large presence of women workers. The women work in poor conditions and are bereft of many social security provisions and statutory benefits like the maternity benefit. In recent times, there has been a focus of workers' welfare boards to provide the necessary social security entitlements. The conditions of work of the women in the construction sector has been analyzed in the paper by Amrita Patel and Swarnamayee Tripathy. Based on empirical work done in Odisha, the evidence brings forth the gaps in the policy to practice trajectory of social security from the perspective of women in the unorganized sector.

We hope the book will provide ideas for reformulation of development and explore ways to overcome social, economic and political injustices.

Asha Hans
Amrita Patel
Bidyut Mohanty
Swarnamayee Tripathy

Bionotes of the Editors and Authors

Amrita Patel died on 27 January, 2020. She was a Researcher, Trainer and Teacher of Women's Studies and has worked on issues of gender budgeting, land rights of women, women empowerment and declining child sex ratio.

Annapurna Pandey teaches Cultural Anthropology at the University of California, Santa Cruz. Her research interests are indigenous women's activism and leadership in the context of state and multi-national corporations, their economic and political empowerment in rural and tribal India. Annapurna just completed a senior Fulbright US Scholarship (2017-18) working in Odisha, India. (adpandey101@gmail.com)

Asha Hans is a former Professor of Political Science and Founder Director, School of Women's Studies, Utkal University, Odisha. She works on gender issues, peace and conflict. She is the founding President of Sansristi, a gender research organization and Director, DRI. (ashahans10@gmail.com)

Bidyut Mohanty was the Head of Women's Studies from 1993 to 2016 in Institute of Social Sciences. Her specialization is in gender studies, development studies and cross-cultural issues. (bidyutmohanty@issin.org)

Bijayalaxmi Nanda is Associate Professor, Department of Political Science, Miranda House, University of Delhi. She has been engaged in teaching and researching in the areas of political theory and gender for over two decades. (bijayalaxmi@yahoo.com)

Deepak K Mishra is Professor of Economics at the Centre for the Study of Regional Development, School of Social Sciences, Jawaharlal Nehru University New Delhi. (deepakmishra.jnu@gmail.com)

Golak B Patra is a Research Scholar pursuing PhD at the Centre for Social Medicine and Community Health, School of Social Sciences, Jawaharlal Nehru University, New Delhi.

Mala Mukherjee is a faculty, Indian Institute of Dalit Studies, New Delhi

Manasi Mohanty is a Lecturer and her areas of interest is migration, gender, politics of development, climate change and energy politics. She was an ICSSR post doctoral scholar in the Department of Political Science, University of Hyderabad. (manashi.mohanty08@gmail.com)

Monica Das was Associate Professor in Economics, Gargi College, Delhi University. Currently she is a Fellow at DCRC (Developing Countries Research Centre), Delhi University. (dasmonica@gmail.com)

Raj Kumar is Professor in the Department of English, Delhi University. His research areas include autobiographical studies, dalit literature, Indian writing in English, Odia literature and post-colonial studies. Research interests are in the areas of political economy of agrarian change, economic transformation of mountain economies, rural livelihoods and agrarian institutions, migration and human development. (bedamatiraj@gmail.com)

Sachidananda Mohanty is Professor and former Head, Department of English, University of Hyderabad. He is the recipient of several national and international awards including those from the British Council, the Salzburg, the Katha and Fulbright. He was Vice Chancellor, Central University at Koraput, Odisha. (sachimohanty@yahoo.co.in)

Sanghmitra S Acharya is Professor at the Centre for Social Medicine and Community Health, School of Social Sciences, Jawaharlal Nehru University. She is currently Director, Indian Institute of Dalit Studies, New Delhi. (sanghmitra.acharya@gmail.com)

Sibabrata Das is a geographer and demographer by training. He is currently a faculty member at the Department of Applied Geography, Ravenshaw University, Cuttack.

(sibabrata2007@gmail.com)

Smita Mishra Panda has a PhD from Asian Institute of Technology, Bangkok, Thailand in 1996 and is currently Professor and Director, Research, Centurion University of Technology and Management, Odisha. (smitafem@gmail.com)

Supriya Pattanayak has her qualifications in social sciences and mental health. She has extensive teaching, research and policy experience and her research interest is in the field of gender and development and social work pedagogy in different contexts. (supriya.pattanayak@gmail.com)

Swarnamayee Tripathy is Professor in Public Administration in Utkal University. She has taught Political Science at Bhagat Singh College, Delhi. (smtripathy2010@gmail.com)

I. Roles, Identities and Agency

1

Multiple Authorship and the Gendered Narrative: *Basanti* and the Woman Question in Odisha

Sachidananda Mohanty

Introduction

The question of multiple authorship and gendered narratives may not have resonance in the era of the digital novel that blurs the notion of authorship and narrative boundaries; and yet a close look at literary examples in this domain is likely to throw up surprising insights regarding the 'woman question' in the colonial era.

This paper will look closely at the Odia novel *Basanti* that was first published by New Students Store, Cuttack in 1931 and had multiple editions.[1] Several issues-both ideological and societal appear to be at the heart of the novel. These include social reforms, religious conflicts, the need for interfaith dialogue, and problems like the system of dowry in marriage, caste hierarchies and the rural–urban divide. Above all, *Basanti* revolves around the larger question of female education and the need for female emancipation. While nine authors wrote the novel, [their names would come later in this article], it is instructive to note that the chapters that are most readable and engrossing are those written by three of the outstanding women writers of the times, namely Sarala Devi, Pratibha Devi and Suprabha Devi, the last two were the illustrious daughters of Biswanath Kar, the Editor of Utkal Sahitya.

The discourse over education and female emancipation has to be read contrapuntally with the rhetoric of domesticity and 'advice for women' texts voiced by Basanti's mother-in-law, Subhadra Devi. One needs to bring in here fruitfully the arguments by Tanika Sarkar who has done pioneering research on women and education in Bengal in the nineteenth century. She has correctly underlined the relevance of female education and other dilemma which the husbands faced. In order to contextualize at the pan Indian level, one can similarly refer to important works of Uma Chakravathi. We also need to remember that the interface of women's narratives and Gandh and other ideological approaches, contain internal problematic that must be carefully thought through.

In this paper, I have drawn from my Introduction to the *Lost World of Sarala Devi*, OUP, 2016. Similarly, our appreciation of the woman question in Odisha gets illuminated by our understanding of the Odia literary feminisms vis a vis the 'conduct book' tradition in the region. Interested readers may see parallel between the latter discourse and the 'advice for women texts' in colonial Bengal.

Basanti is a political novel in the best sense of the term. Located against the backdrop of India's freedom struggle, in the late twenties of the last century, embracing the city and the village, the narrative attempts to find answers to questions that are deeply ideological in nature. Like Rabindranath's *Gora* that questioned the place of women in politically turbulent times, *Basanti* centre-staged crucial debates of the age. The paper shall suggest that while nine authors wrote the novel, three women, most of all, Sarala Devi contributed to the narrative in a uniquely feminist tone and tenor regarding the question of the empowerment of Odia women.

Life and Time of Sarala Devi and Its Influence on the Novel, *Basanti*

Sarala Devi's (1904-1986) ideology and politics were complex and at times contradictory. The difference is evidenced in the views she expressed in *The Rights of Women*, 1934, as well as the nine chapters in the novel *Basanti,* she wrote in 1931, which centre staged female agency, vis a vis the Memorandum she submitted to University Grants Commission as a member of the Senate of Utkal University regarding the need for a separate system of education for women, a problematic category. Nevertheless, Sarala prefigures some of the best thinking of our own times in a remarkable manner.

Sarala Devi lived between 9 August 1904 and 4 October, 1986. Her life and career covered some of the most momentous periods of the 20th century: the consolidation of the British Empire in India, the national Freedom Struggle, the two Great Wars, the Quit India Movement, the National Independence, the Cold War, the Sino-India conflict, the Vietnam War, the euphoria over the creation of the Republic and the subsequent disillusionments. Her essays record these triumphs and tribulations, hope and despair. Seen as a whole, they provide a vital prism through which we can see the many sides of the Indian experiment during the 20th century, essentially from a woman's point of view.

Women as Universal Dependents

While Sarala was not a theorist in the conventional sense of the term, her views on the subject of Feminism were informed by wide readings and an astute understanding of the woman's place in patriarchy; indeed, they appear amazingly close to some of the best thinking of our own times. For instance, while she spoke of women's oppression as a global phenomenon, she was careful to reject the view, as many later feminists did, of 'women as universal dependents' and 'married women as victims of the colonial process.' Similarly, she made a nuanced response to the question of 'women and religious ideologies.' While some feminists made sweeping generalizations about the uniformly oppressive nature of Religion, especially with regard to Hinduism and Islam, Sarala argued that our critique must be context-specific and be informed by particular histories of women in given societies and ideologies. Her view of Islam and woman was exceptionally original. While she was against imperialism; she also saw the dangers of an unbridled nativism.

It is important to look at significant aspects of Sarala's writings in terms of the categories a number of Third World feminists critiqued. Chandra Mohanty's path breaking essay 'Under Western Eyes: Feminist Scholarship and Colonial Discourses' seems to prefigure in a striking manner, many of the insights and seed ideas found in the works of Sarala Devi.

Sarala's contribution is noteworthy in at least five areas: firstly her critical interventions in building up a modern Odisha in the image of a progressive and modern nation; secondly, her use of literature, especially essays and speeches, for social critique and social transformation; thirdly her advocacy of an increasing control of women over their biological and reproductive selves; fourthly, her views on women and the nation, and finally her espousal of women's participation in the larger public arena.

Not many critical studies exist on Sarala Devi and her works, barring newspaper and magazine articles. Three books are worth mentioning in this context: *Mahayasi Mahila—Sarala* in (in Odia) by V. Rajendra Raju, *Sarala Devi* (in Odia) by Ajay Kumar Mishra, and *Alibha Anala Shikha: Sarala* (in Odia) by Banaj Devi.

Sarala's studies in literary feminism were original in approach, insightful, confident in tone and put forth arguments in a systematic dialogic fashion, backed by wide reading and knowledge of the wider world. Her feminist essay, 'Narira Dabi' will remain a classic statement about women's rights that brings to mind the seminal work of Mary Wollstonecraft. Her essay broke free from the conformist feminine discourse of the late 19th and early 20th Century, much of which eschewed the overtly political in favor of the mystical and devotional.

Sarala came from a conservative zamindar background and studied up to class seven. Yet, by her innate intelligence and sheer personal effort, she turned out to be an outstanding littérateur. Although many Odia women excelled in the literary field in the pre and post-independence period, Sarala remains unparalleled as one who combined literary creativity with social activism with remarkable success. Indeed, few women of the region can rival her in terms of the many genres in which she excelled. She scored, above all, as a feminist essayist: she handled the essay form in a manner hitherto unknown in Odia literature. She gave a radical thrust to the essay and gave a direction that sadly few have emulated before or after her times in Odisha.

Sarala's sole unnamed novel remains unpublished. However, she wrote nine chapters of the iconic novel, *Basanti* (Chapters 8, 9, 17, 18, 19, 20, 21, 22 and 27) that show her unique ability as a novelist. The novel was jointly written by nine leading members of the Sabuja (The Romantic) Group, namely Kalindi Charan Panigrahi, Sarat Chandra Mukherjee, Harihar Mohapatra, Annada Shankar Ray, Sarala Devi, Suprabha Devi, Muralidhar Mohanty, Pratibha Devi and Baishnab Charan Das. Sarala's nine chapters stand out for her ability to sketch powerful women characters and deal with issues integral to feminist concerns. Through the protagonist, Basanti, Sarala envisioned her ideal woman, active and intrepid, passionate and independent minded, ready to chart out untrodden paths.

Basanti: A New Novelistic Experiment

First published by New Students Store, Cuttack in 1931, as the second offering by the Sabuja Sahitya Samiti that featured 'nine acclaimed writers of the Sabuja Juga', *Basanti* was reprinted by Pushpita Press, Kazi Bazar in 1968, and again in 1986 by Bhikari Charan Dash, New Students' Store, Kazi Bazar, Cuttack. Dedicated to Biswanath Kar, the Editor of the celebrated *Utkal Sahitya*, the novel was serialized in the pages of the journal during 1926-27. The Prefatory note by Dash (pp. 5-8) outlines the background to the making of this unique book and the copyright agreement signed by 'Kalindi Charan Panigrahi as the Secretary of the Sabuja Sahitya Samiti.' (p. 6). The first edition of the book was published in 1931 with Sarat Chandra Mukherjee as the Editor with the names of 'some women authors left out' (p. 6). This was the first experiment in collective novel writing in Odisha, and perhaps the last. Later there was a move to carry out 'a similar experiment involving Kalindi Charan Panigrahi, Gokulananda Mohapatra and Binapani Mohanty, but the idea fell through.' (p. 8).

Issuing an appeal in the *Utkal Sahitya*, noted writer, Kalindi Charan Panigrahi, outlined the blueprint of the new project. Stating that 'four authors were ready to carry out the task', he said that there was an urgent need to have 'seven to eight or at any rate, four to five authors more.' Such writers had to follow some 'guidelines'. First, following the main plot, they had to write one to two chapters. Secondly, it was important not to have any dissonance with the preceding chapters. Thirdly, while showing the growth in the main characters, care had to be taken to match this growth with the evolution of the minor characters. In other words, there would be no extraneous material. Fourthly, it was permitted to create new characters in the plot, but such characters ought not to eclipse or overshadow the main characters. Fifthly, chapters had to be submitted within the stipulated time. If necessary, the editor could make necessary changes in the chapters in consultation with the authors concerned. And finally, decision regarding specific contributors was to be taken after the list was finalized. And if those agreed had to drop out due to some reason at any time, timely intimation was to be given to the editor so that suitable substitutes could be found in time (p. 11).

The New Woman

The plot of the novel was outlined in the public for the benefit of would be writers. The story relates to the family of Deputy Official BalaramaBabu, whose untimely death rendered his widow Nirmala and daughter Basanti, living at Cuttack, destitute. Before her illness and demise, Nirmala had offered the hand of her daughter Basanti in marriage to Debabrata, the carefree son of a wealthy zamindar, a student at the Ravenshaw College, who frequented the family and had developed closeness to them. Romantic, liberal-minded and honourable, Debabrata got married to Basanti quite against the will of his mother Subhdra Devi who lived in their ancestral village at Balasore.

Basanti studied in the girls' school and was a believer in female education. While Debabrata was sympathetic to the women's cause, he was not in favour of complete independence for women either. For, he believed that such independence would come in the way of conjugal love. (This is a refrain that is found recurrently in the novel). The relationship between the two gradually sours due to misunderstandings and Basanti becomes a near outcaste in the immediate family.

One day, Debabrata happened to discover portions of a letter; suspicious and enraged he sends away his wife to the station, for Basanti had voiced a desire to join the company of a 'stranger'. Her husband was unaware that the 'stranger' was none other than his wife's brother. Distraught but not undeterred, Basanti buys a ticket and proceeds on her journey. After her departure, Debabrata happens to read her diary and comes to realize his folly for having insulted her gratuitously. While Debabrata's mother suggests a remarriage, the repentant son turns down the move and sets out looking for Basanti. Falling ill on the way, in Bengal, he is treated by Binode Bihari who turns out to be Basanti's brother. There is union between Debabrata and Basanti, at Bardhaman. (pp. 12-13).

A careful look at the thirty short chapters of *Basanti* reveals that the nine contributors to the novel carefully conceptualized and wrote their chapters in accordance with the overall design and the outline suggested at the outset. While a degree of tension may be noticed at a few places between the desire to stick to the plot given and the need to expand and develop parallel issues and secondary/minor characters, on the whole, the novel holds together and seems to evolve organically. The role of the editor is clearly seen with regard to the tight knitting of narrative and the manner in which the novelistic vision pans out in the thirty chapters, and leads to an effective and credible ending. The novel moves at a moderate to fast pace and captures aptly the ethos of its times in a realistic manner. Several issues, both ideological and societal, appear to be at the heart of the novel. These include social reforms, religious conflicts, the need for interfaith dialogue, and problems like the system of dowry in marriage, caste hierarchies and the rural-urban divide.

Education, especially female education, is a recurrent and underlying motif in *Basanti.* At Ravenshaw College's discussion forum, for instance, Debabrata Mohanty addresses fellow students on the burning issue of the times, namely 'Independence of Woman' under the auspices of the Samaj Seva Sangha (p. 7). While one section of the audience commends him, another, a more conservative and prurient-minded group, heckles him at the meeting for his open feelings for Basanti and his free-mixing among the sexes. In his hostel room, Debabrata reads Shelley, Keats, Byron, Wordsworth, and Kalidas.(p.33) and is deeply influenced by the progressive message of the British Romantics.

Reading Rabindranath's *Gora* in the Odia Village

Basanti's desire for schooling is seen at many places including on page 33. The question of marriage as the union of like-minded souls, based on mutual affinity and compatibility rather than an artificial and tyrannical bonding brought about by society, is recurrently manifest in the novel. While opposition to Basanti's conversation with Debabrata's friend Ramesh is voiced by the orthodoxy, the narrators remain fully on the side of the female protagonist. In the village at Balasore, on a late afternoon, Basanti reads zealously Rabindranath Tagore's iconic novel *Gora* and tells her friend Nisha: 'While reading *Gora,* I thought we too could do something like them. Indeed, I am sure, together, we could try this out!'

Gora and its progressive message for women becomes inspirational for the two. A new school is begun by Basanti in the village (p. 83) and a library is created soon after (p. 85) along with provision for sports for the village children. In chapter 14, Debabrata congratulates Basanti for her article, 'Women in the Global Scene' that had appeared in the journal aptly called *Nababani,* (*New Message*) (p. 88). Similarly, extracts from the diaries of Basanti and Debabrata are read out, as dialectic exercises by the narrator in Chapter 15 and 16. As index of the characters' inner life, they are instrumental for the education of the mind and the heart.

The discourse over education and female emancipation has to be read contrapuntally with the rhetoric of domesticity and 'advice for women' texts voiced by Basanti's mother-in-law, Subhadra Devi, as the narrator records laconically on page 22:

Following the request of Debabrata, his mother Subhadra comes from the village to take a look at the would--be bride. She stays for two to three days at home and closely watches the habits and conduct of Basanti. In the process, she develops a firm view that it would not be prudent to have Basanti as her daughter-in-law. She has nothing negative to say about Basanti's looks or qualities. But her main unwillingness stems from the fact that Basanti is an educated woman. Subhadra is of the firm opinion that such a daughter-in-law would keep her husband under tight control. After marriage, her son would no longer remain under her influence. Consequently, her stature would be adversely affected. 'Of course, it is always good for the brides to have had a smattering of reading. They could read the *Bhagavata,* read out *Keshava Koili* or *Jema Dei* songs, tear-eyed.' But what is this? English reading, Bengali reading! The reading of newspapers and loud singing! What are these?' Of all things, she is most shocked by the fact that a grown up woman, Basanti has absolutely no sense of shame! While talking to her, she has no decency to cover her head in her saree; she speaks her mind openly! She has notices that Basanti had gone on a morning walk with Suniti, and both of them were shoe-clad Good Heavens!! Her daughter-in-law in shoes! No, she would have no such bride.

The domestic discourse, outlined above, is to be contrasted carefully with the Braja-Basanti conversation in Chapter 19, about women's issues. Written magnificently by Pratibha Devi, it captures the heart of the debates in the novel. Braja, a distant brother-in-law who recently quit studies in the college because of Civil Disobedience Movement, meets Basanti at her residence one winter noon, and asks: 'What is the aim of your life dear sister-in law?'

Remaining pensive, Basanti shreds some paper into bits and says: 'I have no definite goal in life'.

Braja can't hide his surprise. 'Are you not an educated woman?' He asks her, 'How can you not have a goal in life?'

It becomes clear to Braja soon that Basanti's answer was somewhat rhetorical. For most women, she says, follow the directions of their men folk. After all, if the holy books ask women to dissolve themselves into men, where is the question of special aims for women? Pratibha Devi's answer in the chapter in the form of dialogue is close to the views of Sarala:

Braja: To accomplish all this, surely we need to change female education everywhere.

Basanti: Of course, without education, a woman can never enjoy complete independence!

Braja: Well, when you are advocating total independence for woman, you might as well say that she ought to abjure motherhood because that goes counter to her desire for freedom.

Basanti: You have brought in a difficult issue Braja, Who says motherhood is contrary to independence? A woman has never spurned motherhood! On the contrary, she has even gloried in this experience! But wherever motherhood is not a voluntary act, there the woman treats it as a burden and a prison house. And therefore, it becomes a source of aberration. If motherhood leads to the growth of the female self, how can it be bondage? Society has downgraded individuality for the sake of procreation.That is why there is no greatness in motherhood today. Otherwise, there is no opposition between motherhood and independence.

Braja: It seems to me that whatever you wish womankind to achieve basically seems to be of your aspiration and longings.

Basanti: Let it be! I don't wish to quarrel with your judgement.

Braja: Then do you say that to achieve independence is the aim of your life?

Basanti says in a firm voice: Yes!

While Nirmala, the mother of Basanti and Suniti, her Christian neighbour, turn out to be memorable characters, Basanti herself charts out her own life and destiny, away from the home and the hearth. Pushed out of his life by a suspicious husband to Calcutta and Bardhaman, in Bengal, she accepts her fate stoically, and does not return home to unrequited love. This is a pattern in sharp contrast with the notion of the all-suffering wife who seeks to reform her erring husband through self-sacrifice, depicted recurrently in the mainstream literature in contemporary Bengal and Odisha. The reunion with the husband takes place far away from home, in the house of Binode Bihari where a convalescent [and reformed] Debabrata is united with his wife and the new born child. While due concession seems to have been made for this theatrical ending for the wider readership, the novel remains true to its ideological commitment and the heroine wins on her own terms.

As Sarala Devi wrote in Chapter 9 of *Basanti*: Basanti was like the wild current of a river—fast, fresh and flowing. Nothing that was bland and broken had any place in her life. She was of nature born; her soul had been conceived in freedom, in the freedom of a woman. From the very beginning her life had unfolded under this aspect. She had her sights set on higher things; her loving and desiring mind knew no limits. But this did not mean she was aggressive. No. Restraint was an important part of her nature. She never had to struggle to impose control on herself, since by nature she was remarkably self-controlled. The instrument in the deep recesses of her heart rang out new melodies in new rhythms everyday and resonated through her daily life of cares and duties. She never tired of her many chores—from work in the house, to writing, reading and looking after her mother-in-law, to other work. Like the ever-smiling *Sephali* flower in autumn she was always cheerful, basking in the radiance of her own being. (See Chapter 9 inside)

A Political Novel

Basanti is a political novel in the best sense of the term. Located against the backdrop of India's freedom struggle, in the late twenties of the last century, embracing the city and the village, the narrative attempts to find answers to questions that are deeply ideological in nature. Like Rabindranath's *Gora* that questioned the place of women in politically turbulent times, *Basanti* canter-staged crucial debates of the age. While nine authors had contributed, three women including Sarala Devi contributed to the narrative in a distinct feminist tone and tenor.

To sum up: The question of multiple authorship and gendered narrative, explored in this essay, is arguably a complex issue that does not seem to have conclusive answers. We have looked closely at the Odia novel, *Basanti,* authored by nine writers, one of whom Sarala Devi was a significant Gandhian feminist. We have seen that the manner in which Sarala examined the issues of the place of women in the national imaginary was a narrative vision quite unprecedented in its time. Rereading the novel in the present times, with the benefit of hindsight therefore becomes a useful exercise that would tell us much about the way literary women and men in early 20th Century India looked at the question of politics and the novel form.

NOTES

1. For an English translation of this novel, interested readers may see *Basanti: Writing the New Woman,* translated from Odia by Himansu S. Mohapatra and Paul St. Pierre, New Delhi: OUP, 2019. Earlier, a chapter of this novel had appeared in translation from in *The Lost World of Sarala Devi* edited by Sachidananda Mohanty, New Delhi, 2016 by the same translators.
2. It must be added though that in the same representation she advocated better nutrition and training of the mind and the body for female students, and mother tongue and art education for all. See the unpublished Memorandum, the Estate of Sarala Devi.
3. See, Chandra Talapade Mohanty, in *Postcolonial Theory: A Reader*

edited by Padmini Mongia, Delhi: Oxford University Press, 1997.

4. Berhampur: Bijay Book Store, 1995.
5. Bhubaneswar: Orissa, Sahitya Akademi, 2009.
6. Bhubaneswar: Paschima Publication, 1999.
7. I thank Prof. H.S. Mohapatra for a copy of this rare book.
8. See *Basanti,* Cuttack: 1931, rpt. New Students Store, 1986, Preface, 1-16.
9. Mohanty, Sachidananda, *Gender and Cultural Identity in Colonial Orissa,* Hyderabad: Orient Longman, 2008, p. 97; Also by the same author, *A Lost Tradition: Early Women's Writings in Orissa, 1898-1950,* New Delhi: Sage Publications, 2005.
10. *The Economic Times* 2015, HYPERLINK http://www.firstpost.com/business http://www.firstpost.com/business, July 17, 2015.

REFERENCES

Devi, Banaj, *Alibha Anala Shikha: Sarala* (in Odia), Bhubaneswar: Paschima Publication, 1999.

Devi, Sarala, *The Rights of Women,* Cuttack: Hindustan Granthamala, 1934.

Kishwar, Madhu, *In Search of Answers: Indian Women's Voices* (with Ruth Vanita), Zed Books, 1984.

_______. *Gandhi and Women,* New Delhi: Manushi Prakashan, 1986.

_______. *Women Bhakti Poets,* New Delhi: Manushi Publications, 1989.

Mishra, Ajaya, *Sarala Devi* (in Odia), Bhubaneswar: Orissa Sahitya Akademi, 2009.

Mohanty, Chandra Talapade in *Postcolonial Theory: A Reader* edited by Padmini Mongia, Delhi: Oxford University Press, 1997.

Mohanty, Sachidananda, *Gender and Cultural Identity in Colonial Orissa,* Hyderabad: Orient Longman, 2008.

_______. *A Lost Tradition: Early Women's Writings in Orissa, 1898-1950,* New Delhi: Sage Publications, 2005.

_______. *The Lost World of Sarala Devi,* New Delhi: Oxford University Press, 2016.

Mohapatra, Himansu S. and Paul St. Pierre, *Basanti: Writing the New Woman,* translated from Odia, New Delhi: OUP, 2019.

Panigrahi, Kalindi Charan, Mukherjee Sarat Chandra, Mohapatra

Sarat Chandra Ray, Annada Shankar, Sarala, Devi, Suprabha, Mohanty, Muralidhar, Devi, Pratibha, Das, Biashnab Charan, *Basanti*, Cuttack: New Students' Store, 1931; rpt. 1968; 1986.

Raju,V. Rajendra, *Sarala Devi* (in Odia), Berhampur: Bijay Book Store, 1995.

Tagore, Rabindranath, *Gora*, New Delhi: Sahitya Akademi, 2003.

Vanita, Ruth, *Gandhi's Tiger and Sita's Smile: Essays on Gender, Sexuality and Culture*. New Delhi: Yoda Press. 2005.

_______. Co-edited with Madhu Kishwar, *In Search of Answers: Indian Women's Voices from Manushi*, London: Zed Books, 1984, revised edition Horizon Books, Delhi, 1991.

2

Women's Movement for Land and Livelihood: A Case Study of Odisha

Smita Mishra Panda and Annapurna Devi Pandey

Introduction

The visibility of rural women, particularly those belonging to adivasi communities in India and Odisha, protesting against the state in the last decade and a half or so, is being widely reported in the media. There are some studies, though limited, available on the subject (Arnopoulos 2010, Shah 2010, Fontanella-Khan 2014). 'Rural woman' is a generic term and in the chapter at hand, it encompasses populations living in regions and using natural resources in a particular manner typical to that geographical area from time immemorial. However, among the groups dependent on indigenous land, forest and water, the majority are the adivasi communities. It is the voices of such indigenous rural women that have been addressed in this chapter. What is that voice? Does it have any relevance in the context of the current approach to development that we see in India and more specifically in Odisha? Why are the indigenous women resisting? What is the nature of their helplessness if any? Such questions and many more will be explored in the chapter.

It is well known that the problems faced by the indigenous peoples are by and large universal. They suffer from the consequences of historic injustice, including colonization, dispossession of lands, territories and resources, oppression and discrimination, as well as lack of control over their ways of life. Their right to development has been largely denied by colonial and modern states in the pursuit of economic growth. As a consequence, indigenous peoples often lose out to more powerful actors, becoming one of the most impoverished groups in the country (UN 2010). In India, despite the presence of several laws to protect the adivasis and their habitats such as Schedule V, PESA (Panchayat Extension to Scheduled Areas 1996), FRA (Forest Rights Act 2006) and Land Alienation Act (non-transfer of adivasi lands to non-adivasis), all of which have been systematically violated and encroached upon by mega national companies and multinationals for extraction of minerals and other natural resources available on their land. The state is responsible for allowing corporate encroachment on indigenous lands. The profits made by the corporate sector are siphoned out of the area leaving the indigenous population resourceless and puaperized. In the process, indigenous communities are also exposed to a whole range of development-induced changes in their habitats. Indigenous women are worse off as compared to their male counterparts among such communities, as they are largely responsible for providing of household resources (food, fodder, fuelwood and water) and raising their children.

The chapter focuses on grassroots women's resistance and struggles against corporate and state power to save their livelihood sources in the state of Odisha. The paper is divided into six sections. After the introduction, there is a section on the justification for looking at Odisha followed by a section on the conceptual underpinnings which also forms the analytical framework of the study. The fourth section deals with the significance of women's struggle and resistance against the state and corporate power to protect their land and livelihoods. The fifth section looks at two movements and discusses women's agencies and emerging political voices in the State. The last section provides some concluding remarks.

Why Odisha?

The State is one of the poorest in the country, with around

35.69% of the population living below poverty levels (GOO 2015). The ST (22.85%) and SC (17.13%) put together form nearly 40% of the total population of the state. Further, poverty among the ST is 63.52%, SC is 41.39% and OBC is 24.16% (ibid). The adivasis are primarily dependent on forest gathering, swidden cultivation and wage labour for their livelihoods. The irony is that the forests, minerals and adivasis are concentrated in the same region in Odisha. Table 1 gives an idea about the forest and its per capita availability to adivasis over the years. There is a decline from 0.84 ha in 1961 to 0.61 ha in 2011. From the time of independence, deforestation and displacement has impoverished the tribals and other communities dependent on natural resources for their sustenance. Mohanty (2014) very aptly describes Odisha to be a case that presents a crisis of democracy with upper castes and patriarchal domination that has been consolidated through the formation and expansion of the middle class, that provide services to the capitalist extractive economy, while vast sections of the population, especially adivasis, dalits and agricultural workers remain marginalized (p. 46). This process has been accentuated in the recent times of neo-liberal policies, during which the scale and magnitude of mining based industries and pro-corporate mafia have grown to a great extent.

Table 1: Forest Area and Adivasis in the State of Odisha

Year	*Recorded forest area ('000 Ha)*	*Percent of forest area to total geog. area*	*ST popula-tion ('000)*	*Forest area per capita (ST) in ha*	*Total popula-tion ('000)*	*Per capita forest area in ha*
1961	3566	22.95	42,24	0.84	17,549	0.20
1971	6088	39.18	50,72	1.20	21,945	0.28
1981	6640	42.73	59,15	1.12	26,370	0.25
1991	5476	35.24	70,32	0.78	31,660	0.17
2001	5814	37.34	81,45	0.71	36,707	0.15
2011	5814	37.34	95,91	0.61	41,974	0.14

Source: Forest Department, Government of Odisha (2011)

In Odisha, the nature of industrialization is based on the

extraction of natural resources—more specifically minerals. At present, mining operations may have come down due to various reasons, however, the sector has been vibrant in the state of Odisha compared to agriculture which is the only significant determinant of the per capita income and is lagging behind (Mishra 2010). The government of Odisha as of December 2014, has signed 93 MOUs to the tune of 2.15 lakh crores, with industries to set up steel (48), power plants (28), Aluminium (3) and rest in other plants in different parts of the state (Business Standard 2014). Industrialization and growth of the economy is desired in a state like Odisha where poverty and unemployment continues unabated. But the question remains whether the local indigenous communities are being benefited by such development efforts. Minerals (mainly iron ore and bauxite) are by and large concentrated in those areas that are inhabited by the adivasi communities. The extraction of minerals has either led to the displacement of local communities or drastic reduction in the natural resource base (land, water and forests) leaving them homeless, resourceless and pauperized (Padel and Das 2010; Padel 2011). The local communities depend for their survival on forests for collection of NTFP and fuelwood, swidden cultivation on cleared slopes of the hills as well as hunting of small animals.

After the Vedanta case, where the Supreme court stopped the expansion of the UK based company in Lanjigarh, POSCO (South Korean Steel Company) in July 2015 (after waiting for 10 years) has decided to withdraw from its proposed site in Jagatsinghpur district of Odisha. Such decisions by the judiciary and the state have come about primarily because of resistance by local communities who refused to part with their lands. Lanjigarh has bauxite required for the production of aluminium and Jagatsinghpur has iron ore required for steel production. Since the implementation of the Forest Conservation Act 1980, forest land in Odisha has been diverted for non-forest use (shown in Table 2). Forest land diverted for infrastructure and human habitation is much lower as compared with mining which is highest. The actual area mined by the companies may be much more than that allocated by the government. The annual growth rate of Odisha (2014-15) is 7.31% (GOO 2015) Agriculture contributes 15.4%, industry 33.4% and service sector 51.2% to the GSDP in 2014-2015 of the state according to CSO classification (GOO 2015). Although Odisha's economy continues to be in a high growth trajectory, the diversification of the economy leading to a structural shift from agriculture to industry and service-oriented economy, has affected rural indigenous women adversely (Hans 2014).

Table 2: Forest Area Diversion in Odisha (as of 01.10.2015)

Name of the Sector	*No. of Proposals*	*Forest Area Diverted (Hectares)*
Irrigation	83	9712.71
Industry	26	4273.95
Mining	162	21255.56
Energy	06	116.45
Roads and Bridges	39	314.31
Railways	14	2216.29
Defence	04	3865.25
Human Habitation	03	321.94
Others	36	1127.86
Transmission	60	3503.17
Total	433	46707.49

Source: Forest Department of Odisha, 2016

Industrialization in Odisha saw rampant mining in different parts of the state during the last decade. The impact of mining based industrialization has a differential impact on women and men. What is observed is that within the framework of division of labour, women are responsible for the provision of household resources in the form of water, forest products, fodder and fuelwood. With increasing mining activities, there is a decline in the natural resource base of the local communities. The indigenous communities have neither the education nor the necessary skill to obtain alternative means of employment outside their habitats. At best they can migrate to urban centres to find jobs in the labour market as unskilled workers. Mostly men migrate to urban areas to engage in menial jobs. Women are left behind to care for children, old and the sick along with a depleting resource base.

The information sources of research, are primarily civil society organizations and the authors have collected information from rural women leaders and their groups active in their habitats. Intensive individual and group discussions were held in those locations where the struggles and resistance movements have taken place and are still alive. Media reportings was another source of information. Secondary sources of information included relevant published literature and documents available from the government, civil society and other agencies. The first author has been engaged in research on adivasi women's struggles and participation in movements (Lund and Panda 2011, Panda 2014, Lund and Panda 2015). Several insights captured over the last 5 years from the research conducted by Panda have been used in the chapter at hand. The second author has done research on women's activism and leadership (2008).

Conceptual Underpinnings

Grassroots women's struggle and resistance have been conceptualized by several feminist scholars. One of the earlier work is by Chandra Mohanty et. al (1991) in their book *Cartographies of Struggle*, where they have raised pertinent/critical questions of political consciousness and self-identity that are crucial to defining Third World women's engagement with feminism. A feminist reading of anti-globalization is aptly described by Mohanty (2003), who argues for a more intimate, closer alliance between women's movements, feminist pedagogy and cross-cultural feminist theorizing, inter-twinning questions of subjectivity, agency and identity with political economy and the state. She strongly puts forth the thought that community politics can be regarded as an empowering process, particularly where women organize on the basis of collective identity (adapted from Panda 2014).

What is most striking in the struggles and movements of indigenous women in the last decade in Odisha, is their visibility in the public domain and the manner in which they have used their bodies as a weapon to represent collective resistance. Such modes of resistance are becoming more visible in the context of depleting livelihood resources—land, forests and water. Women are losing control over such resources which is becoming a central point of conflict. The analytical approach of this chapter draws on feminist ideas about the effects of class and ethnicity on gender, and how women's experiences of oppressive power relate to their body and ability to act. Second, we relate to studies that have focused on how 'embodied space' is where human experience and consciousness take on material, spatial and symbolic form (Low 2013, 9; Harcourt, 2012). In our case, *indigenous* women are at the outset poor, marginalized, and threatened. Deprived of their land and resources their bodies are mobilised in acts of resistance for survival. The interface situations of 'embodied space' are explored in which indigenous women are actively resisting and struggling against the state and the corporate sector (adapted from Lund and Panda 2015).

In her recent article on 'embodied spaces', Setha Low (2013) investigated a broad range of theories of body and space that are related to people's experienced realities, but, at the same time, can be linked with larger, social and cultural processes. Low defined the body as a physical and biological entity, lived experience and a centre of agency—a location for speaking and acting on the world (ibid.,10). She referred to feminist discourses on body space and, of particular relevance here, the body as situated and 'colonised' (Scott, 1996; Harcourt, 2009). She also made references to Haraway's (1991) thesis that personal and social bodies cannot be seen as natural but only as part of a self-creating process of human labour. 'Her [Haraway 1991] emphasis on *location, a position in a web of social connections, eliminates passivity of the female (and human) body and replaces it with a site of action and of agency*' (ibid., 11, our emphasis). Indigenous women's activism is about how women individually and collectively mobilise their agency. Such acts are context specific. In our study areas, *indigenous* women have no other choice than to expose their bodies physically in political acts. Their struggles are about survival at places which are presently changing to their disfavour. (adapted from Lund and Panda 2015).

In order to facilitate understanding of women's struggles, Harcourt and Escobar (2002) have provided a framework "Women and the Politics of Place" (WPP). An outcome of second wave feminism, it argues that women's diverse experiences of their lived bodies, the local economy and the environment are critical factors for a politics of place that offers the hope of challenging the inequalities of neo-liberal globalization. It is particularly concerned with the political struggles around place that link minority voices with collective action against inequality and repression. It is the body, home, local environs, and community, the arenas that women are motivated to defend, define and own politically. "Women engage creatively with globalization in multiple ways, with particular reference to body politics as core to women's experience of place and politics (ibid 5). WPP reiterates the feminist dictum that the *personal is political.* The protests and struggles of women seen in POSCO and Kalinganagar area is about their engagement with corporate encroachment on their sources of livelihood.

Women's movements have been most successful when they have engaged with the state, through contention and collaboration, without abdicating their own identities and constituencies and have been best served by forging strong linkages with other social movements and groups within civil society without relinquishing their own objectives and identities (Basu 2010: 3).

Women's movements can be both practical and strategic—what begins as struggles to achieve women's practical interests can turn into struggles to defend their strategic interests, and vice versa (ibid 4). Feminism and women's movement have often been alternatively used. Feminism is activism to challenge and change women's gender subordination, whereas women's movements entail women organizing to achieve social change (Ferree and Tripp 2006). Basu (2010) argues that women's movements can address a variety of goals unlike feminism but its constituencies are only female where as for feminism, its constituency can be both male and female. There is however an inter-connection between women's movement and feminism, as the latter is expressed in women's agency, their self-expression, consciousness of their identity and awareness. Further, it is tied to women organizing to advance their own interests. Ray (1999) argues, women's movements are shaped and influenced by political fields, which include actors such as the state, political parties and social movements and broader actors within civil society. Long drawn struggles by women are influenced by external forces as seen in POSCO and Kalinganagar areas of Odisha.

Livelihood is Larger than Life—Formation of Voices of Resistance of Women

In this section, two resistance movements have been described and analyzed, where rural indigenous women are fighting to save their livelihoods in Odisha. The first case is in Dhinkia in Jagatsinghpur district where POSCO (South Korean Company) was to set up a steel plant. The second is Kalinganagar in Jajpur district where a conglomeration of iron ore extraction companies has set up their plants, the main player being the TATA group.

Dhinkia—The Nerve Centre of the Movement

The government of Odisha had signed an MOU with a South Korean company Pohang Steel Company (POSCO), which was signed on 22 June 2005 for setting up an integrated steel plant in an area that will affect eight villages in three panchayats of Jagatsinghpur district in *Kujang Tahsil—Dhinkia, Gadakunjanga and Nuagaon*. The USD 12 billion project would displace 22,000 people and will acquire 2,700 acres of land for the production of 8 million tonnes of steel per annum (Mining Zone People's Solidaddddrity Group 2010). So far the attempts by the district administration to acquire land have been thwarted by strong local opposition starting early 2006, primarily by the POSCO Pratirodh Sangram Samiti (PPSS), a people's organization that spearheaded the movement against POSCO. After the signing of MOU in 2005, the Communist Party of India which has a presence in the area, historically facilitated in organizing the villagers in PPSS (Mishra and Nayak, 2011). The timeline of events in setting up of POSCO were as follows: June 2005, POSCO signs MOU with the Government of Odisha; August 2005, POSCO Pratirodh Sangram Samiti (PPSS) is formed by people, who were to be displaced, to fight against the company; POSCO applies for environmental clearance for captive ports in September 2006 and getting approval in May 2007; In April 2007, Government of Odisha seeks approval from Environment Ministry for diversion of 1,253 hectares of forest land for POSCO; Conditional diversion of land was granted in 2010 by GOI, but government of Odisha was asked to settle the forest rights, to which the latter replied that there were forest dwelling communities; May 2010, clashes begin between the protesters and police and 30 people are injured; July 2010, high court decides to cancel the lease for mining to POSCO; January 2011, environmental clearance comes for POSCO after almost six years. However a petitioner files a case with National Green Tribunal (NGT) challenging the clearance; Dec 2011, violence erupts in Jagatsinghpur as government decides to construct a coastal road in which one person is killed and 25 injured; March 2012, despite Prime Minister Manmohan Singh's assurance to POSCO, the NGT cancels its clearance; May 2013, the Supreme court strikes down the order of the Odisha high court and asks the Central Government to grant mining permission to POSCO; Odisha completes acquisition of 2,700 hactares of land for the project; January 2014, the Environment Ministry gives green signal to POSCO; June 2014, the Odisha government asks the new government (BJP) to hasten the approvals for POSCO. But the then Minister of (Jual Oram) had denied it; March 2015—POSCO realized that it is an uphill task to get clearances with so much of protests from below; July 2015, POSCO decides to move out of Odisha.

In the last decade, women in Dhinkia had been most active and initiated the struggle against the state's decision to acquire land for POSCO. The movement started with a handful of women but later the number reached almost 5,000 from all the three panchayats, says Sulochana Devi· leader of the women's wing of PPSS. There are approximately 3,000 women actively participating in the movement from Dhinkia panchayat alone. Much of their livelihood hinged on 'pana baraja' (beetle vines), fishing and growing paddy (pana, mina and dhana). Typically an adult would earn around Rs 11,000 to 14,000 and children and women workers around Rs 4,000 per month from even a small patch of land (1/20th of an acre). Currently, the betel vines are under threat due to the polluting smoke from the Indian Oil Corporation Limited IOCL refinery. The climatic conditions in the area are conducive for growing a variety of vegetables and fruits. The land is fertile and people do not want to give up their lands for any other alternative. Right from the start, women in the villages have played a significant role in the movement against the company, as they have a stake in the outcome as co-producers for their livelihood. Women have been successful in stalling the activities of the company by physically plugging all the entry points to the area.

According to Sulochana, "POSCO has rolled back because of the women and their tenacity to fight the corporate forces". Women came out of their homes in large numbers to support the movement. Their single point agenda was *POSCO hatao, bitamati bachao* (Remove POSCO and save your lands); *Ame Pana, Mina and Dhana Chadibunahin* (We will not give up our Beetle Vines, Fish and Paddy). Sulochana spearheaded the movement along with the village women belonging to different castes and tribal groups, and kept the pressure against POSCO. They also aimed at putting pressure on the State.

"Women sat on the roads and did not allow anyone to

go inside the area which was cordoned off by the police for POSCO's activities. They have been consistent in their efforts to stop POSCO", says Sulochana. They formed a circle and sat together resisting the entry of any outsider into the area. The police was initially hesitant to use any force to disperse the crowd.

While discussing this aspect with women, what we found was that if there were men sitting in protest, the police would have easily dispersed them by using force and lathi-charge (use of baton). However, after a few days of women's protest police started putting pressure on the protesters. Women continued to be adamant and refused to move. The police fired rubber bullets and also lathi-charged women sitting peacefully in *dharna* (protest) (personal communication with a women's group in Dhinkia, 14 September 2014, Countercurrents.org, 15 May 2010). These physical barriers, along with the psychological impact of the continual threat of arrest, have placed entire communities under siege. Testimony gathered by the research team reveals a pattern of systematic, sustained repression that affects almost every facet of affected communities' daily lives. (IHRC, 2013, p. 34). "Children also came forward and asked the police to kill them as their mothers were always protesting", said Gauri from Dhinkia village. Children went out with their mothers and were active in cordoning off the area along with the adults."Men have supported but women have been most active in the movement" said Laksmi from the same village.

"We will not give up our '*pana baraja*' (betel leaf) as it is our livelihood. Besides old people are not able to work under the sun for government-provided MGNREGS, but can work in the beetle vines in the shade".

"Our biggest struggle besides protecting our lands, was also not to allow the Paradip road that would have passed through our village (Gobindpur) to be constructed. The road was very important for POSCO to make progress in its activities" (personal conversation with Sulochana in Dhinkia village in August 2014). The purpose was to transport the iron ore from mining areas to the port to be further shipped to South Korea for processing into Steel.

Sulochana has taken rubber bullets from the police firing in her chest, which are still lodged inside. She has emerged as a strong leader in the area who at a young age has taken a vow to oust POSCO. She was threatened by the police and state Ministers but refused to bow down before them. There are forty two criminal and civil cases against her.

During the early part of the women's struggle, when they came together in large numbers and collected small amounts of money to buy a mike in 2006-07, men did not support them wholeheartedly. Pro-POSCO people at that time were more in number and taunted the women and asked them to "shave their heads as they will never be able to win against POSCO". There were around 1500 women at that time who drove away the land acquisition officer. After a few meetings with villagers (both women and men), Sulochana was accepted as a leader of the group resisting against POSCO. She made enemies with not only the POSCO people but also, politicians. Their slogan about saving lands and ousting POSCO became even stronger. For three years (2006-10), the movement continued in full swing in which women played a significant role in guarding the village and all their lands. The government stopped food supply to the village. That is the time according to Sulochana the women broke Section 144, and stepped out in large numbers. *"Mahila Durga rupa dharana kale"* (Women took up the role of Durga Goddess, who fights against the evil). They became even more aggressive and took to streets and were not afraid of the police and the pro-POSCO mafia (*Times of India*, March 6, 2013). It was like a do or die situation for them. In the face of such violent protests by women and children, some food supplies were released by the state (videovolunteers.org, June 21, 2013).

Women used to keep vigil all night and wake up very early to keep the police away. Women from Dhinkia were most courageous on the streets and even undressed (nude protests) themselves in public as a mark of protest against the police.

(Personal communication with Sulochona and other women leaders in Dhinkia January 2015, Financialexpress.com, PTI, March 9, 2013). They used cow and buffalo bones as weapons. Pro-POSCO mafia (hired goons of POSCO contractors) threw hand bombs at the women when they were sleeping near the barricade (IHRC, 2013). Over the last 8-9 years, the government has made several attempts to break the struggle against POSCO by resorting to different arm-twisting tactics. "This is the greatest betrayal of the state against its people to use the power of the criminal system to implicate villagers in a large number of fabricated cases to intimidate them, instill fear in them and finally break their collective strength against POSCO" (Alternative Law Forum 2013: 21). This is an example of the state going against its own people. There are 230 cases registered between 2006-10 against 1,200 people out of which around 300 are women (discussion with Sulochana, January 2015). Sulochana mentioned that typically 30-50 cases were filed against one person, so that bail is not possible to obtain. "With so many cases against a single person, it is a kind of house arrest as they are unable to move out of the village". She has not been able to move out of the village for the past eight years in the fear that she would be arrested. Sulochana has severe joint pains and is unable to seek medical support from outside. All her movements are tracked. The President of PPSS was arrested twice and has obtained bail, but Sulochana feels, in order to get bail, she has to allow herself to be arrested first, which is a dangerous proposition for her. Being a woman leader, she has not been able to get much support from the male leaders of the movement, especially with respect to bail against the false cases.

On one instance, on 15 May 2010, Government of Odisha sent 32 battalions (1 battalion has 30 police persons) to Balilutha in Jagatsinghpur district, the entry point for the proposed POSCO project. When thousands of villagers were sitting in peaceful demonstration against POSCO, police attacked them with tear gas, lathis and rubber bullets (Countercurrents.

org, 15 May 2010). They set on fire one temporary shelter in the same site, being used by the villagers. Police beat up the people and injured 200 of them, majority of them being women. They implicated five people in different cases, out of which two were women all belonging to SC and other backward castes. All of them were seriously injured and put in jail for one month. Similarly on 14 December 2011, villagers were attacked by goons and police while they were peacefully protesting against road construction in the coast connecting (Balanton-Chrimes, 2015) Paradip to the proposed POSCO site (personal communication with women leaders in Dhinkia, January 2015). Large number of women, children and men were attacked by the police and charges were arbitrarily slapped on them (Alternative Law Forum 2013).

When we asked about how they participated in the movement (andolan), "This is not an andolan (movement). We are protecting our livelihood", one of the woman activists from the village remarked. "Some families were pro-POSCO and I feel the women did not want to support POSCO, but had to because their husbands forced them to do so", said Sulochana.

People's protest against the company and the relentless struggle by the women has not allowed POSCO to function and make any headway in the area. There were 52 families who were resettled by POSCO in another place. However, they decided to return back after seven years, as they were harassed by the authorities. The people of Patana village accepted them and also helped in their resettlement back in their village. Sulochana was extremely pleased that day and says that "it was my last encounter with POSCO in 2014, as I was convinced that the entire population of the area is against the company". Currently, what is also observed is that political parties of all shades and intelligentsia are coming together in support of the POSCO movement which has further emboldened the women in Jagatsinghpur (Mishra and Nayak 2011).

Kalinganagar—Struggle faded but not in spirit

The struggle in Kalinganagar has a long history. January 2, 2006 was the day when 12 adivasis were shot dead in police firing while they were protesting with several others against the TATA company that had started construction of its Steel Plant. The long standing agitation of the indigenous people got further aggravated when they came to know that the TATAs would start construction of a boundary wall on Jan 2, 2006, without the consent of the local people. The resistance has been going on for a long time in opposition to setting up of different plants including TATA. The main agenda of the struggle is against the displacement of the adivasis from their traditional habitats. Table 3 gives an idea of the amount of land allocated to different industries in Kalinganagar. Among the different industries, TATA is the biggest with 2,500 to 3,000 employees.

Table 3: Land Allocated to Industries in Kalinganagar

S.No	*Industry*	*Land in Acres*
1	MESCO	530
2	Orion	150
3	Maithan Ispat	100
4	Uttam Galva	370
5	NINL	2,500
6	Maharashtra Seamless	500
7	TISCO	2,400
8	Rohit Ferrotech	50
9	Jindal Stainless	678
10	Visa Steel	390
11	Dinabandhu Steel	100
12	K.J. Ispat	50
	Total	7,818

Source: Office of ADM, Kalinganagar (Dash and Samal 2008)

Kalinganagar has a locational advantage of not only being close to the chromite mines in Jajpur district, but also has two National Highways (connecting Kolkata and Chennai) and a railway line. Besides the largest river of the state Brahmani flows through that region. Such advantages in Kalinganagar have attracted a host of industries such as TISCO, VISA industries, Jindal Stainless, Maharashtra Seamless, MAL Industries, AML Steel and Power, National Steel and Power, National Steel and Agro Industries, Tube Investment Industry, Dinabandhu Steel and Uttam Galva Steels, to sign MOUs with the state government. The government has acquired 12,000 acres extending over 83 revenue villages and 10 gram panchayats of Sukinda and Danagadi blocks, where there is high concentration of STs and SCs. Compensation was paid to those who had the titles (*patta*) at the rate of Rs 37,000 per acre. However, most of the people in the area did not have titles and were cultivating the land (with usufruct rights). Government paid Rs 25,000 per acre to pacify them. The same land was sold to the industries like TATA and others at a rate of Rs 3.5 lakhs (almost 5 times) and this further agitated the local communities. Agriculture was the only means of livelihood in the area and with that gone, the indigenous people had nothing to live on. The money received as compensation by the local people was spent within a short period of time. With hardly any skills and education, the people soon found themselves helpless in a pauperized condition.

People's protest gained momentum with the laying of the foundation stone to set up plants by the companies in 2004-06. The indigenous people have successfully come together and formed what is called "Visthapan Virodhi Janamanch", in which both women and men are actively involved. There is a women's wing in the movement. Between 2006-10, 3,000 tribal women from the Kalinganagar area were actively participating in the movement. A tribal (Munda) woman leader Sabari played a significant role by providing leadership to the adivasi women to take the Kalinganagar movement forward. She was the sarpanch of Gobarghati panchayat (1997-98) and was a selfless natural leader according to social activists and media people working in the Kalinganagar area. Her eldest son was killed in the 2006 police firing. She was not deterred by her son's death. Instead, she plunged into the movement wholeheartedly. Her strong activism led to her being arrested by the police as a maoist. She was in jail for about two years. The media reported that she is a confirmed Maoist and justified keeping her in jail. It was one of the most sensationalized news during that time.

Most of the lands (98%) that have been acquired by the industry belong to the adivasi communities. The area also comes under FRA (2006), which implies that those without titles (*patta*) to lands are technically eligible to receive it from the government. Swidden cultivation was practised among the adivasis of the area on the slopes of small mountains. Most of them have disappeared after the companies have acquired them. "Compensation amount have remained the same since 1992 and people are highly dissatisfied with the government" says Sabari.

Both women and men were in the forefront in a road blockade that ensued in 2007 for over a year on the National Highway. In the event, 5,000 women mostly adivasis, came together from not only Odisha, but also, adjoining states of Jharkhand and Chhattisgarh on May 23, 2007 to block the highway unless their 7-point charter of demands were met (Meher 2008). Sabari spearheaded the movement and refused to move out of the road for almost one and a half years (Oral History). At that time, government announced a compensation of Rs 5 lakh for all those who died in the police firing of 2006. Sabari initially refused to accept the compensation for her son who was killed, but after a lot of persuasion by her own people, she gave in with much reluctance. As she was the main leader behind the blockade and also responsible for large-scale mobilization of adivasi women, false cases (15) were fabricated against her by the police (Padhi and Negi, 2018). She was arrested from her cousin's house and was taken to jail and was declared a Maoist, as mentioned earlier. When asked why Sabari did not protest, she said "how does it matter whether I said yes I am a Maoist or no I am not. The police have killed my son". While in jail, Sabari was asked all sorts of odd questions and she told the police that all the cases against her were fabricated. She was taken ill and could not eat and subsequently was shifted to a hospital where her name was registered as Basanti Munda (Oral History). Sabari asked the police why her name was changed, to which she received no response. When she became very serious, the media came to meet with her and she gave the police two options—"kill me or arrest me". She was arrested and put back in jail in Keonjhar town. She was released in 2012 and has been confined to her village ever since.

After Sabari's arrest the women's groups among the adivasi protestors were disheartened and the group was eventually dismantled. Many surrendered and moved to the resettlement colony out of fear. Police actions create fear psychosis among people which the government takes advantage of. Many men in the Kalinganagar area have got co-opted by the companies with the promise of menial job offers and short term contracts. Sabari currently is confined to her village and has the support of only 25-30 families. There is a resettlement colony in Kalinganagar which has around 1,200 households from the Gobarghati panchayat. She still considers herself as leader and is hopeful that the movement will come alive one day. That Sabari was an adivasi woman leader who had opposed the corporate giants of Kalinganagar and was never swayed by monetary attractions, will be etched in the history of industrial development in Odisha.

Reclaiming Livelihoods—Women's Voice Agency

The above account of the two movements and activism demonstrated by rural women tells us about their persistent role in reclaiming their land and livelihood sources. Women belonging to different castes and tribal groups came together in the struggle for a common cause to protect their livelihoods. They were part of those organizations that were formed for resisting against corporate intrusion into the area. The media highlighted the collective action of women as they refused to leave their site of action. By being visible in large numbers and obstructing roads, indigenous women could establish first signs of opposition. Women used their bodies to create medium of resistance in large numbers. Participation of women in large numbers (outnumbering men by a huge margin) represents feminization of public spaces, which is against traditional norms in the villages. Women have broken the cultural barriers and made their voices heard. The collective strength to fight POSCO and the State by women has forced the police use brute force against women. Men who were always visible and had the right articulation and connections with the media and other outsiders have received public attention. However, with the turn of events and rural women's activism in the past eight years, media has begun to report on the significant role of women in the anti-POSCO movement. Although women work in the agricultural fields and betel vines, with their persistent presence in the outer public domain for activism, has led to a re-organization of space. This however does not suggest that men are relegated to the private domain. Visibility of women and their contribution to the anti-POSCO movement was recognized by the community. Similarly, in Kalinganagar despite the fact that industries have been successful in establishing themselves, women's role in the movement against the State and companies is significant in the history of the place. Women's presence in the highway in the road blockade in Kalinganagar for almost a year itself shows the tenacity of women and their protest against the corporate power. Had Sabari not been arrested, the women's group would have continued with their struggle. Whereas, in the case of POSCO, women's collective action moved from strength to strength and fuelled the anti-POSCO movement to greater heights.

Indigenous women are traditionally known to be very active working side by side with their men folks in maintaining their household economy. They are a vital force working as producers in agriculture and forest gathering. Their contribution to the grassroots movement has brought them to limelight and to the attention of print and television media, thus, making them a thorn in the eyes of the State and corporations. There have been other movements where women have come together to fight against the ruling class, establishment or others. The second author has worked among the Kutia Kondh adivasis in Phulbani, Odisha and has written on the emergence of an indigenous women's organization known as Ghumusar Mahila Sangathan (GMS) led by Maka Naik, a Kondh woman, in 1979. With support of other activist groups and student organizations, GMS challenged the State and business officials who were abusing the tribal women in the name of marriage and were later abandoning them. With their protest and political activism, GMS not only, was able to stop this unjust practice but, made the State acknowledge the helpless situation of these women and provide adequate compensation for them and their children's rehabilitation (Pandey, 2008). What is however significant to note, is that the nature of protests and struggles in both POSCO and Kalinganagar areas discussed, where large number of women collectivised for a common cause over a long drawn period was not commonly seen in the history of people's movement in Odisha.

Creation of oppositional spaces of resistance has potential to bring about transformation in the lives of the indigenous women and their households. It is such spaces that have made women carve a niche for themselves. Men have accepted women as leaders and change-makers. It is this newfound space for women who had no such recognition earlier, which has transformed their roles. Furthermore, resistance by women in case of POSCO did not allow the company to go ahead further with its plan. In Kalinganagar, even though women were subdued because of the arrest of their leader, it also proved a crucial point that had they continued with their struggle collectively, the forces of resistance would have been stronger and perhaps the industries would not have been able to make their foothold in the area. In many cases of activism by women earlier researched by the first author, she found that there was strong support by NGOs and other organizations to take their struggles forward (Lund and Panda 2015). However, in the case of POSCO and Kalinganagar, the presence and activism of women as part of the movement itself strengthened the very grassroots organizations, they had formed for the struggle against the state and corporate power. The oppositional space also provided a platform for possible dialogues—both good and confrontational between the women and the State and corporate strength. Our findings on indigenous women's activism resonates with those of other researchers, such as Nagar (2000, 2012), Staheli et.al. (2004), Nagar and Writers (2006), Rai (2008), Padel and Das (2010) and Harcourt (2012), Lund and Panda (2011, 2015).

Concluding Remarks

Indigenous women of both POSCO and Kalinganagar area strategise from marginalized positions and combine their body space with broader aspects of social change in their respective contexts. The opposition created by women have given them a strong political voice to protect their livelihoods. Although the movement in both cases is gendered, however, there is no apparent conflict between genders that would affect the outcome of women's struggles to protect their livelihoods. Differences have occurred where men tend to get co-opted by the company, but that did not distract women from losing sight of their main goal—the struggle to save the sources of livelihood.

In the analysis, body space and spaces of resistance are used as metonymy for social and cultural transformations, and also for challenging/pushing new boundaries, practices and autonomy over their livelihood sources. It draws on the analysis of intersections between the body and body politics, which we refer to as *body space,* indicating how women activists in both POSCO and Kalinganagar areas occupy and shape their trajectories of change through their own bodies, and further combine them with broader aspects of negotiation and possible social transformation. The concept of *spaces of resistance or oppositional spaces* illustrates how women activists may use tacit support from media, intelligentia and civil society groups in their struggle against corporate power. Women have moved from excluded private space to a more included public space which is also politically assertive and strong enough to bring about change.

The active participation of indigenous women in movements against the State and the mega-corporates goes on to show the need to lay importance to representation of marginalized voices in reformulating development. The voices of the indigenous women are generally not heard and often subdued, depriving them of their basic needs and rights and away from any form of decision making. In this, the civil society has increasingly played an instrumental role in opposing the narrow view of development. The alternative view of development proposes critical scholarship in development research, in which the researcher is close to the field and research subjects—focusing on issues such as participation, local indigenous communities, poverty, gender and the environment, gloablization, rights based approach and climate change etc. The alternative view will result in changed ethics of development studies and practice.

REFERENCES

Alternative Law Forum, 2013. *Captive Democracy: Abuse of the Criminal System and Filing False Cases to Curb Dissent against the POSCO Steel Plant in Odisha*. Delhi.

Arnopoulos, S.M., 2010. *Saris On Scooters: How Microcredit is Changing Village India*. Toronto: Dundurn Press.

Balanton-Chrimes, S., 2015. *Odisha's POSCO Project*. Deakin University (Australia).

Basu, A., 1995. 'Introduction'. In: A. Basu, (ed.), *The Challenge of Local Feminisms*. New York: Routledge, pp. 1-21.

Basu, A., 2010. *Women's Movements in the Global Era: The Power of Local Feminism*. USA: Westview Press.

Business Standard (2014) 'MoU Signed Players Invest RS 2.15 Lakh Crores in Odisha'.

Countercurrents.org. 2010. 'Police Attack on Anti-Posco People's Movement—Chronology of Incidents by Posco Pratirodh

Sangram Samiti'.

Das, C.R., 2014. "Tribes and Forests in Odisha: Some Critical Issues", *International Journal of Research and Development: A Management Review*, Vol. 3, No. 3, pp. 29-44.

Dash, K.C. and Kishore C. Samal, 2008. "New Mega Projects in Orissa: Protests by Potentially Displaced Person", *Social Change*, 8(4), pp. 627-644.

Ferree, Marx M. and A.M. Trippe (eds.), 2006. *Global Feminism: Transnational Women's Activism, Organizing and Human Rights*. USA: New York University Press.

Financialexpress.com. 2013. 'Semi-nude sit-in by women against POSCO sparks ourage', PTI, March 9.

Firstpost, 2015. 'End of a $12 Billion Dream? After a decade of delays, POSCO suspends Odisha project' downloaded from, HYPERLINK http://www.firstpost.com/business/end-of-a-12-bn-dream-after-a-decade-of-delays-posco-suspends-odisha-project-2347254.html, on 24.12.2015.

Fontanella-Khan, A., 2014. *Pink Sari Revolution: A Tale of Women and Power in India*. USA: W.W. Norton and Company.

Government of Odisha, 2015. *Odisha Economic Survey*. Bhubaneswar: Government of Odisha.

Government of Odisha, 2016. *Forestry Report of Odisha*. Bhubaneswar: Forest Department.

Hans, Asha, 2014. "Scheduled Tribe Women in Odisha", *Odisha Review*. November 2014, pp. 26-40.

Harcourt, W., 2009. *Body Politics in Development: Critical Debates in Gender and Development*. New Delhi: Zed Press.

Harcourt, W. (ed.), 2012. *Women Reclaiming Sustainable Livelihoods: Spaces Lost, Spaces Gained*. Basingstoke: Palgrave Macmillan.

Harcourt, W. and Escobar, A., 2002. "Women and the Politics of Place". *Development*, 45(1): 7-14.

Harding, S., 2008. *Sciences from Below: Feminisms, Postcolonialities, and Modernities*. London: Duke University Press.

International Human Rights Clinic (IHRC), 2013. *The Price of Steel: Human Rights and Forced Evictions in the POSCO-India Project*, ESCR-Net.

Low, S.M., 2013. 'Embodied space(s): Anthropological theories of body, space, and culture'. *Space and Culture*, 6(1): 9-18.

Lund, R. and S.M. Panda, 2011. 'New activism for political recognition:

Creation and expansion of spaces by tribal women in Odisha'. *Gender, Technology and Development*, 15(1): 75-99.

Lund, R. And S.M. Panda, 2015. 'Struggling bodies and spaces of resistance—adivasi women activists in Odisha, India'. In: Ragnhild Lund, Philippe Doneys and B.P. Resurreccion (eds.) *Gendered Entanglements: Revisiting Gender in Rapidly Changing Asia*. Denmark: Nordic Institute of Asian Studies (NIAS), pp. 147-176.

Meher, Rajkishore, 2009. "Globalisation, Displacement and the Livelihood Issues of Tribal and Agriculture Dependent Poor People: The Case of Mineral-based Industries in India", *Journal of Developing Societies*, 25, pp. 457-480.

Mining Zone People's Solidarity Group, 2010. *Iron and Steal: The POSCO India Story*. HYPERLINK http://miningzone.org, downloaded on 29.12.2015.

Mishra, Banikanta, 2010. "Agriculture, Industry and Mining in Orissa in the Post-Liberalisation Era: An Inter-District and Inter-State Panel Analysis", *Economic and Political Weekly*, Vol. XLV, No. 20, pp. 49-68.

Mishra, B. and B.K. Nayak, 2011."Paan or POSCO", *Economic and Political Weekly*, Vol. XLVI, Nos. 26 & 27, pp. 12-13.

Mohanty, C.T., 2003. *Feminism Without Borders: Decolonising Theory, Practicing Solidarity*, USA: Duke University Press.

Mohanty, Manoranjan, 2014. "Persisting Dominance: Crisis of Democracy in a Resource-rich Region", *Economic and Political Weekly*, Vol. XLIX, No. 14, pp. 30-47.

Nagar, R., 2000. '"Muje Jawab Do!" (Answer me!): Women's grassroots activism and social spaces in Chitrakoot (India)'. *Gender Place and Culture*, 7(7): 341-362.

Nagar, R., 2012. 'Mapping feminisms and difference'. In L.A. Staheli, E. Kofman, and L. Peake (eds.), *Mapping Women, Making Politics. Feminist Perspectives on Political Geography*. London: Routledge, pp. 31-48.

Nagar, R. and S. Writers, 2006. *Playing with Fire (Feminist Thought and Action Through Seven Lives in India)*. Mineapolis, MN: University of Minnesota Press.

Nelson, L., 1999. 'Bodies (and spaces) do matter: The limits of performativity', *Gender Place and Culture: A Journal of Feminist Geography*, 6(4): 331-353.

Padel, Felix, 2011. *Sacrificing People: Invasions of a Tribal Landscape.*

New Delhi: Orient Blackswan.

Padel, F. and S. Das, 2010. *Out of this Earth. East India Adivasis and the Aluminium Cartel*. New Delhi: Orient Blackswan.

Padhi, R. and R.S. Negi, 2018. 'Kalinganagar, Where 'Development' is Threatening a Way of Life'. *The Wire*, January 6.

Panda, Smita Mishra, 2014. 'Right to Rights: *Adivasi* (Tribal) Women in the Context of a Not-So-Silent Revolution in Odisha, India'. In: Catthrine Brun, Piers Blaikie and Michael Jones (eds.), *Alternative Development: Unravelling Marginalisation, Voicing Change*, UK: Ashgate, pp. 191-206.

Pandey, Annapurna D., "Globalization, Swadeshi and Women's Movement in Orissa, India". In Nandini Gunewardena and Ann Kingsolver (eds.), *The Gender of Globalization: Women Navigating Cultural and Economic Marginalization*, US: School of American Research Press, 2008.

Ray, Raka, 1999. *Fields of Protest: Women's Movements in India*. New Delhi: Kali for Women.

Rai, S.M., 2008. *The Gender Politics of Development: Essays in Hope and Despair*. New Delhi and New York: Zubaan/Zed Books.

Shah, Alpa, 2010. *In the Shadows of the State Indigenous Politics, Environmentalism and Insurgency in Jharkhand, India*. UK: Duke University Press.

Staheli, L.A., E. Kofman and Peake L., (eds.), 2004. *Mapping Women, Making Politics: Feminist Perspectives on Political Geography*. London: Routledge.

Times of India. 2013. 'Anti-POSCO villagers vow to oppose plant', March 6.

United Nations, 2010. *State of the World's Indigenous Peoples*. Department of Public Information.

Videovolunteers.org. 2013. 'People Vs POSCO: Violence Against Women', June 21.

The Economic Times, 2015, HYPERLINK http://www.firstpost.com/business, July 17, 2015.

II. Gendered Discriminations

3

Gender Discrimination and the Role of the State: A Case Study of Sex Selective Abortion in Odisha

Bijayalaxmi Nanda

Introduction and Background

Until now Odisha has been at the fringes of discussion and research on sex-selective abortion in India. The estimates of sex-selective abortion are drawn from the Child Sex Ratio (CSR) from the decadal census figures. But a relatively much better CSR of Odisha as compared to India, has perhaps placed the State off the radar of researchers in general and has resulted in complacency among state institutions. What has been missed out is the fact that the rate of decline in the CSR of Odisha has gradually surpassed that of India as a whole. A comparison of CSR of India and Odisha between 1991 and 2011 is an eye opener in this regard. India's CSR stood at 945, 927 and 919 in 1991, 2001 and 2011 respectively. Odisha's figures for the same census years stood at 967, 953 and 941 respectively. Thus, between 1991 and 2001, while India's CSR declined by 18 points, decline in the case of Odisha was 14 points. However, between 2001 and 2011, CSR of India declined by 8 points, while in the case of Odisha it has declined by 12 points. In other words, between 2001 and 2011, while India has made an improvement of 10 points in the declining trend of CSR as compared to the previous decade, in the case of Odisha the improvement has been a meagre two points.[1] While the overall decline since 2001 is of 12 points, the rural and urban break-up presents a more meaningful representation of this decline. While in the rural areas the decline is that of 9 points, in the urban areas it is more pronounced at 20 points.

The district level data of Odisha shows a more disturbing trend. The decline in CSR in 2011, as compared to 2001, is not localized so as to be amenable to a simplistic explanation and an equally simple solution. Out of 30 districts, the decline is noticed in 21 districts, making it a state-wide phenomenon. More disturbingly, decline of greater than 10 points is seen in half of the State, i.e. 15 out of 30 districts. Topping the list are districts of Nayagarh (-49), Anugul (-48), Dhenkanal (-48), Ganjam (-31), Debagarh (-29), Kalahandi (-27), Cuttack (-25) and Sundergarh (-24). In the 2001 Census, all the districts had a CSR of above 900, while in 2011 census there are three districts with lower than 900 CSR, viz. Nayagarh (855), Dhenkanal (877) and Anugul (889). The extent of decline points towards a problem much more deeply rooted than earlier thought of.

Odisha's declining child sex ratio indicates a spread of the practice of sex selective abortion in India to regions which were earlier considered as egalitarian as far as gender discrimination is concerned. The cultural legacy of daughter aversion combined with economic prosperity had been the oft–stated reasons for sex-selective abortion. However, Odisha demonstrated a varied experience and trajectory for this explanation. Agnihotri had pointed out to this phenomenon in 2003 when he stated:

> It is important to highlight here the importance of state specific analyses of the problem. Many a nuance of the state level decline are not revealed in the national perspective. This can be elaborated with the example of Orissa, a state where it was hard to imagine such widespread decline in sex ratios even if the decline is confined to urban areas.... In 1991, only two districts, Kendrapada and Jagatsingpur had low f/m ratios, 942 and 941 respectively. But in 2001 as many as 12 districts had f/m ratios below this level, lowest being in Nayagarh (901). The contiguity of these 12 districts is striking; low f/m ratios show a remarkable cluster and not a scatter (Agnihotri 2003: 4352).

Hans and Patel have also elaborated on this trend:

> The decline in CSR is the main cause of concern as it continues to decline consistently from 967 in 1991 Census to 950 in 2001 Census to even lower 934 as per the 2011 Census (provisional figure). Low CSR shows a remarkable cluster and not a scatter. The districts with the lowest CSR in the 2011 Census data are Nayagarh (851), Dhenkanal (870), Angul (884) and Ganjam (899) (all provisional Census figures). The contiguity of districts with very low CSR in their urban population that is disturbing. There is a set of three adjoining districts Ganjam, Nayagarh and Boudh where the CSR (urban) are below 860 (2001 Census) a figure comparable to female to male ratio (FMR) in some of the districts of Haryana and western UP (Hans and Patel 2012: 40).

The cluster of districts with low child sex ratio that Agnihotri had noticed in 2001 Census, has only expanded in 2011. Apart from the cluster of 12 districts identified with CSR below 941 in 2001 by Agnihotri, 6 more districts contiguous to that cluster are moving to acquire the property of the old cluster rapidly. These districts are Deogarh, Kalahandi, Sundargarh, Sambalpur, Rayagada, Sonepur and Bolangir with a CSR decline ranging from 29 to 12 points in 2011 as compared to 2001. The cluster identified in 2001 is now expanding to engulf majority of the districts of Odisha. However, surprisingly no detailed study has been conducted on this issue.

In this paper an attempt is made to examine the situation especially in the light of state policies, programmes, initiatives, schemes and laws. Unlike Punjab and other northern states like Haryana, Himachal and Rajasthan, on which a rich and varied amount of research, reports and writings on sex-selective abortion exist, Odisha has hardly any. Two significant features are responsible for it: The northern states in India have a history of female infanticide and known for its cultural legacy of son preference. Odisha, on the other hand, has no such historical or cultural legacy. The relatively more equal treatment of sons and daughters (and the status of women) in Odisha as a historical-cultural legacy until the recent past is generally recognised, though there are no well-researched studies on this, except the historical census data on sex ratio which was mostly favourable to females.

Recent studies by some scholars have attempted to throw some light on the possible socio-cultural and economic factors. Mohanty examines the traditional 16th century Odia literary texts to explain how the 16th century in the State was marked by two distinct elements. Firstly, the rice cultivation in Odisha required female intensive labour and secondly, the bhakti movement's resurgence in the region challenged brahmanical patriarchy. Women became the main targets of social reformers who wanted to reform the prevailing social values. Mohanty refers to the Laksmi Purana written by Balaram Das as belonging to this genre. The text, according to her, valorises women's physical labour, economic worth and redefines the caste order in terms of activities rather than hierarchy. The reciting of the Laksmi Purana during rituals by women, children and men led to a radical socialization process. Thus she argues that the Odisha society developed as a fairly gender equal society (Mohanty 2017). This distinction between the wheat cultivation regions being less labour intensive and thereby not providing equal importance to women and the rice cultivation belts recognising women as having economic worth has also been accepted by Miller and Bardhan. Both have tried to explain the deficit in girls in the northern regions vis-a-vis the eastern and southern belt, as being tied to the agrarian society and the relative economic worth of women in that society (Bardhan 1974; Miller 1981).

The deficit of females in Odisha has earlier been attributed to its high maternal mortality. Poverty and its link with mortality in terms with access to health care and other factors have engaged attention. But the kind of correlation that was easily established in Punjab remained unavailable as far as Odisha is concerned. Secondly, the northern states' declining child sex ratio has been noted since 1991 and Odisha then was considered as the better-off state as far as CSR was considered. Odisha's decline in CSR is comparatively recent and therefore there is a paucity of research on the issue.

The paper looks into the commitment of the State to counter the issue through its various schemes and policies, the civil society organizations' other initiatives and activism. Odisha today is known for its resistance movements and the large scale participation of women in these movements. These movements are mostly in the regions which are conflict-ridden and associated with displacement due to the industrialization and mining activities by multi-national corporations. The bearing of the resistance movements on issues concerning CSR is also examined. A qualitative analysis of policy documents and schemes and in-depth interviews with officials, government functionaries and civil society activists informs the paper. The field work was conducted in Bhubaneswar, Cuttack district, Nayagarh district and adjoining areas were studied because of their low child sex ratio and the widespread availability of sex determination facilities in the region. Also some tribal belts in Koraput district were touched upon in the study.

The State Interventions

It was only in 2007 that a media report[2] of female foetuses found in a well near a medical clinic in Nayagarh District brought attention to sex-selective abortion in the State. Due to pressures from the media and civil society initiatives the state government of Odisha started the process of appointing committees and assigning authorities under the PCPNDT Act. It is also to be noted that Odisha was one of the first few states which had expressed a desire to pass a State Act in 1989 when Maharashtra passed its own State Act. However, the state had put the all India PCPNDT Act (1994 and 2002) to cold storage. A state official who was a functionary in the NRHM in 2007 said, "For us the issue of declining child sex ratio is important because it is an issue of mortality. We are concerned about mortality and morbidity and have to curb it at any cost"[3]. The State's preoccupation with mortality and morbidity was due to the fact that Odisha had some of the worst indicators when it came to maternal health and child health in India.[4] Officials were only concerned to deliver on that issue.

The Nayagarh case

Nayagarh district is primarily rural. Even the district headquarters can be classified as semi-urban. However, it is not very far from the urban areas of Bhubaneswar, Khurda and Cuttack. Its child sex ratio has been a cause for concern since 2001 when it was 904. This has further declined alarmingly by 49 points, from 904 in 2001 to 855 in 2011. It, thus, became a point of reference for the State as far as sex-selective abortion is concerned. The early warnings for this inevitable findings, though, were already written on the walls. On 14 July 2007, a young boy rummaging through discarded plastic bottles at Duburi Mundia (hillock) of Ramachandi Prasad discovered polythene bags containing foetuses. He raised an alarm leading to the spread of the news far and wide. By 16th July it became national news.

A fact-finding report of civil society groups says that visits, in-depth interviews and discussions lent credence to the fact that all foetuses were female and more than five months old[5] (which makes it illegal under the MTP Act 1971 as well). This team included mostly child rights groups, and therefore, involved a child-centric approach in terms of its emphasis on foetal rights, right to be born, etc. It shows that women's groups and other initiatives working on women's rights did not engage at this point. The State inaction is also disturbing in the face of such clear evidence.

The judgement of the Orissa High Court on the bail petition of the accused in the case of *Dr. Sudhir Kumar Brahma vs. State of Orissa* on 4 September 2007 is also revealing. The petitioner, Dr. Sudhir Kumar Brahma, had been imprisoned after the appropriate authority and the police found him guilty of sex determination leading to sex-selective abortion. He had appealed for bail under Section 439 Cr.P.C. The judgement on the bail petition begins by referring to the Nayagarh incident. It says:

> Though this is an application under Section 439 Cr P.C filed by the petitioner for grant of bail, the facts on which the case evolved

> not only has created sensation throughout the State as well as the country, but also involves interesting and important questions to be dealt with.... This gave rise to a suspicion in the mind of the general public that probably after sex determination, finding the foetus to be female, the mothers have chosen for aborting the child.[6]

It goes on to say "poor families in the society or for that matter, the conservative and old fashioned parents prefer boys, and girls are seen as a burden and inferior to boys."[7] While dwelling upon gender discrimination the judgement reinforces stereotypes about women's active agency in determining the sex of the foetus, about the 'poor and old fashioned' as the guilty when it comes to sex-selective abortion. The judgement in other parts mentions about medical malpractices and the unethical role of doctors, but accords a certain lesser degree of importance to it in terms of perpetration of the crime while granting bail to the accused. Such judgements abound on the issue reflect the mindset of the judicial authorities who tend to see it in terms of its societal sanctions and women's culpability, rather than the coercion that women face in such situations and the role of doctors in providing this 'service'.

This active nexus and the fact that in Odisha supply of new reproductive technologies led to a demand, which was artificially created by a set of 'middlemen', has also been common knowledge. Interestingly, in a seminar organized by Mamata, a local NGO and Population Foundation of India in Bhubaneswar,[8] a gynaecologist defended the practice of sex determination and sex-selective abortion as a 'social service' offered to parents who could not afford too many children or to women who already had daughters. In this research one was, however, not able to gather any evidence of doctors having offered the service free of charge to the very poor to alleviate them from their 'burden'.[9] The argument about 'social service', therefore, did not have much substance or credibility as far as doctors are concerned. Almost everywhere it was linked to a profiteering motive and based on a complex network of doctors, middlemen, medical technicians, the sellers of machines and families who were seeking the service or were 'motivated' to seek it. In Odisha it is clearly the market driven intensification of son preference through wide availability, affordability and accessibility of reproductive technologies which has led to a decline in child sex ratio.[10] The impunity of doctors who openly offered the services of sex determination and sex selective abortion against the provisions of law also added to the problem.

The PCPNDT Act

Although the Act has been in existence from 1996, it was a Supreme Court's directive in 2001 that led states to implement the Act with some seriousness. In 2002, Odisha was the second state after Rajasthan to start implementing the provisions of the Act. However, it was only in 2007 that the state showed any concrete action under the Act. Media exposure of rampant misuse of reproductive technology in Nayagarh district led to a flurry of activities. The strengthening of the various structures under the Act and the mandatory meetings of supervisory boards and the filing of cases under the Act received attention. Since the committees and appropriate authorities prescribed under the Act were set up hastily, there were inconsistencies and disharmonies with the provisions of the Act. It was also not able to inspire confidence amongst the authorities and people to use the law.

In 2009, with help and support of the UNFPA, the State set up its PCPNDT Cell and strengthened the institutional mechanism for implementation of the Act within the Department of Health and Family Welfare. Series of sensitization and training programmes were organized for key government officials including the District Collectors cum Appropriate Authorities, Judicial Officers, Executive Magistrates, officials of the Departments of Health and Women and Child Development. Various awareness programmes generation of activities also took place targeting women self help groups, young boys and girls in the universities and schools. Posters, pamphlets and other materials were created and distributed highlighting provisions of the Act as well as the value of the girl child. The UNFPA also aided the state government in training decoy customers so that erring doctors could be caught under the Act. It has also engaged in a systematic review of all policies, schemes and programmes of the State regarding the girl-child and women in order to assist the Department of Women and Child Development (WCD). The Department pursued a plan to initiate a woman and girl-child policy in order to mainstream gender concerns in all departments in the State.

Officials implementing the Act at all levels feel that there has been improvement in terms of filing the cases and conviction rates (35 cases and 3 convictions up to 2012 and 66 cases and 4 convictions up to March 2018)[11]. All committees designated under the Act are presently in place. Implementing officials of WCD and Health and Family Welfare departments spoke about the massive sensitization programmes that had been conducted on the issue for the medical fraternity, Accredited Social Health Activists (ASHAs), Judiciary and District Collectors. Posters and other Information, Education and Communication (IEC) materials developed at the state level are generally gender sensitive and give positive messages about the role of the girl child as compared to other states which have pro-life and utilitarian images and messages which are ultimately counterproductive to the issue. There is coordination between the UN agencies and the implementing agencies at some levels.

Middle-level and senior officials of the Health Department did feel that implementing the Act strictly and punishing erring doctors and families will have a deterrent effect. However, some expressed helplessness in the situation by blaming the intense son preference in families and sub-optimal support from district administration and lack of coordination among key actors. They believed that the motivations and perceptions of families cannot change by the implementation of an Act. Some referred to sex selective abortion as a lesser evil if the family already had two daughters. The underlying structural and material factors and the overlapping idea of gender discrimination present in the manifestation of sex-selective abortion was not a part of their understanding.[12] The complexity of working on the issue of gender discrimination and their intersections with policy-making and implementation in the government is precisely this. Their in-depth understanding on gender issues is negligible. They lack initiative to see beyond the rhetoric. Their arguments for change are derived from welfarist notions and do not necessarily extend to ensuring equality and dignity to women and girls. Although there is mention of gender training workshops and capacity building programmes, the analysis of the contents of the programmes revealed a technical approach of assimilating gender into processes without addressing systemic understandings and attitudes. The lack of engagement of active women's groups or feminist groups within the training programmes was evident in the field.

The frontline functionaries like ASHAs and Auxiliary Nurse Midwife (ANMs) in Odisha have not been adequately involved in the monitoring and sensitization programmes regarding the issue. Adequate civil society, women's groups and NGO activities were not noticed in the field. Involvement of elected women representatives and panchayati raj institutions seemed fairly inadequate. The most significant amendment of Odisha Gram Panchayat Act is the reservation of fifty per cent seats for women, giving scope to them in the electoral and decision-making process. As per the 11th Schedule of the Amendment Act, powers and responsibilities to manage 29 subjects have been devolved to panchayats, including monitoring and supervision of health centres and anganwadi centres. Thus the elected representatives, especially women, are expected to extend their hands in creating a gender just society by dissemination of right kind of information, minimizing the impact of stigma and ensuring livelihood.

The women sarpanches, who were part of Focussed Group Discussions (FGDs) for this study, had very little understanding on the issue. Male sarpanches were equally ill-informed. Except for knowledge on the child nutrition programme as part of the Integrated Child Development Services (ICDS) and the midday meals programmes in schools, they were not involved with programmes for the girls and adolescents, like the Sabla or on the issue of child sex ratio and sex-selective abortion. The government authorities at the local level have neither sensitized the PRI representatives nor have they been involved in any manner whatsoever. Similarly the block panchayats and the district panchayats have hardly been involved on such issues. The Village Health, Nutrition and Sanitation Committee had also not been involved. Even if the elected members of Panchayati Raj were acquainted with the issue of sex-selective abortion and declining child sex ratio, they did not consider it as an important subject for their interventions or discussions. It clearly reveals that the issue has not been accorded the priority it deserves at various levels of state administration.[13]

State's Obsession with Two-Child Norm

The State has a two-child norm disincentive for candidates when it comes to qualifying for elections to Panchayati Raj and urban local bodies.[14] Odisha was one of the first two states, apart from Rajasthan, to have taken a lead for such legislative measures to exhibit 'political will' for population control in the early 1990s. The then chief minister, Biju Patnaik, was influenced by the Census report of 1991 which said that India produces population size of one Australia every year. He took up the issue with a missionary zeal to control population by making examples of political leaders in the local bodies' elections in the panchayats and urban local bodies election.[15]

This obsession with controlling population size and growth is common to Indian policy-makers. The theoretical framework which is the feminist understanding on the issue clearly has set the field to bring out its anti-women and anti-poor impact. Moreover in Odisha's demographic context of relatively lower fertility and higher mortality, such restrictive law was not at all called for. Its unimaginative and coercive implications were not considered by the policy makers then. The two-child norm continues to exist in Odisha and Rajasthan even when the states of Haryana, Himachal Pradesh and Madhya Pradesh have withdrawn it. Civil society's advocacy on the issue in Odisha still has not been able to influence the State Government. Research studies through their extensive fieldwork have brought to the fore the gender discriminatory effects of it.[16] It leads to sex-selective abortion and it excludes large sections of the poor and marginalized from participating in elections. It was very encouraging to note that senior level officials in the State had clarity on the anti-women and anti-poor impact of the norm in Odisha. They also had an understanding that it could exacerbate sex-selective abortion. However, an emotive reason was cited for their not being able to suggest the withdrawal of the law since it was launched by the erstwhile chief minister, Biju Patnaik.[17]

A woman respondent of Cuttack district and her husband were actively involved with local issues in their municipal ward where they lived. They worked with the local committees to enhance the communities' control over local resources and decision-making. However, when she wanted to contest for the local elections she found out to her disappointment that she could not do so because of a two child norm applied by the State. In her own words:

> I wanted to contest for the corporator's post of my local ward. When I went to file my papers I found out that I was not eligible to contest for the elections since I had three children. I have three daughters who I am very proud of. But the Government has penalised me for it. Tell me who will now want to have daughters? The present corporator has only one son. He is a known drunkard and wife beater. It does not affect the Sarkar what is happening in our homes and happening to us women. Only we should have two or less children so that we do not increase in numbers. Should the Sarkar not allow me to contest as I have only daughters?[18]

The negative impact of such coercive population control measures on gender have been referred to by Mohan Rao.

He elaborates, "punitive and coercive population policies especially those announced by several states, are an invitation to sex-selective abortion" (Rao 2004).

A large number of respondents who were interviewed for my research in Odisha also explicitly stated this. The women who were interviewed in this region under the study felt that the two-child norm interfered with their right to political participation in the Panchayati Raj and Urban local bodies, it led to rejection and abandonment of wives and daughters by their husbands and fathers, and also exacerbated sex-selective abortion. A confused messaging about the value of women and the girl child is also sent to the society because of this. Many women who held political positions and had not disclosed their number of children or who had children after elections were also nervous and worried about the fallout.

A woman Panchayat member of Kantapada block of Cuttack district said:

> I did not know about this norm. What happens to me now? I have two daughters and one son. May be I will have to resign from my post. I have worked very hard and earned the respect of my community and my family. What an absurd law, which has nothing to do with the competence of an elected person, but how many children she has! I will go to Court if I am thrown out.[19]

Clearly, the contradictions in the policy with gender issues were brought to the fore from the discussions with numerous stakeholders. However, there continues to be resistance from the government to withdraw the norm. This resistance, stereotypical of most policies which deal with population control, reveals the criticality of unearthing and interrogating the State's intentions when it comes to gender.

State's belated initiative on Review of Gender Programmes and Formulation of a Gender Policy

Since the state did not have any scheme specifically for the girl child as other states did, the declining child sex ratio in 2011 has led to the government to consider launching a specific scheme for the girl child in line with the conditional cash transfers offered in other states. The Department of Women and Child Development (WCD) mobilized the support of the UNFPA at this stage. The fact that the Dhanalakshmi scheme existed in the State, even if only in two districts, was not a matter for discussion at all. The UNFPA which had undertaken a desk review of many such schemes and programmes all over the country shared its findings with the State Government. The findings revealed that these schemes had not led to much change on the ground and there was a need to consider the holistic nature of gender discrimination that exists (Sekher 2012).

The WCD then asked for a review of all existing schemes and programmes in Odisha in order to identify their strengths and limitations for addressing the issue of gender discrimination. The approach was to look at strengthening the existing interventions and creating new ones on gender issues to bring about an overall commitment to end gender discrimination. The review that was supported by UNFPA, laid down that any financial incentive that is introduced to counter the unwantedness of daughters should not be linked with support to marriage expenses, or to number of children or girls in families. It should also not be linked to family planning or sterilization of parents which further perpetuates discrimination when the daughter is seen dispensable in the context of a small family set-up. The incentive should be linked to creating assets in the name of daughters and bringing about investment in education. Strong conditions about linkages with education and employment with disincentives in case the financial incentive is misused, would prove useful in this context. Skill building through vocational training and forward linkages with the market for employment by investments by the State may be considered.

The review further suggested that emphasizing on austere marriages, implementing strictly the laws against dowry and introducing tax disincentives on spending on marriages need to be considered. Effective implementation of all gender laws regarding violence and sexual harassment, etc. are necessary. Succession laws, laws regarding property, etc. also need to be reviewed in the context of whether they reinforce son preference. Old age support, innovative pension and social security schemes which reduce parental dependence on children need to be developed. Support for single women will also contribute to changing perceptions about them being a liability. It also recommended that gram panchayats which are proactively creating awareness about the Act should get appreciation letters/awards. Proactive engagement of frontline functionaries like ASHAs, ANMs and PRI functionaries in awareness generation and sensitization should be encouraged. Appreciation letters could be given to the parents of only daughters. Celebrating the birth of a girl child in hospitals, communities and in Panchayats and events like Beti Utsav, as celebrated in other states (Delhi and Haryana), may be considered. Media campaigns highlighting the value of the girl child as well as presenting parents who support and nurture girls as role models for others, should be encouraged. The media should also highlight the role of government authorities and NGOs playing proactive roles in implementing the Act.

There are other equally important measures which will go a long way in countering gender bias and sex selection. These include highlighting the names of the clinics that have been illegally involved in sex determination and sex-selective abortion; quick judgment through fast track courts; counselling services with gender sensitive code of protocol to be established for women survivors and victims of violence; and medical ethics to be included in the curriculum of medical and nursing education highlighting the issue. The Maharashtra model of implementing the Act could be followed in terms of creating inter-state and inter-district coordination committees.

Gender insensitive methods like tracking of pregnancies of women should be discouraged. Tracking pregnancies of women in order to counter sex selective abortion in different states has led to violation of the right to privacy and bodily integrity of women. The study of Nawanshahr district in

Punjab has revealed that this form of tracking also has an implicit anti-poor and anti-rural bias. It is mostly poor women from rural background who are put under this form of surveillance. In Odisha this form of tracking would also be counterproductive as it is the urban areas which have revealed a major decline in child sex ratio. The declining child sex ratio and its primary cause, sex-selective abortion, require a holistic approach to counter it. While addressing the issue it needs to be kept in mind that gender discrimination in any form is a multi-layered and multi-dimensional phenomenon. The urgent countering of sex selective abortion through the measures mentioned above will pay immediate dividends and enhance the status of women and the girl child in all their dimensions.[20]

Based on these recommendations, the WCD decided to launch a women and girl-child policy for the State in 2014. Such policies were in existence in Rajasthan, Gujarat and Uttar Pradesh. The primary concern of such policies was to arrest declining child sex ratio by countering sex-selective abortion. The process of creating the policy was to do so through a series of consultative meetings with various stakeholders which included civil society groups, media groups and law enforcement agencies. Prior to the consultations it was decided that instead of a conditional cash transfer, scholarships for girl students would be floated at the higher secondary level thereby taking care of the two critical indicators, i.e. health and survival of girls.[21]

Civil Society Initiatives

It was in 2002 that 'Sansristi', an NGO dedicated to women's issues started work on the problem of declining child sex ratio and sex-selective abortion. Through seminars, workshops and other research based work they highlighted the issue of declining child sex ratio in the state. They also brought up the complex and nuanced contradictions in policies and programmes like the two-child norm and its adverse impact in terms of exacerbating sex-selective abortion. Professor Asha

Hans, an academician and feminist of repute, spearheaded this along with Amrita Patel, a feminist researcher. Other organizations like National Alliance of Women (NAWO) have also been active on the issues of gender violence. They have asked for the withdrawal of the two-child norm due to its anti-women and anti-poor implications. However, their direct work on sex-selective abortion is limited to an extent.

Women in Resistance Movements

Odisha is also known for its resistance movements where women were actively involved with the freedom struggle. However, the post-Independent era did not see an active women's movement in Odisha from the upper echelons of society. Today women are a large constituent of the resistance movements against the state and the multi-national corporations in Odisha. To quote Padhi and Pradhan:

> When we look at the class and caste character of these women, we find that they are mostly from the peasantry, tribal, dalit or fisher folk communities. Even the landless women have been visible in these struggles. It needs to be noted that in all these communities, women have a direct link to the productive process—whether it is agriculture, fishing, collection of forest produce or even as wage labourers. In a patriarchal society, these women hardly own land or other productive resources, they hardly count in taking decisions in the management of community owned common resources, but they surely are active participants in the economic activities in various ways. Hence their stake in the protection of their land, water and forests are crucial for their own survival. Therefore, they are bound to resist when their resources are being taken away by the corporates aided by the state. It is also important to note that, invariably, in all these struggles, women have expressed the concerns for their children, for the security of livelihood of the future generations. In response to the compensation and rehabilitation packages announced by the government or companies, women have always asked, 'What about the livelihood of the child in my womb?' It is not surprising therefore that we see women always in the forefront of these resistance struggles. They are seen in

> guarding the barricades, sitting on dharnas, taking out rallies, mobilising protest demonstrations and so on. They are also seen facing the batons and guns when the state forces come down heavily upon the protesting people. In fact, it has been noticed that increasingly women are seen in the forefront when the state is determined to crush these movements by sheer brute force. In Kashipur, women were attacked by the police many a time. On the day of police firing in 2000, in which three men were killed and many injured, it is the women who confronted the police when the latter forcefully tried to enter the village (Padhi and Pradhan 2013).

Irrespective of such active involvement of women in resistance movements, women's groups in the city of Bhubaneswar do not have any links with them. The energy and vibrancy seen in these resistance movements is not visible in the NGO-driven activism. When asked about sex-selective abortion, one woman respondent said, "We are against discrimination in any form. Capitalism has brought this form of crime into our state. But we have never been called to participate in any march or rally against this. It is not as if we do not want to be involved in fighting against it". Another respondent said, "We are dealing with our immediate problems, fighting for our own survival but no one from the women's groups comes to stand with us" (Padhi and Pradhan 2013).

Talks with women activists from Bhubaneswar also corroborated the fact that there is no direct support to resistance movements from them. They provided two main arguments for it. Firstly, while the issues raised by the resistance movements are extremely important for women, the mobilization of women in them is not always out of choice. Women and children may be mobilized in the forefront in order to protect the rallies and marches from police firing. This strategy is a patriarchal device that movements have always used. Secondly, the resistance movements may not be committed to principles of non-violence which the women's groups believe in.[22]

The women in the resistance movements also shared their

angst against the men in the movements. According to them while women were the most active members of the movements, decisions about the strategies and methods of conducting the movement is not entirely democratic. The issues raised by women are sidelined to include ideas mostly raised by the male bastion. Women have been alert to this and have protested against it too. However, to understand women in the movement as passive agents would not be a correct assessment of the situation. Women have been active participants of each resistance movement. They have mobilized both women and men for the same. Majority of them are from the poor and landless quarters, yet they are politically and socially aware. While one might question the commitment of the resistance movements to purely women's issues, one can note that the commitment of the women to the movements is sustained by their own involvement, choice and agency. A comparative assessment of women in the panchayati raj system in Odisha reveals that although some of them have been able to engage on their own on issues which are central to women's concerns, some continue to be controlled by men in power and men in their families (Mohanty 2005).

The resistance movements in Odisha offer an example of how effectively people from grassroots can challenge state and business interests. However, the same energy and vibrancy is missing from the women's groups who confront the State in terms of effective implementation of PCPNDT Act or the mobilizing of funds for women's safety, security and enhancement of status. The synergy between the women's groups and the women in the resistance movements would have created better opportunities to be able to counter sex-selective abortion as gender discrimination effectively in the State. However, a strict binary based on issues, class divisions and strategies has kept them both apart. The class differentiation in the leadership of both is to be noted. Most of the women-specific NGOs are led by educated upper class women who are mostly urban based, while the women who are leaders in the resistance movements are essentially uneducated and rural-based.

Although resistance movements do not explicitly seek to counter gender discrimination, they often play an important role in reshaping gender relations. The distance maintained by women based NGOs from women in resistance movements ultimately leads to a failure to take advantage of this reshaping of gender relations and also to examine the strength of channelizing these movements for effectively challenging the state to deliver its promises to women. Across villages in Odisha, it is quite clear that resistance movements have led to women strengthening their bargaining positions vis-a-vis men, offering an improved status to women in society in their specific contexts.[23] However, since it is anti-state and viewed as subversive, it is unfortunately beyond the state discourse to examine why and how women are participating effectively in resistance movements and not able to do so within state machineries such as panchayati raj institutions.

The potentiality of engaging with the resistance movements seem immense, but so are the barriers and obstacles to it. The diversity of issues and a networking in the participation of women's groups was not noticeable in the State. An inclusion of diversity would then have been able to reflect the concern and specificity of each group. A range of issues would have manifested in the confrontation to state authorities or in the demands made to the state authorities. The state would have then perhaps shown greater alacrity in addressing these concerns. The rapidly declining child sex ratio of the state would then have figured in priority concerns.

Tribal Belts and Sex Selective Abortion

A paradox that the Census 2011 has presented before the country is that even egalitarian tribal belts are revealing a lowering of CSR. Odisha presents a classic case in this regard. Out of the fourteen predominantly tribal districts of Odisha,[24] substantial decline in the CSR has been noticed in six districts in the Census 2011. These districts in the descending order are: Ganjam (-31), Debagarh (-29), Kalahandi (-27), Sundargarh

(-24), Rayagada (-16) and Kandhmal (-8). All these districts are contiguous to the relatively prosperous and urban central and coastal districts of the state, which have majorly contributed in pulling down the state's CSR statistics in the Census 2011. The central and coastal districts of Nayagarh (-49), Dhenkanal (-48), Angul (-48), Cuttack (-25), Kendrapara (-14), Jajpur (-11) and Khurda (-10) find place in the notorious neighbourhood of these gullible tribal districts. As we travel away from the central and coastal districts, the influencing effect of these districts on the tribal population seems waning. Examples are the tribal districts of Nuapara (+12), Malkangiri (+10), Keonjhar (+5), Mayurbhanj (+4), Gajapati (+3), Nabarangpur (-1) and Koraput (-4).

An exploratory study of tribal regions in the state through focused group discussions (FGDs)[25] and interviews with tribal families provided some understanding of the issue. Remote tribal regions like Niyamgiri, for example, offered no direct evidence of any form of gender discriminatory behaviour in terms of fertility choices and son preference. However, a change in terms of roles and behaviour patterns was noted. An activist working with the Dongria Kondhs in Niyamgiri pointed out that "while the mass is still untouched by son preference, the power holders like the sarpanch and others do learn about it once they move out of their regions and start socializing in urban regions. The woman sarpanch of Niyamgiri had started manifesting more stereotypical female behaviour in meetings having learnt from the women sarpanches from the coastal belts"[26].

Tribal families with some land or other resources who had managed to send their children to urban regions for education, said that they were keener to send their sons to study, as compared to their daughters, since their sons would support them in old age. This form of 'sanskritization' is not uncommon at all. Patel mentions this in her study on sex-selective abortion. According to her:

> The last category of people are those who send their children to schools, universities, invest in finding white collar jobs for them,

> try to copy middle class consumption patterns and are keen on being seen as sanskritised by emulating upper caste cultural practices....adopting dowry in place of bride wealth is one of the striking practices adopted by this section of the society" (Patel 2007).

Here Patel is making a reference to Other Backward Classes (OBCs) and not to tribals. Writing in early 2000s she does point at caution to the fact that the poorest, which includes dalits and tribals, are gradually moving towards the dominant fertility patterns.

Secondly, the huge influx of women domestic workers from tribal belts in Odisha to different parts of India is also a manifestation of growing gender discrimination. In fact, a large number of the respondents admitted that they had discontinued their elder daughter's education so that she could be gainfully employed and substantiate the household income and support the education of their male sibling. Another issue emerging from sex-selective abortion that had affected the tribal population in Odisha was the supply of girls and women from the tribal belt to northern states like Haryana. Due to dearth of women and girls for marriage as two decades of sex-selective abortion has caught up with the northern states, girls and women are procured for marriage purposes. These girls and women are treated worse than slaves and remain mostly in social exclusion. Their children also do not have the same status as other children who are born from endogamous marriages. Some scholars believe that this may have a positive impact on the larger marriage patterns in India.[27] However, there is no discounting the fact that sex-selective abortion and a growing intensification of son preference has impacted adversely the gender relations in the tribal population of Odisha.

A decline in CSR in the hitherto untouched tribal belts clearly points out to the reach of new reproductive technologies and the emerging practice of sex-selective abortion in the face of a modernizing small family norm. These findings do raise a number of questions about widespread availability, accessibility and affordability of sex determination and sex selective abortion. Another important finding that emerged from the field on this issue, especially in remote areas, is that sex determination was easily available through ultrasound machines being transported in mobile vans, scooters, etc. Abortion after sex determination is conducted mostly through local methods. Every community in the rural region has indigenous methods of providing abortion through use of herbal concoctions, needles and also by quacks. This local knowledge then makes the practice of sex-selective abortion a more silent one which is difficult to trace and control.[28]

Unfortunately, since there has been a deficit of safe and legal abortion facilities in public health systems, local practices which are sometimes hazardous for women's health have flourished in their absence. The emphasis of women's groups to consider the availability of safe legal abortion services for women and girls is very significant in this context. It would lead to an uprooting of such illegal and hazardous practices. These practices not only lead to increased rates of sex-selective abortion, but can also be dangerous and detrimental to women's reproductive health and survival in the long run. In Jharkhand and Chhattisgarh tribal regions are now clearly manifesting the practice. The worrying point about Odisha is that the misuse of reproductive technologies, which is a major factor leading to the decline in CSR, is not being addressed adequately by the state. By the next decadal census, urbanization and growing aspirations of the tribal population will determine to a large degree how the decline in CSR will ultimately play out there.

Conclusion

To sum up, Odisha is a glaring example of the way things will ultimately unfold for the rest of the country as far as declining CSR is concerned. It has been able to provide evidence to refute the well-established theories about sex-selective abortion being an upper class, upper caste, northern patriarchal belt phenomenon. The spread of the practice to rural regions and tribal belts is a testimony to this. It has clearly revealed that the state not only lacks political will to deliver on the issue, but by its contradictory and gender insensitive policies and programmes like the two-child norm, stress on female sterilization and focussing only on reproduction, has exacerbated the phenomenon. The civil society initiatives have not been able to deliver due to their stand-alone interventions and their distance from a hugely successful and vibrant resistance movement in Odisha.

While a public critique of the state's support to MNCs like Vedanta and others like POSCO is a part of the mainstream discussion in both national and international discourses, intensification of gender discrimination by the practice of sex-selective abortion in Odisha is basically being discussed only at the activists and researchers level. Despite all official announcements, programmes and policies, the situation in Odisha, as far as sex-selective abortion is concerned, remains in the fringes. The resistance movements in Odisha are charting new ways to confront the market forces and state apparatuses that are restructuring their living spaces to their detriment. The women's groups and other civil society initiatives have not been able to do so as far as gender relations go in the State.

The declining CSR in majority of districts in Odisha, the extent of the decline and the spread of this trend in hitherto immune tribal districts leave no doubt that the state has underestimated the extent and magnitude of the problem, else its programmes and policies would have delivered a better CSR in Odisha. It needs to put the issue up on its agenda and devise and implement appropriate interventions in right earnest.

NOTES

1. Census 1991, 2001 and 2011. Registrar General and Census Commissioner of India, Ministry of Home Affairs, Government of India.
2. OTV 2007 reporting on television.
3. Interview which was of part study

4. As per SRS (2004-06), Odisha's MMR in 2007 was 303 as compared to Kerala's 95, Tamil Nadu's 111 and India's 254 (See Government of India 2011); As per SRS (2006), the IMR of Odisha was 73 as compared to Kerala's 15, Tamil Nadu's 37 and India's 57 (See Government of India 2007). According to SRS (2014-16) the MMR of Odisha stands at 180 in contrast with Kerala's 46, Tamil Nadu's 66 and India's 130 (See Government of India 2018). As per SRS (2016) the IMR of Odisha is 44 as compared to Kerala's 10, Tamil Nadu's 17 and India's 34 (See Government of India 2017).
5. Orissa Alliance on CRC (2007), *Report of the Fact Finding Team on Female Foeticide in Nayagarh*, Bhubaneswar, URL: http://hindtoday.com/Blogs ViewBlogsV2.aspx?HTAdvtId=743&HTAdvtPlace Code=IND674OR21NAYAG (accessed on 26 July, 2015).
6. Judgement of the High Court of Odisha in the case of Dr. Sudhir Kumar Brahma vs. State Of Orissa on 4th September, 2007, URL: http://legalplug.in/doc/1338997/ (accessed on 21 June, 2014).
7. Ibid.
8. Seminar on the issue of Declining Child Sex Ratio held in 2004.
9. As part of this research, interviews were held with service providers like doctors, technicians, radiologist etc. it was seen that it was mostly private clinics which offer the service of sex determination and sex selective abortion. All of this was available at a price and it catered to a clientele which came to them through middlemen and was based on profit motives. (Source: Nanda 2018).
10. The collection of principles popularly known as Say's law were profoundly influential upon economists of the classical era. The popularly accepted definition of Say's law is that "supply creates its own demand". It never appeared in the writings of Say nor were they accepted as the normative standard until the assent of Keynes. For more details see Tarnell (2011).
11. Information gathered from Legal officer of the PCPNDT cell Odisha government in 2012 during the course of field work 2011-13. As per the latest government report, up to March 2018, 66 cases have been filed, with conviction in 4 cases (See Government of India 2018a).
12. Interviews held as part of this research in state capital Bhubaneswar during 2011-13.
13. FGDs and interviews conducted during field work for this

research conducted in the period 2011-13

14. Two-child norm in Odisha : ineligible to contest elections for rural local bodies if have more than 2 children
15. Interview with the 1991 Census Commissioner of India who said that the chief minister of Odisha took a knee jerk reaction to the increasing population size of India and misunderstood the 'Population Momentum Factor' despite the declining fertility and was not sensitive to the low fertility situation in his state in the conundrum of high mortality of women and children, nor was he aware of its gender insensitive fall out.
16. See Mazumdar and Krishnaji (2001), Visaria (2006) and Buch (2006) for details on how coercive population policies like the two child norm are detrimental to women's rights and can increase the phenomenon of sex selective abortion.
17. Interview with Executive Director Population Foundation of India in 2009 indicated that PFI's advocacy against the two-child norm was successful and State Govt was going to remove the norm; but the C.M. stopped short of the decision due to the emotional attachment to his father's decision.
18. Interview with women respondent of Cuttack district.
19. Interview held in Kantapada Block of Cuttack district for this research study.
20. Draft policy and background paper on status of women and Girl child Policy available at the UNFPA Odisha office Bhubaneswar 2013. The researcher was also part of the process of consultation for the drafting of policy.
21. Consultation meeting held in the period 2012-2013. The researcher was a participant in most of the meetings. Other information was gathered from reports of consultation meetings available at the UNFPA Odisha office Bhubaneswar. The Government of Odisha published the 'Odisha State Policy for Girls and Women-2014', URL: http://wcdodisha.gov.in/Application//uploadDocuments/plugin/doc20170729_123119.pdf (accessed on 17 March 2016).
22. FGDs and interviews conducted for this research during the field work from 2012- 13.
23. Ibid.
24. Kalinga Nagar, Niyamgiri, Dhenkanal and Kujang areas.
25. These districts are Debagarh, Sundargarh, Keonjhar, Mayurbhanj, Ganjam, Gajapati, Kandhamal, Baudha, Nuapada, Kalahandi,

Rayagada, Nabarangpur, Koraput and Malkangiri.

26. The researcher interviewed parents of children who were studying at Kalinga Institute of Social Sciences in Bhubaneswar which caters only to tribal population in 2013 as part of her field work.
27. Interview with Surya Shankar Dash, a noted activist and documentary film maker working with the Dongria Kondh in Niyamgiri.
28. Ravinder Kaur points to the fact that these marriages may also have a positive impact on gender relations since the patriarchal northern values get negotiated by women from progressive regions like Kerala, Odisha, West Bengal and others (See Larsen and Kaur 2013).
29. Information collected through interviews and FGDs conducted in tribal regions in Koraput district and Medical Service providers in other parts of Odisha for this research study.

REFERENCES

Agnihotri, Satish B. (2003), "Survival of the Girl Child: Tunnelling Out of the Chakravyuha", *Economic and Political Weekly*, October 11.

Bardhan, Pranab (1974), "On Life and Death Questions," *Economic and Political Weekly*, 9(32-34), Special Number, August, pp.1293-1304.

Buch, Nirmala (2006), *The Law of Two Child Norm in Panchayats*, New Delhi: Concept Publishing Company.

Government of India (2007), *SRS Bulletin: Sample Registration System*, Vol. 42, No. 1, October, Registrar General of India, New Delhi.

Government of India (2011), *Maternal & Child Mortality and Total Fertility Rates, Sample Registration System (SRS)*, Registrar General, India, New Delhi, 7th July, URL: http://censusindia.gov.in/vital_statistics/SRS_Bulletins/MMR_release_ 070711. pdf, accessed on 10 Dec. 2012.

Government of India (2017), *SRS Bulletin: Sample Registration System*, Vol. 51, No. 1, September, Registrar General of India, New Delhi.

Government of India (2018), *Special Bulletin on Maternal Mortality In India 2014-16, Sample Registration System*, May, Registrar General of India, New Delhi.

Government of India (2018a), *Data on Sealing & Seizer, ongoing Court Cases Convictions under the PC and PNDT Act*, Ministry of Health & Family Welfare, New Delhi, URL: https://mohfw.gov.

in/newshighlights/data-sealing-seizer-ongoing-court-cases-convictions-under-pc-and-pndt-act (accessed on 23 October, 2018).

Hans, Asha and Amrita Patel (2012), "Women of Odisha: Status and Challenges", *Odisha Review*, February-March.

Larsen, Mattias and Ravinder Kaur (2013), "Signs of Change? Sex Ratio Imbalance and Shifting Social Practices in Northern India", *Economic and Political Weekly*, August 31, Vol. XLVIII, No. 35.

Mazumdar, Vina and N. Krishnaji (2001), *Enduring Conundrum, India's Sex Ratio: Essays in Honour of Ashok Mitra*. Delhi: Rainbow Publishers.

Miller, Barbara D. (1981), *The Endangered Sex: Neglect of Female Children in Rural North India*. Ithaca, NY: Cornell University Press.

Mohanty, Bidyut (2005), 'Women and Panchayats in India: Creating a New Space for Leadership in Asia', URL: http://biblioteca.clacso.edu.ar/ar/libros/reggen/pp27.pdf (accessed on 14 May 2017).

Mohanty, Bidyut (2017), 'Missing Women' in China and India. Do girl children have any hope in 2020?' in Richard A. Falk et al. (eds.), *Exploring Emergent Global Thresholds: Towards 2030*, New Delhi: Orient Blackswan.

Nanda, Bijayalaxmi (2018), *Sex-Selective Abortion and the State: Policies, Laws and Institutions in India*, New Delhi: Shakti Books, an Imprint of Har Anand Publications.

Padhi, Ranjana and Pramodini Pradhan (2013), "Women in Resistance Struggles in Odisha", *Mainstream*, Vol LI, No. 33, August 3.

Patel, Tulsi (2007), "Female Foeticide, Family Planning and State-Society Intersection in India", in Tulsi Patel (ed.) *Sex-selective Abortion in India: Gender, Society and New Reproductive Technologies*. New Delhi: Sage Publications, p. 317.

Rao, Mohan (2004), *From Population Control to Reproductive Health: Malthusian Arithmetic*, New Delhi: Sage Publications.

Sekher, T.V. (2012), *Special Financial Incentive Schemes for the Girl Child in India: A Review of Select Schemes*, New Delhi: United Nation Population Fund.

Tarnell, Brown (2011), *A brief look at Say's Law: Attempting to understand its relevance and meaning*, Liberty University, URL: https://mpra.ub.uni-muenchen.de/39365/3/MPRA_paper_39365.pdf (accessed on 15 March, 2016).

Visaria, Leela et al. (2006), "Two Child Norm: Victimising the Vulnerable", *Economic and Political Weekly*, Vol. XLI, No. 1, pp. 1-48.

4

Correlates of Health Care Among Women and Children in Odisha: Understanding Barriers in Access

Sanghamitra S Acharya, Mala Mukherjee and Golak Patro

Introduction

Odisha is a land which transformed a warrior into a compassionate ruler way back in historical times; Emperor Ashoka, denounced war and embraced Buddhism. The State has many temples which inspire worshiping feminine versions of god. Odisha is also the land where women experience poverty, deprivation and marginalization. They are left without education or are less educated., many of them are undernourished, earn less and are not independent to make decisions for their family or self. In contrast, the State has also produced many women of repute in the spheres of freedom struggle, politics and art, film and literature. To name a few, Rama Devi Choudhury (well known as Rama Devi), the legendary freedom fighter and social reformer, who participated in the freedom struggle and inspired the women in Odisha to step into the public sphere. She dedicated herself to the cause of Bhoodan and Gramdan movement of Acharya Vinoba Bhave. Sarala Devi was the first Oriya freedom fighter who would be remembered as the most outstanding literary feminist who contributed to the making of modern Odisha despite her modest educational background. Sanjukta Panigrahi embraced Odissi, the ancient classical dance at an early age and known as its foremost exponent across the world. Parbati Ghosh epitomises Odia Cinema. She has won three national awards in the best Oriya film category. She acted and produced her own films, establishing herself as a pioneer woman director in the country. Pratibha Ray is one of the leading fiction writers in India today, and is also known through her translated works. Tulasi Munda, social activist, has worked to spread literacy among the tribal people and released hundreds of tribal children from being exploited as daily labourers by setting up a school in the mining area. This passion of ensuring education for children is noteworthy also because she herself never got an opportunity to go to a school. Nandini Satpathy, first woman Chief Minister of the State, was also elected as Rajya Sabha member twice. She contributed to Odia literature through her short stories and poems and was conferred the Sahitya Bharti Samman (Discover Odisha. Editorial, 2013).

The State also has a marked geopolitical presence as it shares inland borders with West Bengal, Andhra Pradesh, Chhattisgarh and Jharkhand in the west and opens into the Bay of Bengal in the east. The geopolitical relevance is evident in the historical past of the state. Odisha has significant number of tribal and dalit (Scheduled Castes) populations. All these tribes and castes are indigenous in origin and most of them preserve valuable folk culture. Women have played important roles in preserving this nuance through their active and inactive participation in many ways. This paper, therefore endeavours to understand the conditions of women specially dalits, in Odisha, and highlight the issues pertaining to health and address probable policy regimes. To achieve this objective, demographic, social, and economic and health indicators have been analysed. It also attempts to understand the gaps which remain in attainment of the MDGs and the probable directions towards attainment of the SDGs.

Understanding the Demographic Characteristics

Demographic characteristics are important for understanding the population composition in order to impress and influence policy making and planning process. Unlike its historical magnificent past Odisha has been a State with poor development indicators for a very long time, despite rich mineral resources. The State has about 17% SC and about 23% ST population. Most of them are found mainly in rural areas. Nearly 14 per cent of the State's urban population is SC and only 9 per cent is ST, but in rural area, more than 18 per cent is SC and 26 per cent is ST. Thus, the State has a significant segment of dalit and tribal population (Table 1).

Table 1: Distribution of Scheduled Caste and Tribe Population

STATE	*% SC*	*% ST*	*Name of Districts*	*%SC*	*%ST*
ODISHA Total	**17.13**	**22.85**	Dhenkanal	19.62	13.59
ODISHA Rural	**17.78**	**25.72**	Khordha	13.21	5.11
ODISHA Urban	**13.85**	**8.51**	Puri	19.14	0.36
DISTRICTS			Ganjam	19.50	3.37
Bargarh	20.17	18.98	Gajapati	6.78	54.29
Jharsuguda	18.05	30.50	Kandhamal	15.76	53.58
Sambalpur	18.43	34.12	Baudh	23.79	12.55
Debagarh	16.67	35.33	Subarnapur	25.60	9.37
Sundargarh	9.16	50.75	Balangir	17.88	21.05
Kendujhar	11.62	45.45	Nuapada	13.46	33.80
Mayurbhanj	7.33	58.72	Kalahandi	18.17	28.50
Baleshwar	20.62	11.88	Rayagada	14.41	55.99
Bhadrak	22.23	2.02	Nabarangapur	14.53	55.79
Kendrapara	21.51	0.66	Koraput	14.25	50.56
Jagatsinghapur	21.83	0.69	Malkangiri	22.55	57.83
Cuttack	19.00	3.57	Anugul	18.81	14.10
Jajapur	23.72	8.29	Nayagarh	14.17	6.10

Source: RGI, Census 2011

According to 2011 Census, Odisha has 17.13 per cent SC population, but proportion of SC population varies district wise. Districts like Subarnapur (26%), Baudh (24%) Jajapur

(24%) and Malkangiri (23%) have major concentration of dalit population. All these districts are situated in remote locations or away from the coastal area. Odisha also has nearly 23 per cent of ST population and high concentration of ST population found in Mayurbhanj (59%), Malkangiri (58%), Koraput, Nabarangapur, Rayagada, Gajapati, Kandhamal and Sundargarh districts which records more than 50 per cent population in ST category. It is interesting to note that in Cuttack, one of the most advanced and urbanized districts of Odisha, both SC (19%) and ST (4%) population are lower as compared to other districts. Maximum concentration of dalit and tribal population of Odisha is mainly found in remote and backward districts and not in the coastal area. ST population is extremely low in coastal districts of Bhadrak, Puri and Kendrapara (Fig 1).

Fig. 1: Concentration of Scheduled Caste Population in Odisha (2011)

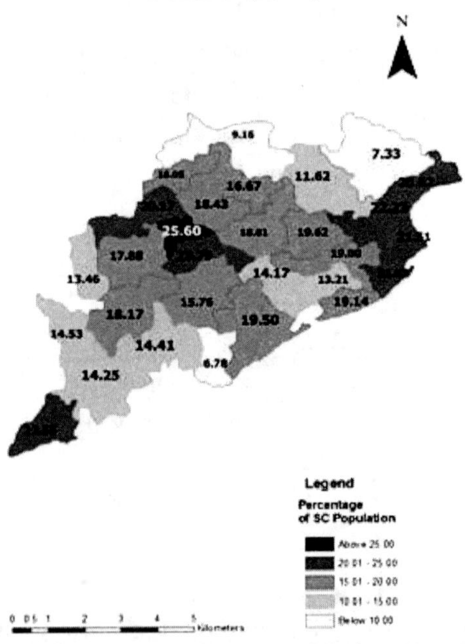

Source: RGI, (2011), Census of India, Odisha, Provisional Tables, Registrar General of India.

Mapping the sub castes in Odisha reflects that Pan/Pano are the largest group constituting about 18% of the total SC population of the State. Dewar and Doms are the next largest caste groups constituting about 11 and 10%. Baghetis are the smallest group comprising of less than 0.5%. Dalits in Odisha are divided into more than 60 castes. Among them, Pan or Pano are numerically dominant and constitute 18 per cent of the total SC population. Traditionally, this community is into basket making. They are divided into many other sub-castes and consider themselves superior to Hadis (scavenger). They are meat eaters but do not take horse meat. Pan community has its own cultural traits where widow remarriage and divorce are permitted. Pan Vaishnava acted as priests among this community and some Pan sub-castes are engaged in specific traditional works like cane weaving, performing of music and working as chowkidars or guards in villages (GoO, 1990).

Dom is the second most important SC sub-caste; they help in cremation of human bodies and burying of dead animals. They also make bamboo baskets, mats and cane goods. Dhobi or washermen is another SC sub-caste which constitutes nearly 10 per cent of the total SC population. Dewar also known as Kaibartya constitutes 11 per cent of the total SC population of the State and they are a fishing community who mainly live in coastal Odisha. These communities preserves some important folk cultures like Horse Dance and worship their boats during spring (Chaitra). They traditionally believe in devi cult (Goddess Vasuli) and the name Dewar has been derived from devi. Ganda (weaver caste), Bauri, Khadala and Kandra are the other main SC sub-castes in Odisha (Table 2).

Table 2: Dsitribution of Constituent Castes of the Scheduled Caste in Odisha, 2011

Constituent Castes	*Percentage*	*Sub Castes*	*Percentage*
Bagheti, etc.	0.48	Gokha	3.16
Bauri	7.47	Hadi, etc.	3.45
Bhoi	1.63	Kandra, etc.	7.63

Chamar, etc.	2.50	Khadala	7.63
Dewar	10.67	Namasudra	2.16
Dandasi	1.00	Pan/Pano	17.73
Dhobi, etc.	9.63	Generic Castes, etc.	1.60
Dom, etc.	10.14	Others	8.52
Ganda	9.30	Ghasi, etc.	1.74

Source: Census 2011

Household Composition, Housing Characteristics and Wealth Index

Like India, Odisha too is predominantly rural. Only one-sixth of households in Odisha are in urban areas, and the remaining are in rural areas. Average household size in Odisha is 4.5 members. It is noteworthy that thirteen per cent of households are headed by women. One-fifth of households are scheduled caste, 23 per cent belong to a scheduled tribe, and 27 per cent are other backward classes (OBC). Thirty per cent of Odisha's households do not belong to scheduled castes, scheduled tribes, or other backward classes.

About one-third of households (32%) live in *pucca* houses and almost the same proportion live in *kachha* houses. Forty-five per cent of households (38% of rural households and 84% of urban households) have electricity. About 80% households (88% rural and 41% urban) in Odisha have no toilet facilities. More than three-fourths (78%) of households use an improved source of drinking water (84% urban and 77% rural), but only 5 per cent have piped water in their dwellings, yards, or plots. Sixty-five per cent of households get their drinking water from a tube well or borehole. Only 18 per cent of households treat their drinking water to make it potable (7 per cent boil the water, 6 per cent use a ceramic, sand, or other filter, 5 per cent strain the water through a cloth, and three per cent use other methods). Eighty-nine per cent of households use solid fuels for cooking.

The wealth index is constructed by combining information on 33 household assets and housing characteristics, such as ownership of consumer items, type of dwelling, source of water, and availability of electricity, into a single index. The household population is divided into five equal groups of 20 per cent each (quintiles) at the national level from 1 (lowest, poorest) to 5 (highest, wealthiest). Since the quintiles of the wealth index are defined at the national level, the proportion of the population of a particular state that falls in any specific quintile will vary across states. Compared to the national average, Odisha's population is poor as 40 per cent of Odisha's population is in the lowest wealth quintile, compared to 20 per cent of India's population. Forty-two per cent of Odisha's households (48 per cent in rural areas and 13 per cent in urban areas) are in the lowest wealth quintile and only 21 per cent are in the two highest wealth quintile combined. Poverty continues to remain the major concern to be addressed (Panda, 1997; de Haan and Dubey, 2005); especially for women in Odisha.

Sex Ratio—Genesis of Gender Differentials

Sex Ratio of Odisha is higher than national average. Odisha has better sex ratio compared to India as a whole and north Indian states. The State records 979 sex ratio which is 989 in rural areas and 932 in urban areas. However, when examined across social groups and rural and urban spaces, there are evident differentials. Notably, urban sex ratio is remarkably low. SC (987) have better sex ratio than total population. Urban sex ratio of SC is lower than that of their rural sex ratio. It indicates that male selective migration in urban areas is prevalent in Odisha. Child sex ratio of total population is 941; it is higher in rural areas (946) and lower in urban areas (913). It is important to note that SCs have better child sex ratio than the total population both rural as well as urban areas. (Table 3).

Table 3: Sex Ratio of Adult and Child Population in Odisha

Total/ Rural/ Urban	*Total Population*	*Scheduled Caste*
Adult Population		
Total	979	987
Rural	989	988
Urban	932	979
Child Population		
Total	941	951
Rural	946	951
Urban	913	950

Source: RGI, Census 2011

Differentials in School attendance among children

In Odisha 83 per cent of children of ages 6-17 years attend school, (86% in urban areas and 82% in rural areas). School attendance is almost universal at the age of 6-14 years (92%) and then drops to 66 per cent. there is no gender disparity in school attendance but in the age group of 15-17 years 63 per cent girls and 70 per cent boys attend schools (Fig 2).

Fig. 2: Children Attending School by Age

	6-10 YEARS	11-14 YEARS	15-17 YEARS
Male	96	92	70
Female	96	91	63

Source: International Institute for Population Sciences (IIPS) and ICF, 2017. *National Family Health Survey (NFHS-4), India, 2015-16: Odisha*. Mumbai: IIPS.

Gender disparity is found in duration of schooling. More than 32% women respondents record no schooling, but 16.3% men respondents are found in this group. The data shows that 19.8 per cent men and 17.7 per cent women respondents record less than 5 years of schooling, 39.2 per cent men and 33.1 per cent women record 5-9 years of schooling, 11 per cent men and 8.8 per cent women record 10-11 years of schooling. The last category reveals 13 per cent men and 8.2 per cent women in 12 or more years of schooling.

Therefore, gender disparity in education is evident in the school age population in Odisha. However, the extent and direction of this gender disparity varies greatly by age and urban-rural residence (Table 4).

Table 4: School Attending Population (6-17 years) in Odisha by Sex and Place of Residence, 2014-15

Population Aged 6-17 Years Attending School (2014-15)				
	Urban %		*Rural %*	
Age in Years	*Male*	*Female*	*Male*	*Female*
6-10 (Primary)	96.9	97.8	96.1	95.5
6-13 (Elementary)	94.9	95.5	94.2	93.6
11-13 (Upper primary)	91.7	92.1	91.2	90.5
14-15 (Secondary)	82.3	76.7	76	71.3
16-17 (Higher secondary)	59.6	57	48.9	38

Source: International Institute for Population Sciences (IIPS) and ICF, 2017. *National Family Health Survey (NFHS-4), India, 2015-16: Odisha*. Mumbai: IIPS.

In urban and rural areas, there is not much difference in elementary school education. In urban areas, girls' school attendance in this elementary level is higher than the boys (96.9 per cent for boys and 97.8 per cent for girls in primary and 94.9 for boys and 95.5 for girls in elementary level). However, in the Secondary level (14-15 years), girls' attendance dropped to 76.7 per cent and boys remained 82.3 per cent; the gap is 5.6. In the higher secondary (16-17 years), boys' attendance is 59.6 per cent, slightly higher than the girls' attendance rate of 57.0 per cent (Table 4).

In rural areas, school attendance of boys and girls always remained unequal. In the primary and elementary level, only one per cent gap is visible, and more than 90 per cent of girls and boys attend school education in primary, elementary and upper primary levels. in the secondary level (14-15 years) male attendance rate is 76 and female attendance rate is 71.3 per cent. In the higher secondary level the gap widens, for male it is 48.9 per cent or nearly 50 per cent and for female it is 38 per cent (10.9%). This influences the autonomy in fertility behaviour (Jeejebhoy, 2001) and health care (Baru et. al, 2015). The differentials are often due to the denial of access to resources and consequent deprivation.

There are large differentials in fertility by wealth and education. At current fertility rates, women in the lowest wealth quintile will have 1-4 children more than women in the highest wealth quintile. Women with no education will have 1-2 children more than women with 10 or more years of education (Fig 3). The wealth quintile data for Odisha for NFHS 4 is not available as yet, therefore NFHS-3 (2005-06) data has been used.

Fig. 3: Education and Wealth Index

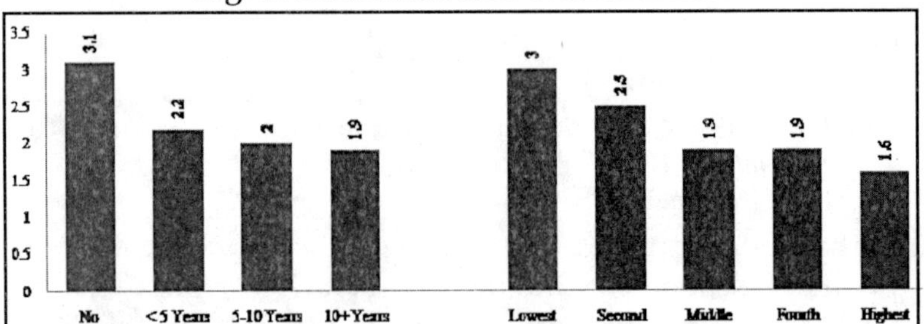

Source: International Institute for Population Sciences (IIPS) and ICF, 2017. *National Family Health Survey (NFHS-4), India, 2015-16: Odisha*. Mumbai: IIPS.

Effective Literacy and Work Participation

The overall effective literacy rate of Odisha is 72.87 per cent. It reduces in rural Odisha to 70.22 per cent and increases in urban Odisha to 85.75 per cent. The rural-urban gap in effective literacy rate is above 15 per cent. Male literacy rate in Odisha is above 81 per cent and in urban areas it is above 90 per cent. On the other hand, over all female literacy rate is 64 per cent and it is further lower in rural areas (60.74%) but better in urban areas (above 80 per cent). Gap in male-female literacy rate is above 18 per cent; but in urban areas it is 10.30 per cent (Table 4). The opportunities available for males are more than the females in much the same way in urban to rural places. The urban male is best endowed in terms of literacy and the rural female is worst off.

Table 5: Effective Literacy in Odisha

Odisha	*% Literate*	*% Male Literate*	*% Female Literate*	*Male-Female Gap*
Total	72.87	81.59	64.01	17.58
Rural	70.22	79.65	60.74	18.91
Urban	85.75	90.72	80.42	10.30
Effective Literacy Rate Scheduled Caste Population, Odisha 2011				
	% Literate	*% Male Literate*	*% Female Literate*	*Male-Female Gap*
Total	69.02	79.21	58.76	20.44
Rural	68.05	78.45	57.59	20.86
Urban	75.18	83.97	66.23	17.74

Source: RGI, Census 2011

Literacy rate among the SCs is lower than that of the total population; but SC males have around 80 per cent literacy rate, while female literacy rate is below 60 per cent. Male-female gap in literacy is above 20 per cent for SC; only in urban area it is 17 per cent whereas it is 10 per cent for total population. If this is contrasted with economic indicators like work participation rate (WPR), then it is noteworthy that despite lower literacy, WPR is almost same (42%) among SC and total population as well as total rural (43.2%) and rural SC (42.5%) population. WPR of rural male (56.53%) is higher than rural SC (56.14) male, though the difference is negligible. It is imperative to note that the WPR of urban SC women is higher than urban total female working population. This points to the low paid works in which comparatively less educated women would be getting engaged (Table 6).

Table 6: Work Participation Rate Differentials in Odisha (in %)

ODISHA	*Persons*	*Male*	*Female*
Total	41.79	56.11	27.16
Rural	43.19	56.53	29.69
Urban	34.81	54.08	14.12
Scheduled Caste	*Persons*	*Male*	*Female*
Total	41.60	55.73	27.28
Rural	42.49	56.14	28.69
Urban	35.85	53.11	18.22

Source: RGI, Census 2011

It becomes important to understand why some get educated but do not participate in work and remain unemployed. The State's propensity to absorb those who graduate from various institutions at different levels varies and results in prolonged spells of vacant positions in different departments. An analysis of unemployment across different social groups beyond the scheduled castes, is imperative at this junction when the overall economic development is the priority of the government. The overall unemployment rate in Odisha is 56, higher among females (76) compared to males (51). Urban unemployment rate is higher (93) compared to rural areas (51). Female unemployment is higher in both rural and urban areas, but it is very high in urban areas (243) whereas male urban unemployment rate is 70. It may be noted that unemployment rate is highest for general population (82) and OBC (62) and lowest for SC and ST (38 and 39). It is more acute for general females (234) compared to their male counterparts (66). Unemployment is higher among ST males (43) compared to the ST females (29); but SC females reveals a completely different picture. SC females record higher unemployment rate compared to their male counterpart. In urban areas, female unemployment is very high across all social groups compared to their male counterparts. Female unemployment is highest for OBC (323), followed by general (285) and ST (245). ST males in urban areas record highest unemployment rate (116) across all social groups. In rural areas, female unemployment rate is highest for general females (215), followed by OBC (78), SC (47) and ST (22). Therefore, unemployment is an acute problem in urban areas of Odisha and women are the worst hit (Table 7). More than half of SC women are unemployed as compared to about one-third ST. There are more ST men (43%) than SC men (34%) who are unemployed despite State efforts to reach out to the poor through MNREGA.

Table 7: Unemployment Rate in Odisha (in %)

Social Groups	*Rural*			*Urban*			*Total*		
	Male	*Female*	*Person*	*Male*	*Female*	*Person*	*Male*	*Female*	*Person*
SC	31	47	34	62	130	75	34	55	39
ST	38	22	33	116	245	142	43	29	38
OBC	52	78	57	74	323	101	55	92	62
General	67	215	80	63	285	87	66	234	82
TOTAL	48	62	51	70	243	93	51	76	56

Source: MLE (2014), *Report on Third Annual Employment & Unemployment Survey (2012-13)*, Vol. I, Government of India, Ministry of Labour & Employment, Labour Bureau, Chandigarh

Odisha has experienced development in socio-economic, political and cultural spheres since the last decade and a half. The economic growth rate has been consistent and above the national average (Pattanayak, 2010). Poverty has reduced from 57.2% in 2004-05 to 37% in 2009-10. The State aims to achieve 9% growth during the 12th Five Year Plan (2012-17) and the budgetary allocation for the 12th plan is over Rs 1.24 lakh crores (MoLE, 2014). However, some issues need attention in this pursuit of achieving economic growth. Since the beginning of the new millennium, the development interventions through targets have been the pathway. The Millennium Development Goals (MDG) adopted by the United Nations, were adopted by countries and thus the states, to follow up and integrate them into national and regional plans and try to achieve those goals in a time-bound manner. The timeline for the MDGs ended in 2015. Most targets remained unattained both for India and for Odisha. Achievements envisioned by the MDGs definitely require an introspection of development, basic human rights, entitlements to the poor and welfare of women in Odisha.

Marital Age and Fertility

In India, legal age at marriage is 18 years for girls; this is the age which is considered as the adult age. However, in Odisha, SC girls are recording lower age at marriage. More than one per cent SC girls are married between 10-14 years of age. When they are 15-19 years of age, 16.46 per cent are married. It is interesting to note that at these two age groups only 2 per cent SC boys get married. This trend is same in both rural and urban areas. Therefore, many dalit girls in Odisha get married at an adolescent age (Census, 2011). The median age at first marriage is 17.9 years among women aged 20-49 year and 23.6 years among men aged 25-49. On an average, men get married six years later than women. More than one-third of women aged 20-24 years (37%) get married before the legal minimum age of 18, and 22 per cent of men age 25-29 years get married before the legal minimum age of 21. At current fertility levels, a woman in Odisha will have an average of 2.4 children in her lifetime. Fertility has decreased during last two decades from 2.9 during 1992-93 (NFHS-1) to 2.5 during 1998-99 (NFHS-2,), in 2005-06, it reduced to 2.37 and in NFHS 4 (2015-16) further to 2.05. Fertility in Odisha (2015-16) is approaching the replacement level. In rural areas it is 2.12 children per woman, much higher than in urban areas where the fertility rate has already reached below replacement level (with a total fertility rate of 1.73 children per woman).

Percentage of ever married SC women and number of surviving children reveals that in Odisha by the end of the child bearing age, more than 25 per cent women would have more than five living children. The most striking finding is that teenage pregnancy is not uncommon here. At the age of 15-19 years, 25.66 per cent women have one living child and 4.37 per cent have two children. More than 1 per cent women have 4 living children at this age. The next age group, 20-24 years records 37 per cent women with one child, 21 per cent with two children and nearly 7 per cent with three children. Therefore, like a low age at marriage, a low age of pregnancy is also noted here. Teenage pregnancy is no doubt harmful for both mother and child; it may be one of the reasons of high infant and child mortality. Around 70% women have up to three children who survive the adversities, social as well as health related. All the programmes directed towards delay in the birth of first child, particularly after 21 years seems to be ineffective or less effective in Odisha. It is appalling to note that more than one-fourth of teenaged girls aged 15-19, and ever married, have one surviving child. High risk pregnancies occurring in higher ages are also more (Table 8)

Table 8: Marital Status and Surviving Children for Scheduled Caste Women in Odisha

Age group	*% Ever married women*	*Number of surviving children*					
		0	*1*	*2*	*3*	*4*	*5+*
All ages	54.44	14.50	16.51	20.38	20.12	14.43	14.06
15-19	16.85	68.02	25.66	4.37	0.84	1.10	0.00
20-24	72.92	33.91	36.52	20.85	6.59	1.38	0.75
25-29	94.94	14.92	22.19	30.50	21.58	8.02	2.79
30-34	98.27	8.58	12.23	24.74	28.30	17.17	8.98
35-39	98.99	6.82	10.12	20.32	26.72	20.52	15.49
40-44	99.11	6.92	10.27	18.41	24.57	20.57	19.26
45-49	99.43	7.11	11.37	18.22	22.53	19.58	21.19
50-54	99.52	8.92	12.60	17.41	20.07	18.10	22.91
55-59	99.69	9.08	12.47	16.24	18.97	18.04	25.22
60-64	99.34	12.09	13.61	15.58	17.13	16.58	25.01
65-69	99.40	12.77	13.23	14.44	16.05	16.39	27.12

70-74	99.03	14.96	14.57	14.16	14.86	15.01	26.44
75-79	98.63	14.50	14.55	13.58	14.45	14.68	28.23
80+	97.48	15.93	15.97	14.03	15.07	14.26	24.74

Source: RGI, Census 2011

An insight into the economic status of women who get married and contribute to the fertility reflects some interesting trends. Only 10.4% are in the highest wealth quintile (WQ), while more than four times of this share, 44% are in the lowest quintile. More than 46% ever-married urban women are in the highest wealth quintile as against about 8% who are in the lowest quintile (Fig 4). This also suggests rural feminization of women in Odisha.

Fig. 4: Women by Wealth Index and Place of Residence

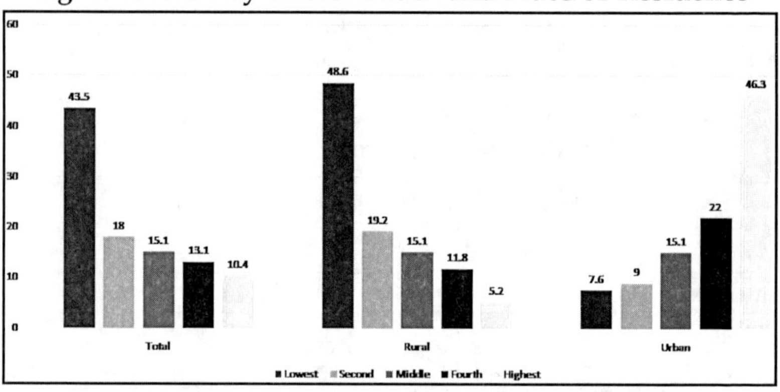

Source: International Institute for Population Sciences (IIPS) and ICF, 2017. *National Family Health Survey (NFHS-4), India, 2015-16: Odisha*. Mumbai: IIPS.

Disparity in Health Facilities Across State

The health services in Odisha, like the other states, function through a three-tier system in the public sector and a parallel system in the private sector. Odisha provides health service delivery, through health care facilities—sub-centres, primary health centres, community health centres and district hospitals in the public sector; and uni-clinics, polyclinics and super-speciality hospitals in the private sector (Table 9). There are also health facilities run by the trusts-charitable and non-charitable, non-governmental and community based organizations. Access to healthcare facilities is determined by the propensity more than the severity of the illness (Baru et al, 2015; HMIS, MoHFW, 2013).

Table 9: Health Care Service System in Public and Private Sector

Public Sector	*Private*
Sub Centres	Uni-Clinics (Single Specialist/ General Physician)
Primary Health Centre	Polyclinics (Multi- Specialist Centres)
Community Health Centre	Specialty Hospitals/ Polyclinics
Tertiary Hospitals/ Medical College / Research Institute	Super-specialty Hospitals/ Medical College/ Research institute

Source: IIPS and MoHFW (2010) *District level Household and Facility Survey 2007-08 Orissa.* International Institute for Population Sciences, Mumbai, Minstry of Health and Family Welfare, New Delhi.

Ante-natal care is one of the important components of maternal and child health care and these services are provided during pregnancies to avoid complications. Indian government as well as private health care centres provide ANC, but government health centres offer subsidized services and thus, most of the women (54%) access ANC from government health centres. Odisha is no exception; in this state nearly 60 per cent women get ANC from government sources. Women of Odisha heavily rely on subsidized services and only 15 per cent of them have received ANC from private centres, whereas in India, 36 per cent women receive ANC services from non-governmental sources. It confirms that government health care centres are the single important source of health care services in Odisha. It is the same across all the districts. However in some districts, like Khordha (34%) and Bhadrak (37%) private centres are a popular source of ANC services. Therefore, in Odisha, women mainly receive ANC services from government centres. Very few receive services from community based health facility; Raygada (15.8%) and Koraput (12%) are the only districts where a significant percentage of women receive ANC services from community based health care centres. Aggregate data shows Odisha records better access to ANC service compare to rest of India because 23.2 per cent women have received full ANC whereas in India only 19 per cent women are found in this category. Access to full ANC is above 60 per cent in all the districts except Kendujhar (46%), Mayurbhanj (44.7), Gajapati (33.8%), Bhadrak (48%) and Nabarangpur (48.5). (Appendix A)

Percentage of Women (15-45 years) Receiving Ante-natal Check-up from Private Institutes in Odisha (2007-08)

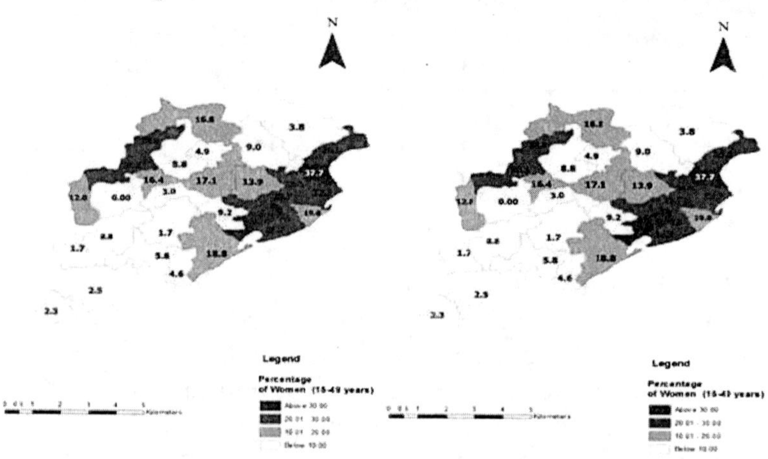

It is evident that 16% pregnant women do not avail ANC services and more than 30 per cent of home deliveries are not attended by skilled health workers. Low birth weight is very high in Khandamal. Some districts like Cuttack, Khordha, Baudh, Gajapati, Rayagada and Koraput perform poorly in terms of service delivery, performance and access. The two reasons identified are outreach and drop outs. There is drop out in accessing first to the third ANC services; and immunization (HMIS, MoHFW, 2013). It is evident that the districts where higher proportion of governemnt institutions are visited for ANC, the use of private health facilities is lesser. The contrast is visible also in terms of proximity to the neighbouring state of West Bengal where the presence of facilities is higher than the districts in the west (Figs 5a & 5b),

The analysis reveals vast regional disparity and indicates that poorly performing districts are predominantly inhabited by scheduled castes. Districts with more than 20% SC population (see Table 1) have 40-70% institutional delivery. Subarnapur with highest share of SC population, is also one of the districts with the lowest sex ratio (966) but has 93% institutional delivery. The district with highest sex ratio 1031 females per 1000 males, Gajapati, has 63% institutional delivery. Cuttack with lowest sex ratio has 95% in contrast (Table 10). Thus, it is imperative to understand this association and the differences between social-group to find out who are excluded from health care services.

Table 10: Female Aversion and Health Care Utilisation

State/ District	*Sex Ratio (Census 2011)*	*Institutional Delivery (NFHS-4, 2015-16)*	*District*	*Sex Ratio (Census 2011)*	*Institutional Delivery (NFHS-4, 2015-16)*
Odisha	972	85.4	Anugul	941	90.3
Districts			Nayagarh	938	92.5
Bargarh	976	92	Khordha	902	85.1
Jharsuguda	946	95.2	Puri	968	97.8
Sambalpur	969	90.7	Ganjam	998	91.5
Debagarh	980	85.3	Gajapati	1031	63.3
Sundargarh	957	88.2	Kandhamal	1008	72.7
Kendujhar	977	72.7	Baudh	984	82.6
Mayurbhanj	980	85.6	Subarnapur	966	93.3
Baleshwar	953	91.9	Balangir	984	87.1
Bhadrak	974	87.7	Nuapada	1007	84.7
Kendrapara	1014	94.2	Kalahandi	1001	74.5

Jagatsinghapur	963	97.6	Rayagada	1028	71.7
Cuttack	938	94.7	Nabarangapur	991	64.3
Jajapur	972	94	Koraput	999	68.4
Dhenkanal	961	90.1	Malkangiri	997	67.8

Source: International Institute for Population Sciences (IIPS) and ICF, 2017. *National Family Health Survey (NFHS-4), India, 2015-16: Odisha*. Mumbai: IIPS.Census 2011, India

Health Care Utilization

Health care utilization reveals that 61.8 per cent women (15-49 years) have accessed three or more times ante natal cares but only 48.3 per cent got the first ANC during first trimester of their pregnancy. More than 83 per cent have got IFA tablet, 40.9 per cent received post natal check-up. However, the percentage of institutional birth is very low in Odisha, only 35.6 per cent had institutional birth and only 44 per cent births are attended by health personnel. It is also seen, contraceptive use is also very low, only 47 per cent is using it. Social group wise segregation reveals that OBC and others have better access to ante-natal and post-natal cares. Opportunity of having post-natal care is slightly lower for ST (83%) and SC 83%) compare to others (84 %). Access to institutional delivery is lowest for ST (72.5%) followed by SC (86.2%); on the other hand, more than 92.5 per cent upper caste people have accessed this facility. SC records only 86.8 per cent of births are assisted by health personnel and in case of upper caste population more than 66 per cent births are assisted by trained health workers. Usage of contraception is above 36.0 per cent for all social groups except STs (35.8%). Apart from contraception use, distribution of IFA tablet also shows uniformity across social groups. More than 90 per cent SC and OBC women have got IFA tablets, even 91.8 per cent ST women have got it. Therefore, in Odisha, distribution of IFA tablet depicts a success story (Table 11).

Table 11: Maternal Heath in Odisha

Maternal Heath Indicators	*ST*	*SC*	*OBC*	*Others*	*Total*
Percentage who had four or more ANC Visits	59.9	58.5	65	64.3	62
First ante natal visit during first trimester	59.9	63.5	67	66.5	64.1
Given or bought IFA	91.8	89.7	90.3	90	90.5
Women with post-natal check-up	83.4	83.4	86.6	84	84.5
Currently use contraception	35.8	39.8	35.5	34.5	36.2
Last birth at Health Facility	72.5	86.2	92.5	92.5	85.4
Birth assisted by health personnel	75.7	86.8	92.8	92.5	86.6

Source: International Institute for Population Sciences (IIPS) and ICF, 2017. *National Family Health Survey (NFHS-4), India, 2015-16: Odisha*. Mumbai: IIPS.

Note: All numbers are a percentage of population

As a result of the available facilities and the utilization of heath care services, the evident outcome in the form of mortality among infants and children suggests that a lot still needs to be organized and put in place. Comparing with other social groups gives an idea of the position which SC women are likely to be in terms of the health facilities accessed and utilized. The scheduled caste women in Odisha are worse off than their counterparts in the country as well as the State as a whole. Neo-natal mortality is seven percentage points higher than India and marginally lower than that of Odisha. Post neo-natal and infant mortality are about six percentage points higher than that of Odisha. However, child mortality (19.5%) and under 5 mortality (92%) are lower than Odisha by 9.4 and 3.9 percentage points.

Odisha records 28.2%-Neo-natal; 11.5%- Post neo-natal; 39.6 -Infant; 8.8 - child mortality and 48.1%- Under five mortality. Odisha records slightly lower mortality rates for infants and children compared to India as a whole. Social group wise analysis shows that ST records highest Post Neo-natal Mortality (16.3%) followed by OBC (10.5%) and it is lowest for SC (8.7%). Neo-Natal Mortality results in loss of more than 35.5% infants among the STs and OBCs. However, it is comparatively lower for SC and lowest for upper castes or others (21.6%). Infant mortality, child and under five mortality rates are lowest for others but high for other social groups. Under five mortality rate is extremely high for ST (65.6%) followed by SC (45.7%) (Table 12). Therefore, in Odisha, SCs and STs experience higher mortality rates for infants and children. This needs to be understood in the light of less than one-third, 30.2% births occurring in a health facility and less than 40% being assisted by a skilled birth attendant (Table 11). The vulnerable populations do not seem to be facilitated enough for accessing the required care.

Table 12: Infant and Child Mortality in Odisha across Social Groups

Social Groups	*Neo Natal Mortality*	*Post- Neo natal Mortality*	*Infant Mortality*	*Child Mortality*	*Under Five Mortality*
SC	28.3	8.7	37	9	45.7
ST	35.5	16.3	51.8	14.6	65.6
OBC	26.2	10.5	36.7	6.4	42.9
Others	21.6	9.8	31.5	3.8	35.2
Odisha	28.2	11.5	39.6	8.8	48.1
India	29.5	11.3	40.7	9.4	49.7

Source: International Institute for Population Sciences (IIPS) and ICF, 2017. *National Family Health Survey (NFHS-4), India, 2015-16: Odisha*. Mumbai: IIPS. (Table 35, page-75)

Note: All numbers are a percentage of population

The frequently pregnant women among most vulnerable population groups, SCs, STs, urban poor, for instance are exposed to physical vagaries and are often devoid of means to assist them in equipping the body for procreation. This is more than true for women in Odisha. Nearly more than half the women, who are SC and ST, are thin with BMI less than 18.5. Nearly 15% of ST and more than 13% of SC women are severely thin with BMI less than 17. It is noteworthy that 3.5% women in Odisha are obese with more than 30 BMI. Less than 1% of ST and little of 2% SC women are also obese (Table 13).

Table 13: Women with Specific Body Mass Index (BMI) and Anaemia in Odisha

Women with Specific Body Mass Index (BMI)				
Social Groups	*<18.5 (total thin)*	*<17.0 (moderately/ severely thin)*	*25.0> (overweight or obese)*	***30.0> (obese)***
SC	30.4	13.2	12.4	2.2
ST	36.5	14.6	5.5	0.8
OBC	23.5	9.6	18.9	3.7
Others	16.3	6.4	28.8	7.6
Total	26.4	10.9	16.5	3.5
Women with Anemia by Social Groups				
Social Groups	*Mild (10.0-11.9 g/dl)*	*Moderate (7.0-9.9 g/dl)*	*Severe (<7.0 g/dl)*	*Any anaemia (<12.0 g/dl)2*
SC	42.9	11.3	0.9	55
ST	46.9	15.3	1.2	63.3
OBC	38.2	7.9	0.5	46.7
Others	34.6	5.4	0.5	40.4
Total	40.5	9.8	0.7	51

Source: International Institute for Population Sciences (IIPS) and ICF, 2017. *National Family Health Survey (NFHS-4), India, 2015-16: Odisha*. Mumbai: IIPS.

Note: All numbers are Percentage of women age 15-49 with specific body mass index (BMI) levels.

Similar trends are noted for anaemic conditions among women. Anaemia is a general problem in Odisha; more than 51 per cent women have anaemia. NFHS-4 has divided anaemia into mild, moderate and severe. More than 40.5 per cent women have mild anaemia. It is higher for SC/ST women, 46.9 for STs and 42.9 for SCs, as compare to OBC and the others. Nearly 10 per cent women in Odisha have moderate anaemia. About 15 per cent ST and 11.3 per cent SC and 5.4% Other women have moderate anaemia. Occurrence of severe anaemia is highest among SC and ST women. More than 63 per cent ST and 55 per cent SC have anaemia while 40.4 per cent others have it (Table 13; Fig 6). Anaemia levels are such despite more than 90% women in Odisha receiving iron folic acid (IFA) tablets as part of the ante-natal care services. Less than 90% SC women received IFA (Table 11). A point to ponder is that while women from other vulnerable communities receive this service almost at par with the other women, why is it that the SC women lag behind? There are indications of probable exclusion of these women from rendering the service which is reflected in such an outcome.

Fig. 6: Women (15-49 Years) with Anaemia

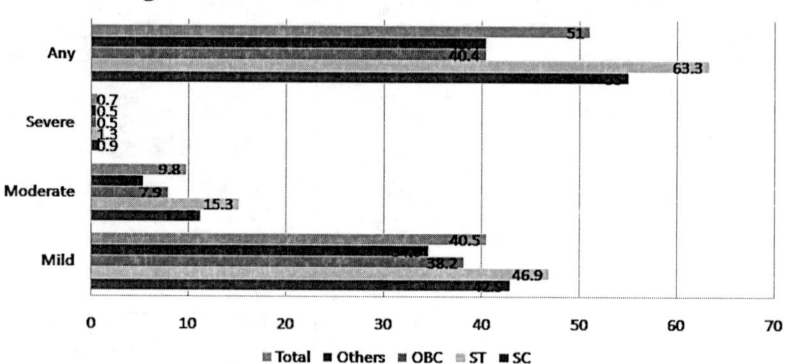

Source: International Institute for Population Sciences (IIPS) and ICF, 2017. *National Family Health Survey (NFHS-4), India, 2015-16: Odisha*. Mumbai: IIPS.

Experience of Violence

Amidst childbearing in anaemic conditions, poor BMI and inadequate health care services, the additional burden which women bear is that of violence, both within and outside the domestic spheres. Most women do not report violence. Only one per cent of the cases that are actually filed end in convictions. The 2009 report of the UN Special Rapporteur on Violence against Women accounts that dalit women in India are raped and beaten by higher castes in the course of their daily lives, such as while working in the field, going to the market or doing domestic work. All of it has impact on health in 2007; the report of the UN Committee Elimination of Discrimination against Women (CEDAW) addressed the issue of dalit women in India. Perception of the dalit woman as the *'other'* is the outcome of patriarchal and brahminical values entrenched in society. It leads to exclusion, invisibility and structural and domestic violence which is the experience of dalit women. Even among women, she is perceived as *'other'* and is at the tail end of the social ladder. It is manifested in her condition of total social, physical, economic and political vulnerability; and evident in the struggle for basic needs such as food or water, and in the submission to sexual violence for the sake of employment. Most dalit families are landless and precariously dependent on the dominant castes for wage labour (Stephen, 2009). Violence perpetrated by one's own spouse can be more devastating than that committed by unknown person because the spouses, according to marital norms, are expected to be caring towards the other. Perpetration of violence by the spouse has its genesis in patriarchal upbringing of the men. It may also be caused due to dissatisfaction in work place, earnings, inability to find work or appropriate work which gets manifested in the reasons linked with domestic indicators such as those revealed through the National Family Health Survey data- not caring for children, not respecting the in-laws, and not cooking good food. Therefore, attitude towards women and girls, define the perpetration of any kind of violence towards them (Jeejebhoy, 2001; Verma et al, 2016) and needs to be addressed through a multi-dimensional strategy.

NFHS-4 data reveals that more than 36.6 per cent women in Odisha face emotional, physical and sexual violence, 35.2% face physical or sexual violence, 8.5% face sexual violence, 33.3% experience Physical violence and 12% face emotional violence. SC and ST women face all sorts of violence higher than OBC and Other women. Occurrence of physical and sexual violence is extremely high among these women; here more than 39.3 per cent women face it. The experience of violence is highest among ST women. About 41.4% experience emotional physical or sexual violence. As regards physical violence, most of it is perpetrated against SC women (37.0%) closely followed by ST women (40.0). They also experience most emotional violence as compared to women from other groups. (Table 13). Poverty related factors such as unemployment, and low wages are likely to be linked with the negative behaviour of the spouses resulting in violence.

Table 14: Experience of Spousal Violence by Women across Social Groups

Social Group	*Type of Violence*				
	Emo-tional	*Physical*	*Sexual*	*Physical or sexual*	*Emotional, physical, or sexual*
SC	15.3	34.8	9.5	37	39.3
ST	14.8	37.9	10.6	40	41.4
OBC	10.8	32.2	8.1	33.8	35.2
OTHERS	8.8	28.1	5.9	29.8	30.6
TOTAL	12.3	33.3	8.5	35.2	36.6

Source: International Institute for Population Sciences (IIPS) and ICF, 2017. *National Family Health Survey (NFHS-4), India, 2015-16: Odisha*. Mumbai: IIPS.

Note: All numbers are a percentage of. ever-married women aged 15-49

Women, Sanitation and Health

India spends 6 % of its GDP annually to meet the health burdens due to lack of basic sanitation and hygiene to its population (UNICEF, WHO et al., 2008). Total census households increased from 98.73 lakh in 2001 to 127.59 lakh in 2011. Total population also increased from 3.68 crore in 2001 to 4.19 crore in 2011. Basic sanitation, toilet coverage is one of the minimum parameters set out by the government to be achieved by 100% by 2015. But the toilet coverage is poor. Currently, a little less than one crore households (98.55 lakhs) are not covered with toilets. Over 80% households which have toilets, are not using them. This is a major challenge for Odisha to achieve sustainable sanitation.

In 2001, households not covered with toilets were 85.1% (83.33 lakh HH). Households having toilets in 2011 reduced to 77.6% (98.55 lakh HH). Though the households not having toilets in percentile terms shown as decreased from 85.1% to 77.6%, during 2011-2011, in absolute numbers, this has increased from 83.33 lakhs HH to 98.55 lakhs, during the same period. Over 28 lakh household got added during the same period from 2001 to 2011. The growth rate of the toilets in households in Odisha, is yet very dismal. In percentile terms, households not having toilet have decreased to 77.6% in 2011 which indicated the rate of increase in toilets is only 7.5% during 10 years. This further indicates that there is a long way to go before Millennium Development Goals in Odisha are achieved. In a year about 1,40,000 toilets get constructed for individual households. Therefore, Odisha will have to wait till 2080 to achieve the goals of basic sanitation rights to all, which were originally to be met by 2015. This is despite of the fact that, India has had the world's largest toilet movement under the total sanitation campaign, *Nirmal Bharat Abhiyan* and *Swachch Bharat Mission* on a subsidized mode. The State Government has undertaken a number of innovative steps like *SANJOG, NGP (Nirmal Gram Puruskar)* and others to scale up the toilet coverage matching to the MDG goal. However, demand for the toilet, an important health related household asset, is not increasing. Crores of rupees earmarked by the Government on subsidies under this head, as poor household's is unused entitlements remain inaccessible to most people. Women, thus remain the worst affected as they have to compromise with their privacy and continue to defecate in the open and expose themselves to the vagaries of nature as well as ill-intentioned men. Most rapes have been reported to occur while women go out of their house to attend the call of nature. They often have to wait for a person to accompany them to enable easing themselves. To prolong the use of toilet, they consume lesser water than required; and suffer related illnesses. In addition, they are also the providers of cleaning services. More than 90% of the sanitation services are rendered by women. Therefore, while providing the toilets is important, signpathy with the women as workers is essential. While providing solutions to sanitation it is important, the government, civil society and research institutes need to think of solutions for toilets from technical, economic, behavioural and cultural perspectives of people who use as well as who provide services, majority of whom are women.

Policies and Programmes for Women in Odisha

Odisha government has initiated many welfare programmes for women: *Mission Shakti* for economic empowerment of women; *Swadhar Shelter Home* to provide shelter, clinical and legal support to women in crisis. *Swadhar* takes care of abandoned widows, victims of trafficking, natural calamity and terror, domestic violence and mentally challenged. HIV affected women get shelter, medical aid and legal help, *Ujjawala* provides shelter and help in rehabilitation of trafficked girls. *Adolescent Anaemia Control Programme* not only distributes IFA tablets among girls, but also tries to delay early marriages, improve nutritional status of adolescent girls and give special emphasis on deworming. It also creates awareness through *Kishori Swasthya Mela*. Health infrastructure especially transportation during emergency and in remote areas needs to be strengthened. The government has launched *"Amo Doli"* in Rayagada district of Odisha under which 183 remote villages will be provided with a specially-designed mode of transportation. This programme aims at helping people residing in hilly areas where no approach road to a village exists. These will be kept either at village welfare committees or with ASHA workers. After reaching the nearest motorable point, the villagers can call ambulance by dialling 102 for pregnant women and 108 for emergency services to shift a patient to the nearest hospital. Odisha government also has many centrally sponsored women specific programmes like SABLA, MAMATA, *Kishori Shakti Yojana* and so on. The Women and Child Welfare Ministry also addresses the issues of child marriage, domestic violence, trafficking and construction of women hostels.

Summary and Conclusion

There are eight districts where concentration of scheduled caste population is more than 20 per cent; and six districts where the scheduled tribe population is more than 50 per cent. Gajapati has highest concentration of ST population (54.3) per cent, but it has lowest concentration of SC population (7 per cent). On the contrary Puri district which has the lowest concentration of ST (0.36 per cent) has nearly 20 per cent SC population. It is appalling to note that more than one-fourth of teenaged girls aged 15-19, and ever married, have one surviving child; and high risk pregnancy occurring in higher ages are also many. Poor performing districts have higher concentration of SC and ST population. There are lesser poor ever married women in urban areas as compared to rural areas. Less than one third SC and about one tenth ST women had institutional delivery; and less than half of SC and less than one fifth of ST women had delivery assisted by skilled health personnel. Neo-natal infant, child, and under five mortality is high among the SC and ST. More than half of SC and ST women have less than 18 BMI and are anaemic. Nearly half of them experience spousal violence which is emotional sexual and physical in nature

Gender disparity widens with the increase in the number of years of schooling and thus between the literates too. Women with less education and less wealth are likely to have more children than those with more education and more wealth. Disparity in effective literacy is highest among rural scheduled caste women.

Unemployment rate among SCs and STs is around 40 per cent. However, gender gap is wider among SCs than STs. Among SCs the gap is about 20 per cent with 55 per cent women remaining unemployed. In contrast the gender gap among STs is about 14 per cent with 43 per cent men remaining unemployed. The gap between rural and urban women unemployment is huge.

Though Odisha as well as central government have launched many welfare programmes for women and girls, none address the specific needs of social groups in the context of region. SC and ST women and girls are the worst victims of child marriage and teenage pregnancy, due to poverty and lack of infrastructure. These women face high infant and child mortality, lesser access to ANC and PNC services, suffer anaemia and low body mass index. They experience acute health deprivation compared to other social groups. It is interesting to note that women work participation is low across all social groups in Odisha and unemployment is very high among women of all social groups. Moreover, education level is low. Thus, low economic empowerment makes women more vulnerable. Data on domestic violence reveals that more than 40 per cent SC/ST face violence in homes. There is to have necessity ensured employment and skill building for employability. This will call for addressing the drop-outs at various levels of education. Providing toilets must be priority for most rural girls to continue schooling. In addition, some mechanism whereby those attending to their siblings while parents are away at work, can free them from this and other household chores. Anganwadi centres may be doubled up as also care centres. Occupational hazards encountered by women as low paid daily wage earner, sanitation worker, for instance, is compounded by the vulnerability to sexual violence they are exposed to. Another important issues is that of protection from violence. Creating enabling environment to raise their voices against the spouse requires support from the family and community as much from the state machinery. Mind set of young boys has to be developed so as to empathize with girls and women. Thus, gender issues needs to be analysed from socio-demographic and economic specificities. This will be the pathway to follow for attaining the unfulfilled MDGs to move towards Sustainable Development Goals (SDGs).

REFERENCES

Baru, Rama, Arnab Acharya, Sanghmitra Acharya, AK Shiva Kumar and K Nagaraj (2015) 'Inequities in Access to health Services in India—Class, Caste and Region' in Kapila, Uma (ed.) *Indian Economy Since Independence: A Comparative and Critical Analysis of*

India's Economy, 1947-2015. Sixth Edition, Academic Foundation, New Delhi.

Cook, Kay (2009) 'Not Measuring up- Low-income Women Receiving Welfare Benefits' in Taket Ann et al (eds.) *Theorising Social Exclusion*. Routledge, London, pp. 55-67.

Haan, Arjan and Amresh Dubey (2005) 'Poverty, Disparities, or the Development of Underdevelopment in Orissa', *Economic and Political Weekly*, May 28-June 4: 2321-2329.

Discover Odisha (2013) Editorial. http://mybhubaneswar.com/iconic-women-of-odisha and http://www.oriyanari.com/id58.html March 8. Accessed on 21 Dec 2015.

GoO, (1990) *Gazetteer of India, Orissa State*, Vol. I, Chief Editor: Nrusinha Charan Behuria (Chapter-I), Gazetteer Unit, Government of Orissa.

IIPS and MoHFW (2010) District level Household and Facility Survey 2007-08 Orissa. International Institute for Population Sciences, Mumbai, Minstry of Health and Family Welfare, New Delhi.

IIPS and ICF (2017) *National Family Health Survey (NFHS-4), India, 2015-16: Odisha*, International Institute of Population Sciences, Mumbai.

Jeejebhoy, Shireen J (2001) 'Women's Autonomy and Reproductive Behiaviour in India' in Sathar, Zeba A and Phillips, J F (eds.) *Fertility Transition in South Asia*. Oxford University Press, Oxford, pp. 204-238.

MLE (2014), *Report on Third Annual Employment & Unemployment Survey (2012-13)*, Volume I, Government of India, Ministry of Labour & Employment, Labour Bureau, Chandigarh.

Odisha HMIS (Ministry of Health and Family Welfare) April-October, 2013.

Panda, P K (1997) 'Female Headship, Poverty and Child Welfare—A Study of Rural Orissa, India'. Centre for Development Studies. Thiruvananthapuram. August.

Pattanayak, Subhas Chandra (2010) *Sambad Survey*, http://orissamatters.com /2010/10/05 /3159 -mdg-survey/October 5.

Odisha HMIS (Ministry of Health and Family Welfare) April-October, 2013; Ministry of Health and Family Welfare 2005-2006. National Family Health Survey 3.

RGI, (2011), *Census of India, Provisional Tables*, Registrar General of India, http://www.censusindia.gov.in/2011-prov-results/prov_results_paper1_india.html.

MOLE (2014) *Report on Third Annual Employment & Unemployment Survey (2012-13)*, Volume I, Government of India, Ministry of Labour & Employment, Labour Bureau, Chandigarh.

Stephen, Cynthia (2009). Feminism and Dalit Women In India, 16 November, Countercurrents.org.

Verma, R K, Pulerwitz, J, Mahendra V, Khandekar S, Barker, G, Fulpagare, P (2006) Challenging and Changing Gender Attitudes among Young Men in Mumbai. *Reproductive Health Matter*, 14(28): 135-143.

Appendix A: Health Facilities and Utilisation Disparity (%)

District	*Government Health Facility*	*Private Health Facility*	*Full ANC*	*District*	*Government Health Facility*	*Private Health Facility*	*Full ANC*
Bargarh	67.9	20.3	64.3	Nayagarh	75.0	9.2	62.9
Jharsuguda	53.9	22.8	74.3	Khordha	57.1	34.4	74.8
Sambalpur	76.6	8.8	68.2	Puri	67.0	26.7	65.9
Debagarh	75.5	4.9	66.1	Kandhamal	63.7	1.7	56.2
Sundargarh	41.9	16.8	67.7	Baudh	37.3	3.0	57.7
Kendujhar	61.6	9.0	46.1	Sonapur	78.8	16.4	63.0
Mayurbhanj	50.7	3.8	44.7	Balangir	70.5	0.0	56.5
Baleshwar	54.1	26.0	64.3	Nuapada	71.8	12.0	60.2
Bhadrak	53.6	37.7	47.9	Kalahandi	65.2	8.8	62.2
Kendrapara	66.5	22.7	75.2	Rayagada	34.6	5.8	52.4
Jagatsinghapur	79.0	19.8	69.6	Nabarangpur	23.6	1.7	48.5
Cuttack	64.0	27.7	69.3	Koraput	42.5	2.5	51.1
Jajaur	64.4	28.8	60.4	Malkangiri	26.4	2.3	34.2
Dhenkanal	74.3	13.9	60.4	Odisha (15-49)	58.9	15.3	23.2
Anugul	63.5	17.1	57.4	India	54.5	36.3	18.8

Source: Table 4.2 Antenatal care by District. Percentage of women (aged 15-49) who received any antenatal check-up (ANC) during pregnancy by source and place of ANC by district, Orissa, 2007-08, District level Household and Facility Survey 2007-08 Orissa. International Institute for Population Sciences, Mumbai, Ministry of Health and Family Welfare, New Delhi.

5

Women and Underage Marriages in Odisha: A Developmental Perspective

Monica Das

Universal discrimination against women can be seen as what I would like to term 'apartheid of gender'. Due to the ensuing gendered discriminations of varied dimensions that are universal, women constitute an acutely marginalized group. As for India to be specific, every single day the media abounds with news of atrocities on women and the callousness with which they are met with by people at the helm of affairs. Be it rape or killings, bride burning, maternal/infant mortality, female feticide, the Khap diktat, that is primitive to the core and such other matters, they all speak of the highly abject state that our women are in.

The pointer turns towards a cultural construct and a negative mindset of the people. This turns out to be the predominant reason that explains the abuse against women. The natural corollary of this being gender inequity. It is almost common knowledge that this has its roots in socio-cultural conditioning of society spanning many many years. The outcome of all this is manifest in a gendered social practice-underage marriage, popularly and legally construed as 'child marriage'. Such a social practice is highly detrimental to the growth and development of women in particular and the country in general.

Age at marriage and development of self-identity of women are inextricably interlinked. Social scientists have argued that early marriage prevents women from attaining their rightful education, accessing employment and training opportunities, developing social relationships with peers, attaining balanced health and participating in civic life. Precisely speaking, underage marriage keeps women away from the process of development leading to a gender-unequal society.

Talking of the link between gender inequality and development, one can find that the former holds back the growth of individuals, the development of nations and the evolution of societies to the disadvantage of both men and women. Gender issues are not simply about women's issues. Understanding gender means understanding opportunities, constraints and the impact of change, as they affect both men and women. To quote Todaro, the eminent social scientist,

> Development should be conceived of as a multi-dimensional process involving major changes in social structures, popular attitudes, as well as acceleration of economic growth, reduction of inequality and the eradication of absolute poverty. (Voth, 2004).

Todaro continues to argue that development is a physical reality and a state of mind in which society has, through some combinations of social, economic and political process secured the way of obtaining a better life (Todaro, 1981: 56).

National Family Health Survey (*NFHS-IV, 2015-16*), estimated that the percentage of women in the age group 20-24 married before the age of 18 years is 26.8 which was 47.4 in *National Family Health Survey* (*NFHS-3, 2005-06*)[1], thus showing a decreasing trend. Of these, 2.7% girl child had tied their marital knot before they were 16, and 5.6% were married when they were between 16 and 17 and 11% got married between 17 and 18. There are 12 states in India that show a higher prevalence of child marriage than the national average of 11.9%. These are West Bengal (25.6%), Tripura (21.6%),Bihar (19.7%), Jharkhand (17.8%), Dadra and Nagar Haveli (17.5%), Assam (16.7%), Andhra Pradesh (16.6%), Rajasthan (16.2%), Gujarat (13.1%), Telangana (12.9%), Maharashtra (12.1%) and Arunachal Pradesh (12.1%). NFHS-IV survey reveals that the prevalence of girl child marriages in the age-group 15-19 years is significant in rural areas. However, underage marriage has been observed in some urban pockets of certain states. Some of these states are Haryana (41%), Tamil Nadu (37%), Maharashtra (33%) and Manipur (32%). It has also been found in the survey that 40% of underage marriages have happened in poorer families.

Thus, social structures and popular attitudes are major influencing factors so far as the status of women in Odisha and India is concerned. This impacts the development process through its adverse effects on the socio-economic parameters. For presenting the scenario pertaining to underage marriages that are noticed in the state of Odisha, a study of the Empowered Action Group states (EAG states) (eight in number including Odisha) has been taken up in the paper. The identification of states has been done in the *Annual Health Survey of India, 2012*, on the basis of high fertility and high mortality. These high focus states with high fertility and high mortality account for about 48% of the total population in the country.

The Annual Health Survey (AHS), conceived in a meeting of National Commission of Population in 2005, was confined to 284 districts (as per 2001 Census) of the 8 Empowered Action Group States. All 30 districts of Odisha have been included in the survey (AHS, census 2011). The study uses district-level data as well, for a more comprehensive analysis. The Annual Health Survey 2013 fact sheet Odisha categorically states that

> Decentralized district-based health planning is essential in India because of the large inter-district variations. In the absence of vital data at the district level, the State level estimates are being used for formulating district level plans as well as setting the milestones thereof. In the process, the hotspots (districts requiring special attention) very often get masked by the State average. This statistical fallacy compounds the problems of the districts acutely, more so in the health sector. (*Annual Health Survey Bulletin 2012-13*)

The paper makes an attempt to understand the socio-economic consequences of underage marriage through the pages of literature and research studies. It also explains the policy interventions made by the State and recommends certain policy measures.

Conceptualizing Underage Marriage

According to the Prohibition of Child Marriage Act 2006, the case of any girl married below 18 years of age and that of any boy married before 21 years, is considered a "child marriage", which is a cognizable offense. Since marriage is consummated in an age lower than the minimum age advanced in law such marriages have been explained as 'underage marriages' by sociologists. Such underage marriages have long term negative consequences for both boys and girls in terms of educational outcomes as well as transitions to the labor market and family formation. Especially, the adverse effect of underage marriage on girls is grave. This includes educational setbacks, lower employment prospects, exposure to violence and abuse—leading to negative physical and psychological outcomes. Besides the risk of early childbearing many child brides have little say within their marital households. In India, child marriage has been declining slowly over time, but the number of girls and boys getting married before their respective legal ages remain large with 12.1 million child marriages reported by Census 2011. In particular, child marriage has serious health repercussions on girls, such as frequent pregnancies, miscarriages, maternal and neonatal mortality, and early motherhood. (*MWCD Annual Report, 2014-15*)

Further analysis of NHFS-4 reveals that the highest prevalence of child marriage is reported amongst scheduled tribe girls (15%) followed by scheduled castes (13%). However, when we analyzed child marriages amongst the top 10 states with the highest prevalence of child marriage we find that this phenomenon is occurring across caste groups. For instance In Arunachal Pradesh, 72% of the sample aged between 15-19 years who had child marriages belong to scheduled tribes while 38% of the other castes girls in Maharashtra reported the highest percentage of married girls before 18. Furthermore, while Bihar, Gujarat, and Telangana report a very high prevalence of child marriage amongst OBC girls, West Bengal has the highest prevalence of child marriages amongst SC girls.

Moreover, it would be still more startling to note that out of 15 lakh girls who are married under the age of 15, 20% (3 lakh girls) have already borne children at least once (2001 census). Some mention of narratives from my book *The Other Woman* has been used to articulate these facts.

The Indian social reality is that a woman is best perceived in the confines of domesticity. Marriage being obligatory for the Indian woman and especially so for the Hindu woman as sanctioned by the shastras (ancient texts), their lives revolve around the institution of marriage and their position, as well as their family's position, is determined with reference to it.

Socio-economic Dimensions of Underage Marriage Through Literature

Bringing in the question of socio-economic structures and popular attitudes as influencing factors, a literature interface with the socio-economic phenomenon of underage marriage has been attempted. Literature is a brilliant way of articulating reality. It can bring to the notice of the common reader the socio-economic reality. People generally read fiction and media reports separately. That fiction is not divorced from reality is the point that I wish to maintain. Literature can be said to be the looking glass of society and has an innate quality of capturing snapshots of the good and bad happening around us.

So the articulation through fiction is important. The ensemble of stories in my book *The Other Woman* brings out the problem of 'shortchanging' women which definitely has its adverse impact on the socio-economic status of women. Girls are often reduced to being seasonal brides and almost always return home in a year or less, abandoned by the groom, impregnated, and has no forwarding address for the in-laws. But the offense of bigamy is non-cognizable and hence a number of bigamous marriages go unchallenged. The problem is not only relevant in the 21st century, but I should say, more relevant now than before (Das, 2009).

This helps to bring out the fact that patriarchy is an

endemic, historical and cultural practice that assumes 'male' as the 'norm' and the female as the 'other'. Again, this has a lot to do with the socio-cultural practice of underage marriage. The malady of a male-dominated society has a cultural context. What follows is the many direct and insidious ways of inflicting abuse on women. However, what caught my attention is the abuse of a different kind—abuse through the practice of underage marriage. As per the Report of the National Commission on the Status of Women in India 1979, the incidence of bigamy and polygamy was higher among Hindu Tribals than Muslims. Although there are movements to end polygamy, some orthodox members of the Muslim community seek to preserve the practice. Coupled with this is the rising trend of bigamy and polygamy that has a far-reaching adverse socio-economic impact. Quite interestingly this has an overlap with the fact of underage marriages. (Das, 2009)

My book *The Other Woman* has an ensemble of stories which relate to issues pertaining to underage marriage and Bigamy / Polygamy. I would particularly like to mention Mahasweta Devi's *China*, where the woman who is deceived and deserted by her man, is rendered vulnerable and left with a total lack of identity. *Recoil* by Jayakanthan is a pointer to 'closet bigamy'. The case of an under-aged woman in a pre-marital liaison is portrayed in *Kishori Charan Das, The Visitor*. *Body Offering* by Makarand Paranjpe is about sexuality and the exhilaration of falling in love. This has special significance in view of the recent legal provision where adultery has been decriminalized. These stories also point to the fact that bigamy and polygamy interestingly so, have an overlap with child marriage. Child marriage is the worst form of exploitation. Worst because, it happens right in front of our eyes, sometimes in the name of tradition, sometimes in the name of patriarchy and sometimes in the name of security and future of the girl child.

Review of existing literature reveals some interesting findings on this aspect of marriage. Husbands of older women and women with less education are more likely to have multiple wives than husbands of younger women and women with higher levels of education. Spouses of women aged less than 30 have about 1.35 partners whereas husbands of women aged 30 or more have 2.22 to 2.51 partners. One interesting finding is that women across religious groups—Hindu (1.77 partners), Muslim (2.55 partners), Christian (2.35 partners), Buddhist (3.41 partners) have reported that their husbands have multiple wives. It is more common for the husbands of women belonging to scheduled castes and tribes to have multiple wives than women belonging to 'other' groups. (Yelamanchili and Parasuraman, 2010)

According to UNICEF, around one-third of women aged 20 to 24 in the developing world were married as children. Child marriage is also common in other South Asian countries and some African nations. According to the International Centre for Research on Women, if present trends of child marriage continue, more than 142 million girls worldwide will be forced into early marriage during the next decade—the equivalent of 38,000 girls every day (*ICRW Report 2013*)[2].

Social Reality of Underage Marriage in India

Bigamy, especially underage bigamy, adds to the list of the different ways in which abuse occurs and women are often rendered insecure, abandoned and hapless. According to the Census of India report of 2001 on marital status released in 2005, it reveals that 11.7 million Indians are married underage, and almost the same number, ten million Indian women alone, are living in bigamous marriages. So if one thought child marriages are largely history in India or fast disappearing, the 2001 census report has a different story to tell.

Another interesting fact is that among those enumerated as married at the time of the census, women outnumbered men by five million (Census, 2001)[3]. More pressing becomes the problem when we look into the possibility of underage marriage having an adverse impact on Human Development Index (HDI), Gender Development Index (GDI) and other socio-economic parameters, because when we consider the three determining factors of HDI, literacy, life expectancy and level of earnings the predicament of women becomes too obvious. Girls below age 18 (legal age of marriage of women) who get married are shortchanged on all the three counts mentioned above. They cannot attain literacy and education nor enjoy good health, or longer life expectancy, what to speak of obtaining skill for earning a livelihood. It goes without saying that they would be saddled with marital responsibilities and the daunting burden of motherhood & repeated childbirth.

Girls forced into early marriage face many challenges. Often they must drop out of school to raise children, which diminishes their future opportunities. Girls are withdrawn from schools when they reach puberty with the excuse of *paraya dhan* to be protected till her marriage. And depending on the girls' developmental stage, pregnancy can be a tremendous physical burden. More than 70,000 girls aged 15 to 19 die due to complications relating to childbirth every year (UNICEF)[4]. Even children whose mothers survive face challenges of their own, including being underweight and suffering, delayed physical and cognitive development.

Women's identity in Odisha

Odisha has a population of 41.9 million and is the eleventh largest state in the country[5]. A substantial proportion of the population (40%) belong to the disadvantaged communities (22.8% ST and 17.1% SC)[6]. About 6% of the population belong to minorities with Muslims constituting 2.1% and Christians 2.4%.[7] Nearly one-third of the population live below the poverty line[8].

Although the overall sex ratio of the state has improved from 972 to 979, the child sex ratio has declined from 953 to 941 with marked rural, urban and regional and differences as per Census 2011. The scheduled caste (SC) and scheduled tribe (ST) population in the State, on the other hand, have comparatively better sex ratios (987 and 1029, respectively). The elderly women constitute 9.5% of the female population which is the seventh highest among large states of India. Further, women with disabilities in the state constitute 2.74% of the female population which is also higher than the national average of 2.01%.

The infant mortality (male 52, female 54 per 1,000 live births) and under-five mortality (male 70, female 74 per 1,000 live births) rates have remained higher for girls as compared to boys and many districts (24 out of 30) witness wide gender gaps[9]. More than two-third girls (67%) aged 6-59 months and six out of ten women (61.2%) in the reproductive age are anaemic. The Maternal Mortality Ratio (MMR) of the State has declined from 258 (2009) to 235 per 100,000 live births (2012) but is still the fourth highest in the country.[10]

Overall literacy rate of the state is 72.9%, with 64% women being literate, but the literacy rates of women vary widely from 35.8% in Nabarangpur to 81.6% in Khurda district and the women from ST communities are least literate (41.2%). Further, Census 2011 data reveal that the gender gap in overall literacy rate has reduced from 24.8 (in 2001) to 17.6 points. The enrolment ratio among girls in primary schools has substantially increased from 58.2% (2000-01) to 99.6% (2011-12). The drop out rate has declined sharply from 41.4% (2000-01) to 0.6% (2011-12) and at upper primary level from 61.1% (2000-01) to 2.23% (2011-12). But the drop out rate of girls at the high school level is high at 51.8% (2011-12) and in case of SC and ST communities, the rate is even higher at 61.8 and 62.7%, respectively.

The share of women workforce in the organized sector has increased marginally (from 14.9% in 2005 to 16.8% in 2011) but more than three-fourths are found working in the agriculture sector and 66% of marginal workers are women in Odisha.

The study in hand that gives a comparative picture of the EAG states of India and presents a picture that is far removed from the mission envisaged under MDGs (Millennium Development Goals–India). As for Odisha, the picture is rather dismal. In the context of violence, 42% of women (15-49 years) are subjected to either physical or sexual violence in Odisha against 35% women in the country. Odisha stands at 10th position with respect to crimes against women, 7th for dowry murder and 8th position in terms of rape cases. As per the statewide incidence of IPC crimes under sexual offenses during the year 2014, Odisha stands at 7th position, MP at the top and Sikkim at the bottom among all states and union territories (Sharma and Sunita 2015).

Graph 1 below, gives a comparative picture: HDI and its dimensions for Indian states. This graph shows Odisha ranks the lowest.

Graph 1: Status of MDGs in India

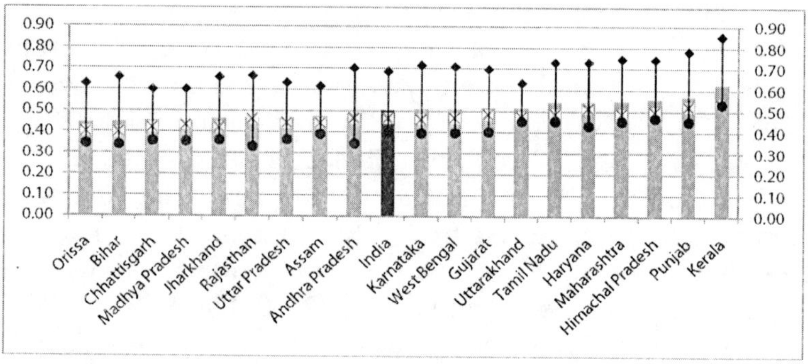

Notes: Vertical bars (orange color for states and red for India) indicate the HDI; dark black circles (inside the bars) indicate the education dimension index; cross within white squares, the income dimension index; and dark black diamonds (outside the bars), the health dimension index; and the states are arranged in ascending order of their HDIs.

Source: Inequality-adjusted Human Development Index for India's States, UNDP 2011

Underage Marriage and Women in Odisha

Talking of child marriages in Odisha, we find 21.3% of girls of 20-24 age group had married before they attained 18 years and 10% of 15-19 years of girls had child marriage. UNICEF Report states that 13% of men got married before they are 21. Completion of secondary education is much lower amongst married teenage girls than the unmarried girls amongst 15-19 age group across all states. State level analysis further indicates that prevalence of underweight amongst 15-19 years married girls who were below the legal age of marriage, is found higher in Dadra and Nagar Haveli (68.9%), Gujarat (50.9%), Daman and Diu (44.0%), Rajasthan (43.9%), Nagaland (41.4%).

Further, NFHS–IV reveals that 21.3% of the currently married women in the age group of 20-24 years has tied the knot before the legal age limit. The high tribal component in the population of Odisha perhaps compounds some of the problems. Citing one example from the extremely backward and tribal-dominant district of Kandhamal—the percentage of girls being pushed into child marriage is 35.5(currently married women aged 20-24 who were married before the age of 18 years (DLHS 2007-08). A host of complex socio-economic problems including abject poverty and a poor female literacy rate—less than 30% among tribal women contribute to these dismal numbers (DLHS 2007-08).

It is observed that underage marriages on an average are not very high in Odisha, the figure for which stands at 4.6. Currently for the married women of 20-24 years who had underage marriage, the percentage is low and at 28.8 that stands much below the other six states. The mean age at marriage is 22.4, the highest amongst all eight states indicating that on an average the incidence of underage marriage is low, which is a good indicator. Women aged 15-19 years who were already mothers or pregnant at the time of survey constitute 44 per cent of girls of that age. The drop out rate among girls in Odisha is 13.5% which is highest among all eight states. This is an important indicator denoting a possible adverse impact on development. (Table 1)

In terms of the age cohorts, Odisha's figures indicate that females married in greater numbers than males, in both age cohorts of 15-19 and the age cohort of below legal age. The respective figures for Odisha stand at 83.3 and 72.0. As compared to the other seven states, Odisha has highest incidence of under-age marriage in the age cohort of 15-19. It is observed that in all eight states, females had underage marriages in greater numbers than that of males. (Table 2)

Table 1: Odisha vis-à-vis other states) Status of Underage Marriage in the EAG States

	*(1) Marriages among Females below legal age (18 years) (%)**	*(2) Currently Married Women aged 20-24 years married before the legal age*	*(3) Mean Age at Marriage Female*	*(4) TFR*	*(5) Women aged 15-19 years who were already mothers or pregnant at the time of survey (%)*	*(6) Female Drop out (Age 6-17 years) (%)*	*(7) Unmet need for Spacing (%)*	*(8) Total Unmet need (%)*	*(9) IMR*
Bihar	16.5	52.4	20.1	3.6	47.7	4.3	17.3	33.5	52
Chhagtisgarh	4.7	34.7	21.1	2.8	48.9	6.2	14.1	24.8	50
Jharkhand	12.6	48.3	20.6	2.9	46.7	6.5	11.8	22.6	38
MP	10.4	46.1	20.9	3.1	48.5	8.2	10.8	21.6	65
Odisha	4.6	28.8	22.4	2.3	44	13.5	8.1	19.1	59
Rajasthan	16.3	54.1	20.4	3.1	38.6	11.4	8.1	12.6	57
UP	6.3	35.8	21.5	3.4	43.1	10.8	12.4	24.1	70
Uttarakhand	2.3	22.7	22.2	2.1	41.6	6.5	8.4	18.1	41

Source: Computed from AHS of Census, 2011.

Table 2: Percentage of Underage Marriage Out of Total Married in Age Cohort (15-19)

	Aged 15-19		*Below Legal Age*	
	Male	*Female*	*Male* <21	*Female* <18
India	21.4	78.6	24.4	68.8
Uttarakhand	18.9	81.1	20.7	70.2
Rajasthan	28.4	71.6	30.9	67.1
UP	25.2	74.8	29	67.8
Bihar	21.5	78.5	25.2	67.1
Jharkhand	19.1	80.9	23.1	70
Odissa	16.7	83.3	18.7	72
Chhatisgarh	18.9	81.1	21.6	67.3
MP	25.1	74.9	28.6	65.5

Source: Computed from Census, 2011

In comparison, only three districts in Odisha have 10 to 20 per cent of women married underage, whereas the corresponding figure for Bihar is 17 districts. In 27 districts of Odisha, there is low incidence of underage marriage which is less than 10%. (Table 3)

Table 3: Number of Districts and the Percentage of Women Married Below Legal Age in the EAG States

State	*(1) 30 and above (%)*	*(2) 20 to 30 (%)*	*(3) Number of women marriage underage 10 to 20 (%)*	*(4) Less than 10 (%)*	*(5) Total Dist*
Bihar	5	8	17	7	37
Rajasthan	5	5	13	9	32
UP	2	3	9	56	70
MP	0	7	13	25	45
Jharkhand	0	5	7	6	18
Chhattisgarh	0	0	0	16	16

Odisha	0	0	3	27	30
Uttarakhand	0	0	0	13	13
Total	12	28	62	159	261

Source: Computed from AHS of Census, 2011

All the above findings are rather thought-provoking and should propel us into action. These findings help to corroborate the fact of the deplorable state of women in the EAG states and specifically in the state of Odisha. However, there are many other factors that need to be looked into for ensuring women's autonomy. These are right to land, control of local markets, and access through education and training to occupations that enhance self-esteem. Needless to say that apart from all the above, another inherent factor that needs to be kept in mind for prospective analysis is the socio-cultural factor of androcentrism.

Androcentrism is the practice conscious or otherwise of placing male human beings or the masculine point of view at the centre of one's view of the world, its culture, and history. The opposite of Androcentrism is gynocentrism. The term 'androcentrism' was introduced by Charlotte Perkins Gilman in a scientific debate in 1911. She described androcentric practices in society and their consequences in her investigation on the 'man-made' world. Androcentrism is understood as a societal fixation on masculinity whereby all things originate. Under androcentrism, masculinity is normative and all things outside of masculinity are defined as the 'other'. According to Gilman, masculinity as a pattern of life & masculine mindsets claimed universality while female ones were considered as deviance. Feminist anthropologist Sally Slocum argues that there has been a long-standing male bias in anthropological thought. This perhaps is the reason for women's neglect. This neglect is observed in India at the micro-level and is more pronounced in the EAG group of states of which Odisha is a part.

All the above, concerning neglect of women, finds its

echo in ancient Indian literature as well. In the context of the imposition of child marriage in the Indian society by the patriarchal order, a quote from Sarojini Naidu's poem would do good to understand the thought behind the core cultural practice of underage marriage in India. Her poem depicts all this in a candid and beauty-laden manner. The second paragraph of the poem helps to bring out how beautifully the prospective girl bride counters the societal norm by stating what she thinks of this bondage and how she seeks to free herself from it all. The poem beautifully upholds the independent spirit of a girl child in India. Following are the extracts of the poem written by Sarojini Naidu, poet and freedom fighter.

Honey child, honey child, the world is full of pleasure,
of bridal-songs and cradle-songs and sandal-scented leisure.
Your bridal robes are in the loom, silver, and saffron glowing,
Your bridal cakes are on the hearth:
O whither are you going?
The bridal-songs and cradle-songs have cadences of sorrow,
The laughter of the sun today, the wind of death to-morrow.
Far sweeter sound the forest-notes where forest-streams are falling;
O mother mine, I cannot stay, the fairy-folk are calling.

The above poem depicts the strong spirit of some women who are raring to go. This spirit needs to be emulated by many more women. Role models definitely serve to bring about the necessary changes.

The pertinent question that arises here is, could there be a link between these menacing indicators concerning Odisha and its low HDI (Human Development Index) ranking? An in-depth study on this is called for. This is just a poser.

Policy Interventions by the State

The Indian State has in many ways tried to address the issue of child marriage through its National Policy for Children. Replacing the outdated National Policy for Children 1974, the Government of India adopted a new policy in April 2013. MWCD is the nodal ministry for overseeing and coordinating the implementation of this policy. Within its objective to strengthen the overall child protection framework, the policy provides for tracking, rescuing and rehabilitating out of school children, including married children and ensuring them access to their right to education.

The MWCD has proposed a national strategy on child marriage dated 14 February 2013 that reflects the commitment of the Government of India to curb child marriages. It has suggested ensuring linkages with the Integrated Child Protection Scheme (ICPS) structures and statutory bodies to ensure detection and prompt referral of cases that require care and protection. One of the strategic directions is 'In cases in which children have already been married, they should not be discriminated when accessing services such as health, nutrition, education, and employment programmes'. According to MWCD's Press Note on Child Marriages in India dated 20 November 2013, a draft plan of action was discussed in a Regional Consultation at Lucknow on 8 July 2013 and in a National Consultation at New Delhi on 18 July 2013. It is being finalized based on the deliberations at these consultations. In its last draft, it did not have a timeline and any clarity on the allocation of funds to implement the Plan.

Some other programmes and schemes that are in place are Rajiv Gandhi Scheme for Empowerment of Adolescent Girls; Kishori Shakti Yojana (Adolescent Girls Scheme); Nutrition Programme for Adolescent Girls (NPAG); Dhanalakshmi, Conditional Cash Transfer Schemes in the States; Poorna Shakti Kendras (PSKs); Integrated Child Protection Scheme (ICPS); Bal Vivah Virodh Abhiyan (Campaign against Child Marriage).

Women and Child Related Schemes in Odisha

The Odisha state policy for girls and women 2014 has the mission which states about creating an enabling environment for girls and women that promotes equal opportunities, eliminates discrimination, ensures holistic development and empowerment and enhances capacities. The above not withstanding, we find that a lot remains to be done to meet the MDG's (Millennium Dev Goals), apart from other goals in general.

Schemes, programmes and policies are all in place, but a little reading in between the lines reveals a lot of lacunae that is present in the system and all too obvious. The very fact that all these provisions are not yielding the desired result speaks volumes about the hiatus that needs to be bridged and that too early. It would do well to go into a perusal of the developmental issues that have been raised already.

Despite the policies and programmes being in place a satisfactory level of development still remains a far cry. Development eludes us over and over again. Many would like to believe that the pointer is towards non-participation of women due to socio-cultural constraints existing in society. The saga of women's eternal suffering can be alleviated only by reformulating development strategies and working on an alternative paradigm of development that has a special focus on women. The onus lies on society, civil societies, and individuals. It can be taken as an indictment on the society if women are not empowered to be agents of change at this crucial juncture. Here, two magic words mentioned below, have the potential of acting as a panacea for this menacing illness of women's backwardness. These two are, if I may say so, one is education and the other socio-economic empowerment of women. These two in their turn have a strong potential to work their way into the morass of the misery of women and make a dent on the much talked about deep-rooted cultural construct and the mindset of the people.

There are a plethora of remedial measures for alleviating women's conditions. However, a few points are most imperative: Following are the points put in a nutshell. Some of these are- affirmative action, delivery system in place, community policing—neighbourhood watch scheme, village committees, peace committees etc. and use of technology that cuts down human interface, thereby reducing corruption. Besides the above, the following points may be borne in mind to bring about necessary changes for bettering the lives of women.

a. Advocacy at the grassroots level, regarding the adverse impact of child marriages on family welfare and women and child welfare.
b. Shifting the common perception regarding a girl from a 'girl woman' to a 'girl child' in the truest sense of the term.
c. Advocacy in general, especially in the rural areas focusing on the fact of the prospects of economic dividends that would accrue to the family by giving importance to the girl child in terms of education and nutrition
d. Community government partnership initiative (CGPI) at the grassroots level in order to promote the interest of the girl child.
e. To promote the concept of HSR (Human Social Responsibility)—An appeal to the human psyche.
f. Gender sensitization and training

Conclusion

The idea is to end the chronic conundrum with regard to women in Odisha. Proper objectivity demands that we dismiss meaningless meandering in addressing issues. Right perspective is what is needed now. Coupled with this is required a visionary angle on the part of decision makers. Governmental initiatives notwithstanding, women have to stand up for themselves and also take men along to voice their opinion and make things happen the gender-friendly way. There is no gainsaying the fact that the visionary angle should have the interests of posterity in mind. It is, after all, a question of our future generations, the younger folk of our country and our state, for whom we need to leave behind a better world. Quoting Pericles:

> What we leave behind is not what is engraved in stone monuments, but what is woven into the lives of others.

NOTES

1. NFHS-IV(2015-16)
2. NFHS-III (2005-06)
3. https://www.icrw.org/files/publications/Pages-%20Girl%20 Insights%20Report%20FINAL.pdf
4. Census 2001
5. http://www.unicef.org/philippines/mediacentre_10139.html
6. Census 2011
7. *Economic Survey 2012-13*, Government of Odisha
8. Ibid.
9. http://www.desorissa.nic.in/pdf/small-area-estimation-technique.pdf
10. SRS 2013
11. Ibid.
12. Integrated Child Protected Scheme. Child protection- a shared responsibility. Reducing child vulnerability: This will be integrated with other programmes like NREGS, SHGs, PDS, child day care, education. Strengthening family – family counselling. Promote Non-institutional care. Intersectoral linkages and responsibilities. Create a network of services at community level. Establishing standards for care and protection. Building capacities. Managerial Subsidy to MVSN (Mahila Vikash Samabaya Nigam). Training programme of MVSN. Mishan Shakti a WSHGs (Women Self's Help Group). Training support for Mahila and Shishu desks. Protection of women from domestic violence. Support for DNA testing. Support to social welfare board. Functioning of gender cell. Madhu Babu Pension Yojna. National Family Benefit Schemes (NFBS).

REFERENCES

Young Lives India and National Commission for Protection of Child Rights (NCPCR), New Delhi India. September 2018, *Report on India Child Marriage and Teenage Pregnancy*, http://ncpcr.gov.in/showfile.php?lang=1&level=1&sublinkid=1671&lid=1677.

Annual Report 2014-15, Ministry of Women & Child Development, Government of India.

Yelamanchili and Parasuraman, 2010, Polygamous Marriages in India, an international conference held from April 15-17, 2010 organized by PAA at Dallas, Texas.

Sharma and Sunita (2015), Women Exploitation: Violence against Women in India, *International Journal of Indian Psychology,* Vol. 3, No. 7.

Voth, D.E. (2004), 'An Overview of International Development Perspectives in History: Focus on Agricultural and Rural Development', *AGEC 4163, International Agricultural and Rural Development.*

Todaro (1985), *Economic Development in the Third World,* Longman, p. 56.

Das, Monica (2009), *The Other Women,* Harper Perennial—Imprint of HarperCollins Publishers India.

Dass, Cheryl, Gale Summerfield and Dzodzi Tsikata (2014), 'Feminist Economics', *Land, Gender and Food Security.*

Chang, Mariko Lin (2012), *Shortchanged: Why Women Have Less Wealth and What Can Be Done About It,* Oxford University Press.

Sylvia, Walby (2011), *The Future of Feminism,* Polity Press, Cambridge.

III. Development and Equality

6

Poverty and Food Security in Rural Odisha: The Gender Dimension

Deepak K Mishra

Introduction

Odisha, which continues to be among the least developed states of India, has been known in the past for its mass poverty, hunger, malnutrition and low levels of development. However, in the past two decades Odisha has also been noted as among the relatively faster growing states of India. Poverty levels in Odisha, though still higher than the all-India average, has shown a remarkable decline in the recent years. However, behind the story of this turn-around, lies the continuation of the structural causes of poverty and deprivation. This chapter examines the interconnections between gendered access to food, resources and institutions, and the prevalence of food insecurity and poverty in Odisha. Using evidence from both secondary and primary sources, this research argues that gender relations are central to the understanding of poverty and food security scenario in the state.

With the sweeping economic reforms initiated since the early 1990s, states were expected to compete with each other to be attractive destinations for capital, which in turn was expected to unleash a set of internal reforms enforcing fiscal discipline, accountability and efficiency. Because of the reform measures adopted by Odisha, it has also been projected as the poster boy of neo-liberal reforms. Several initiatives at the state and at the central level have been launched in recent years that emphasized the role of private investment in mining and extractive industries in transforming the economy of the State. While the relatively faster growth in per capita income is being seen as an outcome of such a policy shift, the conflicts surrounding dispossession of a large number of farmers, tribal and other marginalized social groups, incidents of farmer suicides and widespread agrarian distress, seasonal outmigration of poor labourers and relative neglect of social sector development have raised doubts regarding the distributional implications of such development policies. The presence of multiple marginalities, based on economic identities such as those based on occupations and, access to market and state institutions as well as those based on social identities such as those based on caste, religion, ethnicity and gender, among others, requires a careful analysis of the structures that create and perpetuate deprivations across dimensions. Capabilities are an interlocked set, deprivation along one dimension has a spill-over effect on other dimensions as well (Nussbaum 2001). Thus, these multiple marginalities create multiple forms of deprivation and exclusion which intersect each other. Even when the economy is growing comfortably, the structural inequalities of the past, in the absence of strong countervailing measures by the State and the civil society, might perpetuate the pre-existing disparities or might create newer forms of deprivations and marginalizations. This chapter contextualizes the gender dimensions of poverty and food insecurity as an important vantage point to understand the social embeddedness of neo-liberal economic transformation in Odisha.

2. Gender, Poverty and Food Security: The Interconnections

Food security exists when everyone has access to sufficient and nutritious food at all times. It incorporates the dimensions of availability, accessibility and utilization. It has long been pointed out by Sen (1981) that while the lack of availability of food definitely worsens the food security position of households, physical availability alone cannot guarantee access to food. Economic access is a key dimension that is often overlooked in macro-level analysis of food security. Thus, the analysis of food security in any society has to take into account the availability of food, through production or import, its distribution through market and state-administered public distribution system, the earning capacity and ability to purchase food that define economic access of households and individuals, and the conditions under which food is actually used, that includes issues of health and sanitation. Studies across the world have demonstrated that gender disparities in access to food and nutrition are significant, particularly in the developing economies (Harriss 1990).

The gender dimension of food insecurity encompasses a wide range of issues and concerns, including but not limited to:

> the gendered access to land and other productive resources; participation in and control over food production and food gathering activities; access to earnings through self-employment and wage income; access to institutions that help in accessing food, earnings and other resources that are vital for access to food.

Thus, food security of individuals is mediated through several institutional realms: those of the family and community; the market and the state. The changing discourses around gender relations and food security has been summarized by Rao (2005) in the following words:

> Until the 1980s, the issue of food security was exclusively linked with food production. Following the occurrence of a series of famines in the 1970s and 1980s, Sen (1981) attempted to explain the links between people and food through a focus on a range of entitlements: ownership (through trade, production, own-labour or inheritance); exchange (through market-based trade or transfers from the state, such as public works, social security and food subsidies) and legal. So, starvation can result from a fall in endowments (such as land alienation), unfavourable shifts in exchange entitlements (as seen in food price and wage fluctuations) and the difficulties of implementing legal rights. Property rights particularly are fuzzy and mediated by family

> and kinship ties, and a strict focus on legal rights, can jeopardise women's rights to land, often unrecorded. The difficulties posed for women due to the legal framework of individual titling followed in most countries have in fact led to a rethinking of this strategy, with the World Bank now recognizing the importance of flexible and locally managed systems for guaranteeing secure access on the ground (Rao 2005: 2514).

To the extent that food is produced within the households, access to it is likely to be decided within the production-unit, i.e. the households, which more often than not is controlled by the males. Linkages are established between women's participation in the production of food and their control over the output, particularly in the context of tribal societies (Krishna 2005). Women tend to have better access to food items collected from the forest and common property resources. However, there are instances where women continue to participate in the production processes, but simply because their contribution is less valued socially, they do not necessarily control the use of the output produced. There is enough evidence to argue that commercialization of agriculture creates several barriers to access to food. Once agriculture gets commercialized, food crops are typically substituted by non-food crops. The decisions to use inputs and the products become part of commodity production process and hence are mediated through cash. Once the market mechanism takes over, the role of women gets constrained because of the bar on women's access to the public sphere.

Commercialization typically results in increasing control of men over the commodity and cash flows. A further implication of these transformations is that access to food is mediated through the market and hence the ability to earn (cash) income, and the fluctuations in market prices, come to play a vital role. Women's access to gainful employment either through self-employment or wage labour then plays a critical role in determining their access to food. The norms controlling women's mobility, autonomy and employment also influence their access to earnings and by implication to food. In India, social norms tend to devalue women's employment and in relatively better-off households, many women tend to withdraw from the labour market[1]. Those women who do not earn income independently, tend to be dependent upon their male relatives for having access to food through the market. It is also true that when they have access to some earnings, they do not necessarily control it.

When the State attempts to improve access to food, nutrition and earnings, it is still targeted to families and the norms of participation in these programmes are again tied to the local social customs. Typically, women have less access to institutions of the State. Notwithstanding the significant improvements in women's access through reservations in the panchayati raj Institutions and women-centric programmes (such as JSY, ICDS, etc.), state institutions continue to be beyond the easy access to a significant number of women in India. Women's access to a range of resources and programmes, like health care, sanitation, education, public distribution system, subsidized energy schemes, etc., has a direct or indirect bearing upon their food and nutrition security. To the extent that women have unequal access to these programmes, the distribution of benefits from the state intervention reflects the prevailing gender bias rather than overcoming it. However, programmes targeting specific vulnerabilities of women and NGO interventions, such as those through SHGs, have been able to break these barriers in diverse contexts.

Intra-family distribution of power, income and wealth as well as the community norms regarding 'proper' gender roles within the family governs the way available food is distributed within the households. The stereotyping of women as the care-givers and those who ought to sacrifice for the family, the husband and others, and internalization of such a value system by women themselves, often lead to a gross violation of access to adequate and nutritious food, even when there is no absolute shortage of food. However,in the event of food shortages and poverty, such norms lead to a skewed distribution of food against women and the girl child.

The Poverty Regime in Odisha

A Neo-liberal Turn Around?

In recent years, Odisha's economy has seen a remarkable transformation. The economy of Odisha registered an average annual growth rate of 8.82 per cent during the 10th plan period and 7.05 per cent during the 11th Plan period (Government of Odisha 2015). The state's economy has in fact grown at a slower rate than that of India as a whole, if the entire post-reform period is taken into account (for example, during 1993-94 to 2013-14 per capita NSDP grew at a rate of 4.53 per cent per annum which was lower than that for India as a whole). However, during 2000-01 to 2009-10 per capita NSDP in Odisha grew at a faster rate than that of the Indian economy. This relatively robust growth has resulted in a structural transformation of the economy. The share of agriculture, the mainstay of a majority of workers in the State has gone down to 15.4 per cent in 2014-15, while the share of industry and service sector has been 33.4 and 51.2 per cent respectively. During the post-reform decades, mining and quarrying sector has grown at an annual average growth rate of 8.44 per cent as against 3.1 per cent at the all-India level[2]. During the 1990s, this sector expanded at an annual rate of 12 per cent per annum. Manufacturing, which had registered a growth rate of 7 per cent in the 1980s, has not grown appreciably in the post-reform decades. The growth of the service sector has, however, improved in the post-reform period, particularly during 2002-03 to 2012-13. It is important to note here that banking and insurance sub-sector has increased at a rate of 12 per cent during the post-reform period.

The implications of such growth dynamics can be understood when the changes in employment structure are taken into account. According to 2011 census, the workers' participation ratio in Odisha was 41.8 per cent, which was marginally higher than the national average of 39.8 per cent. It is important to note that between 2001 and 2011 the share of marginal workers in the total workforce increased substantially from 33 per cent to 39 per cent, while the share of main workers declined from 67 per cent in 2001 to 61 per cent in 2011 (Government of Odisha 2015). The rising share of marginal workers captures the increasing stress on the employment front. These changes in the employment structure has distinct gendered patterns as well. The workers' participation ratio was 56 per cent for the males and 27 per cent for the females. The percentage of main workers among total workers declined from 67.2 per cent in 2001 to 61per cent in 2011. The share of main workers among male workers was 73.9 per cent while that among the female workers was only 33.9 per cent. During 2001-11, the share of male main workers declined from 81.7 to 73.9 per cent, but that among female workers also declined from 35.4 to 33.9 per cent. While the share of agriculture in the NSDP declined sharply, the share of total workers in the agricultural sector, declined slowly from 64.7 per cent in 2001 to 61.8 per cent in 2011. Thus, while the economy on the average has been growing, there has been a less robust growth of gainful employment, particularly for those who are less educated and are from the rural areas. In agriculture, there is a sharp decline in NSDP per agricultural worker, which has, in all likelihood, created enormous distress for a large section of the rural population. An important aspect of the changing employment structure is that between 2001-11 there was a decline in the share of cultivators to total workers (from 30 to 23 per cent). But the fall is due to a decline in the absolute number of female cultivators.

It is under these conditions of increasing precariousness of employment in a situation of relatively robust economic growth that the questions of poverty and food insecurity in Odisha need to be looked at. Agricultural productivity growth has been much below the potential. Although there has been some diversification of the cropping pattern, particularly in terms of rise of the area under cotton and vegetables, paddy continues to account for more than 90 per cent of the area under foodgrain production. Of the total area under principal crops, only 28.30 per cent was under irrigation, against the all India average of 44.90 per cent. The low productive agricultural sector, however, was the major source of livelihood in rural Odisha. Nearly 70 per cent of rural workers were in agriculture in 2011. Among the agricultural workers, which include both cultivators and agricultural labourers, the share of agricultural labourers has gone up from 54 per cent to 62 per cent during 2001 to 2011. Further, among the cultivators, a substantial majority belongs to the small and marginal landholder category. Thus, in broad economic terms, the poverty regime in Odisha is characterized by low-productive, mostly rainfed, subsistence paddy cultivation, rising landlessness and dependence on insecure, intermittently available low-paid wage work and high dependence on the informal credit market.

Poverty: Spatial and Social Concentration

Poverty in Odisha, measured through per capita consumption expenditure, continues to be high, but the State has seen one of the fastest decline in poverty-from 57.20 per cent in 2004-05 to 32.59 per cent in 2011-12. During the same period, rural poverty declined from 61 per cent to nearly 36 per cent (Table 1).

Although Odisha is considered a poor state in comparison to other states, the diversity in the nature and extent of poverty in Odisha is less explicitly recognized. With the recent changes in the economy, where the economic transformation of a particular kind is deeply embedded in the local economies[3], this diversity has further been complicated.Poverty in Odisha is spatially and socially concentrated—there are distinct regional patterns in the concentration and inter-temporal trends in the incidence of poverty (Mishra 2011). Among the three NSS regions, poverty is highest in the southern region, followed by the northern region and is the least in the coastal region. Often the state-level trends in poverty reduction mask the regional dimension. For example, although poverty has declined in all the regions between 2004-5 and 2010-11, what is remarkable is that poverty levels in the southern and the northern regions are persistently higher, in fact, more than double than that in the coastal region[4].

At a very broad level, (and taking the risks of generalization) at least four different stylized spatial contexts within Odisha can be outlined in which poverty gets perpetuated in Odisha[5]. *Firstly,* in the relatively fertile, agriculturally developed districts of Odisha located mainly in the coastal belt and also in the Hirakud command area in north Odisha (Bargarh and Sambalpur), poverty is typically concentrated among the agricultural labourers and marginal farmers. In this context, poverty is closely linked to landlessness, denial of access to or unfavourable access to agricultural input and output markets as well as the lack of gainful employment within and outside agriculture. *Secondly,* in the rain-fed districts of interior Odisha (Balangir, Sonepur, Nuapada, etc.), poverty dynamics is closely linked to the seasonality of agricultural activities, low productivity in agriculture, lack of employment and frequent droughts. *Thirdly,* in the tribal-dominated, interior districts of southern Odisha (Koraput, Gajapati, Malkangiri, Nabarangpur and parts of Kalahandi, for example) poverty dynamics is more closely related to forest-based livelihoods. Apart from low productivity and the gradual disintegration of indigenous agricultural systems, land alienation (both through large-scale displacement caused by mega-development and conservation projects as well as through indebtedness) has a more prominent role in this region. *Finally,* in those parts where predatory mining and industrial activities has created a class of vulnerable peasants and wage labourers suffering from a livelihoods shock caused by economic and environmental damage (Jharsuguda, Sundergarh, Kalinga Nagar area, Keonjhar), a relatively new dynamic of poverty and insecurity is being generated that is more closely linked with urban, non-farm livelihoods and labour market dynamics[6]. Of course, there are general features that are part of the poverty regimes in all these spatial contexts, but for a comprehensive analysis, the gender dimensions of poverty and food insecurity need to be understood in relation to such specificities.

Table 1: Poverty Head Count Ratio (Per cent) in Odisha and India, 1973-74 to 2011-12

(*in percentages*)

Year	*Reference Period**	*Odisha*			*India*		
		Rural	*Urban*	*Total*	*Rural*	*Urban*	*Total*
1	*2*	*3*	*4*	*5*	*6*	*7*	*8*
			Expert Committee Methodology				
1973-74	URP	67.28	55.62	66.18	56.44	49.01	54.88
1977-78	URP	72.38	50.92	70.07	53.07	45.24	51.32
1983	URP	67.53	49.15	65.29	45.65	40.79	44.48
1987-88	URP	57.64	41.53	55.58	39.09	38.2	38.36
1993-94	URP	49.72	41.64	48.56	37.27	32.36	35.97
2004-05	URP	46.8	44.3	46.4	28.3	25.7	27.5
			Tendulkar Committee Methodology				
1993-94	MRP	63	34.5	59.1	50.1	30.8	45.3
2004-05	MRP	60.8	37.6	57.2	41.8	25.7	37.2
2009-10	MRP	39.2	25.9	37	33.8	20.9	29.8
2011-12	MRP	35.69	17.29	32.59	25.7	13.7	21.92

Note: *URP—Uniform Recall Period Method, MRP—Mixed Recall Period Method

Source: Economic Survey of Odisha, 2013-14.

Regional and social concentration of poverty reinforce each other—SC and STs have higher rates of poverty than others, but ST/SCs of interior Orissa have a remarkably higher probability of being poor than their counter parts in coastal Orissa[7] (de Haan & Dubey 2005; Shah et al. 2005; Panda 2008; Mishra 2009)[8]. This spatial and social concentration of poverty in Orissa is rooted in the historical processes of economic transformation and stagnation. The structural inequalities in the distribution of assets and entitlements mirror the underlying processes of social hierarchies, discrimination and exclusion. The agrarian economy of Orissa and the way it has been transformed since the colonial period provides clues to the regionally and socially differentiated poverty regime in rural Orissa. As Mohanty (2014) points out, Odisha's class-caste structure shows remarkable stability in a period of comparatively rapid economic transformation. The same caste groups that dominated Odisha some 20 years back continue to dominate the state's economy and polity. Unlike many other parts of the country, there has been little dynamism in the state, so far as mobility of the lower and middle castes is concerned.

Table 2: Poverty in Rural Orissa: Social Groups and Regions 2004-05 to 2011-12

Region	*Rural*				
	ST	*SC*	*OBC*	*Other*	*All*
2004-05					
Coastal	78.40	55.18	41.84	34.03	44.64
Southern	89.34	79.15	72.45	53.29	80.70
Northern	82.41	79.59	63.64	42.79	71.58
Orissa	84.43	67.89	52.60	37.06	60.78
2009-10					
Coastal	40.80	37.70	15.63	25.45	25.30
Southern	78.71	62.42	34.67	21.67	52.35
Northern	57.55	41.87	28.05	24.27	41.66
Orissa	66.03	47.11	25.62	24.54	39.20
2011-12					
Coastal	53.13	33.19	17.37	12.74	21.65
Southern	69.02	58.91	27.79	23.17	48.00
Northern	59.44	34.71	29.17	8.55	39.97
Orissa	63.52	41.39	24.16	14.20	35.69

Note: Poverty lines for rural Odisha are taken as (Tendulkar Methodology: Mixed Recall Period in Rs. per capita per month) Rs. 407.78 for 2004-05 (61st round), Rs. 567.1 for 2009-10 (66th round), and Rs. 695 for 2011-12 (68th round) from GoI, Planning Commission (2009) 'Report of the expert group to review the methodology for estimation of poverty' for 2004-05; GoI, Planning Commission (2012) 'Press Note on Poverty Estimates, 2009-10' for 2009-10; and GoI, Planning Commission (2013) 'Press Note on Poverty Estimates, 2011-12' for 2011-12.

Source: NSS unit level data of Consumption Expenditure Survey of respective rounds.

It is precisely in the two poorest regions of Odisha (northern and southern), where an overwhelming majority of scheduled tribe and scheduled caste population lives. For Odisha as a whole, the incidence of poverty among the ST and the SC is higher than that among the others. Between 1993-94 and 2004-05, poverty ratio, in fact, has increased among the STs and SCs in the northern and southern districts. This spatial and social concentration of poverty among the tribals and dalits living in interior districts of Odisha is the outcome of the historical processes of exclusion and discrimination that have been among the pronounced features of the social economy of the region[9]. However, the exclusion from and unequal access

Table 3: Food Consumption, Expenditure and Nutrition Characteristics in India and Odisha, 2011-12

Indicators	*Odisha Rural*	*India Rural*	*Odisha Urban*	*India Urban*
Average MPCE (Rs.)	1003	1430	1941	2630
% Share of cereals in total expenditure	17	11	10	7
% Share of food in total expenditure	57	53	45	43
Monthly per capita quantity of cereal consumed (kg)	13.4	11.2	11.4	9.3
% in total quantity of cereal consumed of				
Rice	94	55	81	50
Wheat	6	39	18	47
Other cereal	1	6	0	3
Calorie intake (kcal) per day per capita	2215	2233	2191	2206
% Of calories from cereals	69.7	57.4	59.6	48
Protein intake (gm) per day per capita	53.4	60.7	55.9	60.3
Fat intake (gm) per day per capita	27.1	46.1	37.7	58

Source: Based on NSS 68th Round (2011-12) Reports.

to state-initiated anti-poverty measures also has a significant bearing on such outcomes (Shah et al. 2005).

The general scenario of food consumption pattern is depicted in Table 3. While the average monthly per capita consumption expenditure in Odisha is less than that of India, the share of food expenditure in total expenditure and the share of expenditure on cereal in total food expenditure is much higher in Odisha. Cereal consumption in Odisha is dominated by rice, more remarkably in rural Odisha. While average protein and fat intake in Odisha is much less than that of India as a whole, the gap is less severe in calories intake per capita per day and a higher share of calorie comes from cereals. Thus, the production and consumption of rice need to be examined more closely to understand the food security scenario in Odisha.

Unfortunately, the secondary data on consumption poverty does not provide an adequate understanding of the intra-family distribution of food and nutrition. However, given the dominant patriarchal norms prevalent in the society, there is a distinct possibility that women and girl children suffer more in the context of abject poverty and malnutrition. Another dimension that should be noted in the backdrop of the discussion above is that women's access to food or livelihoods is likely to vary within Odisha as well. For example, those who are living in a context of commercial agriculture with significant use of hired labour in agriculture, the crucial aspect could be the terms under which they are incorporated into the rural labour market, while those who are located within the context of self-cultivation the patriarchal norms governing use of family labour is more likely to have a determining influence.

Contextualizing Female Disadvantage in Odisha

Sharp disparities in opportunities and outcomes between males and females have come to be an enduring feature of the social life in Odisha. Although scholars referring to spatial embeddedness of gender relations in the Indian context often refer to the north-south divide in India (also expressed as the wheat-rice difference, referring to the role of cropping patterns and associated work opportunities) (Raju 2015), the relatively high levels of gender disparities in Odisha can be thought of as a counterexample to such generalizations. A detailed analysis and assessment of gender disparities in Odisha is beyond the scope of the present paper. However, even a cursory look at selected dimensions of gender equality captures the patriarchal bias in this State. However, it is equally important to note that gender relations are far from uniform within Odisha—apart from caste, ethnicity and region which play an important role in defining and differentiating the status of women.[10]

Table 4: Infant and Under-five Mortality Rates in Odisha by Sex

	NFHS III (2004-5)	*AHS (2010-11)*	*AHS (2011-12)*	*SRS (2011)*	*NFHS IV (2015-16)*
IMR					
Boys	75	59	56	55	40.5
Girls	59.4	66	63	58	39.6
Total	67.7	62	59	57	40
U-5MR					
Boys	103.7	80	76	70	49.4
Girls	84.4	84	81	74	47.8
Total	90.6	82	79	72	48

Source: NFHS III and IV, Census of India.

Life expectancy at birth in Odisha for male and female are estimated at 64.3 years and 67.3 years respectively, which are lower than the national average of 67.3 years and 69.6 years respectively. The state also reports a higher IMR (51) than that of the country as a whole (40) in 2013, although there has been a steady improvement over time (Government of Odisha 2015). Odisha's record in reducing Maternal Mortality Ratio (MMR), which was 235 per one lakh live births during 2012-13 (compared to 178 in India), has been far from satisfactory. The gender disparities in IMR and under-5 mortality rates, presented in Table 4, suggests that the IMR and U5MR for girls in Odisha are higher than that for boys, though NFHS III results suggest the reverse.

According to NFHS-III, in 2005-06, 18.3 per cent of women were moderately or severely undernourished compared to 12.5 per cent of men, and girls in the age group 6-59 months were more anaemic (66.6 per cent) than boys (63.5 per cent). Also as per NFHS-III, within the age-group 15-49 a higher percentage of women were thin than that among the men. NFHS IV data suggests that under 5 mortality rate among the girls in Odisha continues to be higher than that for the boys, despite significant improvements in the mortality rates (Table 4). Such pervasive gender discrimination is noticeable in other spheres of health and well-being as well (Table 5). Only 64 per cent of women are literate in Odisha, while literacy rate for males is 82 per cent. The female literacy rate among the marginalized communities and less developed regions within Odisha is much lower. de Haan and Dubey (2005) have drawn attention to the enduring discrimination against women in Odisha, by examining a number of demographic, economic and social indicators. According to the Annual Health Survey (2010-11), nearly one third of currently married women in the age group of 20-24 years were married before the legal age of 18. Further, NFHS IV data suggests that among the women belonging to 15-49 years in Odisha, 35 per cent were subjected to either physical or sexual violence. In a study based on NFHS II data, Sahoo & Raju (2007) report that 28.8 per cent of ever-married women in Odisha were beaten or physically maltreated, as against the all-India average of 19.4. Further, working women are more likely to face violence than those who are not working.

The vulnerabilities faced by women in the sphere of resource ownership and employment gets further accentuated during periods of crisis such as floods, cyclones and other disasters. An ethnographic research on surviving disasters in a village in Odisha noted that 'caste, class and gender do not operate on their own; they intersect to intensify women's vulnerabilities before, during and after multiple disasters' (Ray-Bennett 2009: 19).

Table 5: Nutritional Status of Women and Men (Age 15-49): 2015-16

Region	*Percentage of population whose BMI is below normal (BMI<18.5 kg/m²) (NFHS IV 2015-16)*							
	*Women**				*Men*			
	Urban	*Rural*	*Total NFHS IV (2015-16)*	*Total NFHS III (2005-6)*	*Urban*	*Rural*	*Total NFHS IV (2015-16)*	*Total NFHS III (2005-6)*
India	15.5	26.7	22.9	35.5	15.4	23.0	20.2	34.2
Orissa	15.8	28.7	26.5	41.4	12.6	21.4	19.5	35.7

Note:*Excludes pregnant women and women with a birth in the preceding two months.
Source: NFHS-IV, 2015-16.

Of particular significance is the condition of female-headed households. Female-headed households themselves could be diverse and depending upon the family structure, other social characteristics, such households may experience different degrees of poverty and undernutrition. According to (Panda 1997), nearly 10 per cent of households in rural Odisha are headed by female. In a detailed analysis of the levels of poverty across households, Panda found that per capita consumption-levels in female-headed households is nearly half of that among male-headed households, indicating a strong relationship between female-headed households and poverty, regardless of the poverty measure or welfare measure used. Parappurathu et al. (2015) in a study in eastern India that included four villages from Odisha noted that male-headed households are more likely to have a diverse diet.

While noting the pervasive female disadvantage across multiple dimensions, it is important not to miss out the significant differences among women across caste/class groups. Secondly, it is also important to note that while outcome disadvantages are important in themselves as indicators of women's status, it is the process disadvantages which need to be focused on as long-term and fundamental structures that generate long-enduring gender discrimination (Jackson and Palmer-Jones 1999).

Gendered Poverty and Food Security

Gender and Land Rights

Engels in his *Origin of Family, Private Property and State* has linked the issue of property rights over land to the subordination of women. Boserup has drawn attention to the linkages between changing farming systems and womens' status in society. Of particular significance is the transition from slash and burn agriculture to plough based system, where women's role in socially valued, productive activities gets reduced.

Land rights for women, help in overcoming poverty and undernutrition, but more importantly, it helps empowerment of women through increased bargaining power within and outside the households (Agarwal 1994a; Agarwal 2003).

Property rights over land mean a bundle of rights including 'access' (the right to be on the land); withdrawal (the right to take something from the land, such as water, firewood, or produce); management (the right to change the land in some way, such as to plant crops or trees); exclusion (the right to prevent others from using the land); and alienation (the right to transfer land to others through rental, bequest, or sale' (Doss et al. 2014). In any given context, these ownerships of land might mean all or most of these rights, though 'they are not necessarily bundled together, and women may have fewer rights over land than men. Women may have access, withdrawal, and even management rights, but are less likely to have exclusion and alienation rights' (Doss et al. 2014). Access to productive assets like land, undoubtedly enhances the possibilities of earnings and control over food items produced on the land. Land is also an important social resource and is often a precondition to access non-tangible resources like 'trust' and 'influence'. Rights in land, especially among poor households, argues Agarwal (1994)' could reduce women's own and, more generally, the household's risk of poverty and destitution. The reason for this stems partly from the general positive effect of giving women access to economic resources independently of men; and partly from the specific advantages associated with rights in land resources'. However, it is important to note that the reason behind women's access to land cannot simply be reduced to its instrumental role in raising productivity and enhancing nutrition. Secondly, the interrelationship between land ownership and food and nutrition security is far from being automatic and is highly context dependent.

Table 6: Share of Female Operated Holdings in Odisha

Farm-size Class	*Share of Female Managed Operational Holdings in*			
	2004-5		*2010-11*	
	Holdings	*Area*	*Holdings*	*Area*
Marginal	2.95	2.79	3.41	3.20
Small	2.57	2.56	2.99	2.96
Semi-medium	2.30	2.29	2.98	2.95
Medium	2.30	2.27	3.06	3.07
Large	2.62	2.22	3.50	2.52
Total	2.76	2.50	3.29	3.05

Source: Agricultural Census 2004-05 and 2010-11.

Unfortunately, the data on land ownership is not available by gender. Women in general do not have land ownership rights in Odisha. An approximation can be made from the data on female-managed operational holdings that is available from the Agricultural Census. Female-managed operational holdings accounted for 2.76 per cent of all operational holdings in Odisha in 2004-05, which has gone up to 3.05 in 2010-11 (Table 6). The share of women operated holdings in areas is smaller than their share in holdings, indicating that average size of women operated holdings is smaller than the rest. The average size of female operated holdings is 0.96 ha in 2010-11, as against the average size of 1.03 ha in the case of male operated holdings. It is interesting to note that the share of women operated holdings is highest among the marginal holdings, followed by the large and medium categories. Different mechanisms of access to land might be at work at different scales of farm operations. Of the total female managed operational holdings in 2010-11, nearly 46.57 per cent are operated by ST women and 10.54 per cent are managed by SC women.

It is important to take note of the processes of dispossession that have been an intrinsic part of the neo-liberal development strategy, particularly in the context of Odisha. A large number of projects for mining, industrialization, infrastructure development, commercial plantation and conservation have displaced people from their land. Many of these projects are located in interior Odisha, in districts having substantial tribal populations (Mishra 2011). The primitive accumulation has already created a large mass of people, displaced from their traditional habitats and livelihoods, and forced to be dependent upon precarious livelihoods. Such processes have a long-term disempowering effect on the poor and the vulnerable populations in general, but this is also a gendered process. Because, notwithstanding the inroads that commercialization and private property rights have already made into the tribal areas, women's participation in the subsistence economy used to be considerably high in these regions. Once the foundations of the livelihoods are snatched away, women farmers in particular, become disinherited peasants: those who continue to work, but without any effective control over the production. The loss of village commons and access to other natural resources not only increases women's work burden substantially, but it also adversely affects their access to food.

Women and Work in Rural Odisha

Given the overwhelming significance of rural labour market dynamics for poverty in Odisha, the nature of employment available for women and the terms under which they are employed has a crucial implication for their earning capabilities as well as the welfare implications of work. Needless to add, a substantial majority of female workers work as unpaid family workers or as wage labourers, though the worker participation rate is lower than that of the all-India level (Table 7). Close to 70 per cent of female workers are employed in agriculture, and the share of females employed as self-employed is not only higher in Odisha than at the national average, it has increased during 2004-05 to 2010-11 as per NSS data, a trend that needs to be seen in the context of the shifts within the agrarian economy. Among the female subsidiary status workers in 2010-11, 73.07 per cent are self-employed, while 26.42 per cent work as casual labour. Of all female subsidiary workers, 73 per cent were in the farm sector.

Table 7: Employment Characteristics of Rural Females

Labour Force Characteristics	*Orissa (Rural)*		*India (Rural)*	
	2004-2005	*2010-11*	*2004-2005*	*2010-11*
Labour force participation PS+SS (female) in Odisha	25.1	25.1	28.7	25.3
Share of female Self-employed as per PS+SS status	61.9	66.1	63.7	59.3
Share of female regular employees as per PS+SS status	2.1	3.4	3.7	5.6
Share of female casual labour as per PS+SS status	35.9	30.5	32.6	35.1
Share of agriculture workers in total female workers as per PS+SS status	74.6	69.31	83.3	74.9

Note: PS+SS refers to both principal and subsidiary status.
Source: NSS rounds.

Data from another large-scale survey outlines the broad context of such participation of women (Table 8). The patriarchal control over women's employment patterns can be easily deciphered from the data presented here. In the case of Odisha, the say of husbands is significant in the case of 77 per cent of females, which is much higher than that in the country as a whole. While nearly 52 per cent of women are willing to work, if suitable jobs are available, nearly 51 per cent of them are not allowed to work even if suitable jobs are available—a share that is much higher than the rest of India. The poverty-employment relationship has to be seen in the light of such overwhelming patriarchal control of the decision to work.

Table 8: Women's Autonomy in Work, India and Odisha

Indicators		*India*	*Odisha*
Ever worked for pay/wages	No	58.9	70.4
	Yes	41.1	29.6
Ever worked for MGNREGA	No	62.8	72.9
	Yes	37.2	27.1
Who has most say: decisions about your work	Self	44.1	32.7
	Husband	52.2	66.9
	Senior male	1.7	0.1
	Senior female	1.7	0.2
	Others	0.3	0
Willing to work: if suitable job found	No	34.8	48.2
	Yes	65.2	51.8
Allowed to work: if suitable job found	No	34.2	50.9
	Yes	65.8	49.1

Source: Based on IHDS II.

Insights from Field Survey

In this section, the question gendered poverty and food insecurity has been explored with respect to very specific contexts: agrarian transition and seasonal migration. Choice of these two 'case studies' is based on the relative importance of these two modes of livelihoods for a large number of poor women. As mentioned in the earlier sections, agriculture in Odisha is facing a severe crisis and in the rain-fed regions, this crisis of livelihoods is much more pronounced. The process of seasonal migration, which has emerged as a durable survival strategy for a large number of labour households in interior, rain-fed Odisha, is linked to the crisis of agrarian livelihoods

Table 9: Distributions of Individual Migrants by Age-group and Gender

Sl. No.	District	Village	*All age-group*		*Below 15 years*		*15-30 years*		*Above 30 years*	
			Male	*Female*	*Male*	*Female*	*Male*	*Female*	*Male*	Female
1.	Balangir	Tentuliunda	110 (52.13)	101 (47.87)	28 (56.00)	22 (44.00)	38 (48.72)	40 (51.28)	44 (53.01)	39 (46.99)
		Sorgul	106 (43.09)	140 (56.91)	32 (46.38)	37 (53.62)	30 (33.33)	60 (66.67)	44 (50.57)	43 (49.43)
		Total	216 (47.26)	241 (52.74)	60 (50.42)	59 (49.58)	68 (40.48)	100 (59.52)	88 (51.76)	82 (48.24)
2.	Kalahandi	Dongapakhan	111 (62.01)	68 (37.99)	7 (46.67)	8 (53.33)	41 (65.08)	22 (34.92)	63 (62.38)	38 (37.62)
		Khaliapali	77 (53.10)	68 (46.90)	8 (34.78)	15 (65.22)	21 (48.84)	22 (51.16)	48 (60.76)	31 (39.24)
		Total	188 (58.02)	136 (41.98)	15 (39.47)	23 (60.53)	62 (58.49)	44 (41.51)	111 (61.67)	69 (38.33)
3.	Nuapada	Tuthibar	89 (53.94)	76 (46.06)	26 (57.78)	19 (42.22)	25 (45.45)	30 (54.55)	38 (58.46)	27 (41.54)
		Botha	89 (48.63)	94 (51.37)	16 (41.03)	23 (58.97)	42 (47.73)	46 (52.27)	31 (55.36)	25 (44.64)
		Total	178 (51.15)	170 (48.85)	42 (50.00)	42 (50.00)	67 (46.85)	76 (53.15)	69 (57.02)	52 (42.98)
Grand Total			582 (51.55)	547 (48.45)	117 (48.55)	124 (51.45)	197 (47.24)	220 (52.76)	268 (56.90)	203 (43.10)

Note: Figure in parentheses refers to percentage.
Source: Mishra (2015).

in Odisha. The role of state and non-state agencies has also been described on the basis of field experiences.

The Agrarian Dynamics

Based on recent field investigations[11], a few aspects of women's participation in the agrarian economy of Odisha are being described here. Women's participation in agriculture is relatively high in the tribal-dominated southern districts of Odisha. Given the overwhelming dominance of patriarchal norms, women's participation also differs across caste lines. In overall terms, Odisha's agrarian economy is dominated by paddy cultivation, which is a labour-intensive crop. Consequently, a large number of women participate in their family farm or as agricultural labour. In the irrigated paddy-cultivating belts of Odisha, seasonally migrant labour is employed for transplantation, weeding and harvesting, many of whom are women. In recent years, there have been some significant changes in the agrarian economy of Odisha, which include, diversification of crop cultivation to vegetables in the irrigated region, rising cost of inputs, particularly pesticides and fertilizers, rising labour costs, increasing environmental problems, and declining profitability of paddy cultivation. The areas under cotton cultivation has expanded in the rain-fed region. In some parts of the state, such as Kalahandi and Koraput, new areas have been brought under irrigation and a new agrarian economy of multiple cropping of paddy is being introduced[12].

However, except for a few households producing vegetables and in some parts rice, most rural households have diversified into the non-agrarian economy in one way or the other. The better-off households have typically diversified into transport, trading, real estate, construction, services and education. While those at the bottom have joined the non-farm labour market within the villages, in nearby towns and also through circular migration. This has several implications for women within the labour and cultivating households. On the one hand, the relative tightening of the (male) rural labour market, many more women have joined as casual wage labour in agriculture and also in the non-farm labour market. MGNREGA, despite its limitations has acted as a floor in rural wage labour market, where there is a credible chance of being employed atleast for a few weeks. Consequently, women's wages in the rural labour market has increased, though there are considerable variations across the districts.On the other hand, women of cultivating families have been drawn to work in the family farms as a means to reduce labour costs or because the men have moved out for employment elsewhere. This spatial relocation of family labour and the associated risk minimization strategies, point to a selective feminization of agriculture, both in the case of subsistence as well as commercial agriculture. However, the empowerment effects of such participation remain an open question. The increasing share of women as subsidiary or marginal workers points to the distress phenomena underlying such employment outcomes.

The other aspect of the on-going commercialization of the agrarian economy is that in the backdrop of withdrawal of state support to agriculture, the role of the commission agents-traders-input dealers has become central to technology adoption, input-choice, credit availability and marketing of products (Mishra 2008). These agents and traders are increasingly significant source of credit, inputs and information, and often enter into interlocked transactions involving purchase of products after harvest.This process is essentially male-centric and often involves bargaining and negotiations in shops, market places and in nearby towns. Small and marginal farmers are as such at a disadvantageous position. Women cultivators, in the absence of support from males, face discrimination in such kind of a transformation of agriculture.

The increasing participation of women in both family farms as well as in the casual labour market might seems as a positive development. However, this increased participation is often under conditions of distress and hence, it should be seen in relation to work intensity. Under conditions of environmental degradation, the work burden of women increases (Mishra and Mishra 2012), and it adversely affects the food security of women and children. Under such conditions, participation in work does not necessarily increases well-being (Jackson and Palmer-Jones 1999).

Seasonal Migration

Seasonal migration of labour from the rain-fed agricultural belts of Odisha's KBK (Kalahandi-Balangir-Koraput) region, has been a durable strategy of the poor since decades. Now this kind of migration has also been noticed in other parts of the state. Seasonal migration is typically underestimated in secondary data, and there is hardly any evidence to judge its impact on poverty. What, is of course, clear that bondage and unfreedom of labour have been defining characteristics of most, if not all, seasonal labour contracts (Mishra, 2016).

There are different streams of seasonal migration, ranging from migration to the urban informal sector in Chhattisgarh, to construction work in Kerala, Tamil Nadu and Maharashtra, but the dominant stream in the region is that of migration to the brick kilns within and outside Odisha. Migration to brick-kilns is generally through labour contractors, with families and in labour groups. As labour movement to brick kilns dominates seasonal migration from the study region, where family labour is preferred, it was seen nearly 72 per cent of workers moved in mixed groups comprising of males and females. Nearly 10 per cent went in either exclusively male or female groups. Typically, the male head of the household takes an advance from the labour contractor or his agents and commits the labour of the entire family. Payments are made against groups of three called *pathuria*, with one male, one female and one child. The data presented in Table 9 indicates that females constitute as high as 48.45 per cent of all seasonal migrants and in the villages dominated by migration to brick kilns, their share is even higher.

The seasonal migration process involves several elements

of bondage, such as: working off of debt through labour, virtually no freedom to bargain wages with the employers directly, no control over or information regarding destination of migration, no freedom to change employers before the contract period is over, restriction on mobility at the work site, poor working and living conditions, physical violence etc. However, women workers are specifically vulnerable in such kinds of labour contracts. Not only do they not enter into the bargaining process with the labour contractors, they virtually have no control over their labour-power during the contract period. They live under extremely unhygienic conditions, in make-shift *chawls* at work sites, and survive on *kanki* (broken rice, usually sold as chicken feed). Seasonal migration of this kind is simply the last resort to escape hunger in the lean season, and it adversely affects the health of the workers. There have been cases of physical torture, sexual harassment and rape against the owners and their henchmen. The travel to the destination and return journey has also been traumatic experiences for some migrant women. Those who do not go for seasonal migration, typically shoulder a bigger work burden in terms of taking care of the old and disable members of the family and household chores. Thus, under conditions of extreme poverty and vulnerabilities, livelihood 'choices' like seasonal migration accentuates women's exploitation.

State and NGO Interventions

State interventions through PDS, employment guarantee, provision of rural infrastructure like roads and sanitation, basic services such as health and primary health care plays significant role in reducing poverty and malnutrition. Odisha's performance in this regard has been mixed. While significant progress has been made in some areas, abysmal records in many other areas remain a cause of concern. Similarly, NGO intervention through self-help groups has been hailed as a success story. A comprehensive overview of these interventions is beyond the scope of this study. However, a few tentative observations on the impact of state intervention on poverty and livelihoods diversification from a gender perspective, need to be highlighted here. Firstly, notwithstanding all the leakages and corruption involved, universal PDS in the KBK region has helped poor households in general to avoid starvation. The performance of ICDS and other targeted programmes for women have improved in comparison to the past, and it has started showing impacts in terms of better access to health care[13] (Thomas et al. 2015). It is important to underline the fact that programmes that have deviated from the strict neo liberal prescription (universal PDS coverage rather than targeted PDS, for example) and have created institutional capacities at the local level have performed better.

Apart from schemes such as ICDS, the government of Odisha, with support from the DFID (Department for International Development) has initiated a specific plan Nutrition Operation Plan which focuses on the 15 'High Burden' districts of Odisha viz. Angul, Bhadrak, Bolangir, Guajarati, Jharsuguda, Kalahandi, Kandhamal, Keonjhar, Koraput, Malkangiri, Nawarangpur, Nuapada, Rayagada, Sambalpur and Sundargarh, with the an objective to bring down malnutrition from current levels of the children by four years. The specific aims are to reduce i) the per cent of underweight children from 41 per cent to 25 per cent focusing on scheduled tribe with an average annual reduction of 3.5 percent; ii) Stunting from 45 per cent to 35 per cent with an average annual reduction of 2.5 per cent; iii) Wasting from 20 per cent to 10 per cent with an average annual reduction of 2.5 per cent. In terms of access to ICDS, NFHS figures do not report substantial gender bias against the girl child in Odisha (Department of Women and Child Development 2009), however, at the moment the gendered impact of such intervention seems not to be the focus.

The performance of MGNREGA, however, remains uneven and less impressive than other states. As per official statistics, the average number of days of employment generated per household under MGNREGA in Odisha was 57 in 2006-7 and it has declined to only 33 days in 2011-12, which is lower than the national average of 43. Many states such as Andhra Pradesh, Himachal Pradesh, Madhya Pradesh, Tamil Nadu, Kerala, Karnataka and Maharashtra have shown a better performance on this count. Of the total households in MGNREGA in Odisha, only 6 per cent completed 100 days of employment in 2006-07, and this got reduced to less than 1 per cent in 2011-12. So far as social groups-wise participation is concerned, in Odisha, the participation of SCs in the scheme declined from 23.65 per cent in 2006-07 to 2011-12, while that of STs remained around 35-39 per cent during the same period. The share of women in the scheme, however, declined from 57 per cent in 2006-07 to only 33 per cent in 2011-12[14]. The fact that improvements in delivery of some programmes are better than others suggests scope for improvement within the delivery mechanism; but more importantly, there may be demand-side factors such as political mobilization of the poor and role of the media and civil society in creating pressure for better implementation of programmes, which might explain such diversity of outcomes. An example of inter-governmental initiatives that might help the conditions of seasonal migrants is the establishment of Migrant Assistance Centres, through a joint initiative of the governments of Odisha and Andhra Pradesh (Borhade 2016).

Viewed from the field-survey experiences, NGO interventions have undergone a change in the last two decades, at least in the study areas. From activities that directly supplemented or substituted state's efforts at creating alternative and sustainable livelihoods, the NGO activities are more about lobbying, and influencing state-initiated programmes. Regarding approaches, the dividing lines between NGOs and state interventions has shrunk considerably. Market-enabling interventions have taken precedence over other programmes. All these changes have significant implications for women, who have been the focus of NGO interventions in the region. Self-help groups remain the core strategy of many NGOs and in some cases, at least it seems to be working in reducing dependence on informal lenders. Creation of alternative livelihoods have not worked everywhere, but where it has, the vulnerability of women, particularly those belongin to the migrant labour households seems to have decreased.

Conclusion

The question of food security and poverty is embedded in the larger political economy of economic transformation of Odisha. As Odisha's development strategy involves opening up of the state's mineral and other natural resources for exploitation by private capital, both domestic and foreign, the labouring poor are being gradually incorporated in what essentially constitutes a 'low road to capitalism' (Basile 2013). A gendered view of this process not only highlights the differential impact of such a transformation on women and the girl child but more importantly, it opens up the possibility of examining the transition through the intersecting transitions in the spheres of state, market, community and family. This chapter highlights the ways through which economic transformation under neo-liberalism creates and sustains older and newer forms of vulnerabilities for the poor in general and for the women in particular. It is important to note that in a period of gradual decline in the incidence of consumption poverty, the spatial and social concentration of poverty has remained more or less unchanged. As poorer households attempt to cope with this onslaught on their livelihoods by opting for diversification across space and time, women face additional burdens of work, within and outside the domestic spheres.

NOTES

1. There are, of course, lots of variations across space and social groups. For a discussion on women's employment and its interface with socio-economic characteristics see Raju (2015).
2. In 2012-13, metallurgical products accounted for nearly 41 per cent of total exports from Odisha in value terms whereas minerals accounted for around 18 per cent. The main mineral export from Odisha is iron ore. Thus, extractive industries are significant to understand the interlinkages between the economy

of Odisha and the global economy (Das and Mishra 2015).

3. Odisha's recent economic growth has been mainly driven by mining and mineral-based industries. The spatial concentration of these activities in and around specific locations within Odisha has meant very different kinds of opportunities and vulnerabilities faced by the poor populations in these districts. It is important to note that industrialized districts such as Jhargsuguda, Sundergarh and Anugul; or mining areas such as Mayurbhanj and Denkanal have emerged as the most prosperous districts in the recent period on the basis of per capita district domestic product, on the other hand agriculturally prosperous districts such as Balasore, Bhadrakh and Bargarh have shown a decline in their relative positions. For a discussion on the regional dimension of Odisha's economic development see, Das and Mishra, 2015.
4. However, the *Odisha Economic Survey 2014-15* argues that economic growth in Odisha has been inclusive: 'Poverty declined in all National Sample Survey regions (i.e., coastal, northern and southern regions) and among all social classes (i.e., ST, SC, OBC and others) of Odisha.' This implies inclusive growth in Odisha. Though there has been significant poverty reduction among ST and SC communities and in northern and southern regions, the incidence of poverty in southern and northern regions as well as among ST and SC communities still continues to be high and remains a matter of concern'.
5. It is possible to support the first three types of poverty regimes from the NSSO and other secondary data, to the extent the dominant characteristics are found in the three NSS regions: coastal, northern and southern Odisha (see Shah et al. 2005).
6. These stylised contexts are far from exhaustive. There are specific vulnerabilities that has created poverty traps for specific groups such as fisherman communities, people living along the coastlines, artisan groups and others losing their traditional occupations.
7. The regional differences are not just limited to divergent initial conditions, the trends in poverty reduction shows remarkable differences as well. The Coastal region, which has the least poverty ratio, has experienced a significant decline in the HCR-from 45 per cent in 1993-94 to 27 per cent in 2004-05. During the same period, the southern region, which has the highest incidence of poverty at 73 per cent in 2004-05, has experienced

an increase in poverty by 4 percentage points. The Northern region has witnessed the biggest rise in the incidence of rural poverty from 46 per cent in 1993-94 to 59 per cent in 2004-05 (Panda, 2008).

8. Alternative estimates of poverty also indicate a similar picture. As pointed out by de Haan and Dubey (2003), NCAER (1999) data suggests that 'Orissa in 1994 had the highest percentage population below the poverty line: 55 compared to the all-India average of 39 per cent, with—perhaps even more striking—a poverty gap of 0.30 compared to the national of 0.18, and the lowest average per capita income per year: Rs. 3,028 compared to the India average of Rs. 4,485 (poverty line for Orissa was set at Rs. 2,330; mean income of the poor was Rs. 1,319)'.
9. An important aspect of Odisha's social history has been the gradual (and discriminatory) assimilation of the tribal population with the caste Hindu society. The interior districts of Odisha, with relatively high concentration of scheduled castes and tribes, continue to be the battleground for these tendencies of assimilation, exclusion and autonomy.
10. Extent of calorie deprivations, for example, vary significantly across MPCE classes and castes (Gupta and Mishra 2013).
11. The evidence presented here are from three different rounds of household surveys conducted in villages of Odisha. Two rain-fed villages, one each from Koraput and Nuapada were surveyed with a focus on paddy cultivation, under the project *Resource, Greenhouse gases, Technology and Jobs in India's Informal Economy: The Case of Rice, 2010-13*. Seasonal Migrants from six different villages, two each from Balangir, Kalahandi and Nuapada, were studied under the ICSSR-sponsored project *Seasonal Migration, Poverty and Livelihoods Diversification in Rural Orissa, 2010-13*. Two villages- one each from Bargarh and Balangir district were surveyed under the ICSSR-sponsored project on *Agrarian Transition and Rural Transformation in India: A Study in Comparative Political Economy* (2013-16). Insights from all these surveys are being selectively presented in this section.
12. While the availability of irrigation has increased agricultural productivity and has led to agrarian prosperity of a kind, it has also created a new structure of deprivation. Migrant cultivators from outside the region, and non-tribal households, have acquired a high proportion of irrigated land.
13. The Economic Survey reports: 'The coverage of households

having access to safe drinking water (taps, hand pumps and tubewells) was 75.3 percent as per the 2011 census. The Integrated Management Information System (IMIS) reports that 2.7 percent rural habitations in Odisha were not covered under drinking water supply programmes in 2009. As per 2011 census about 78% of all households do not have sanitation facility in their premises. The Total Sanitation Campaign (TSC) has been implemented to provide toilets in rural areas and encourage people to improve sanitation conditions. Physical achievements under this programme have been encouraging. By 2013-14, 58.1 percent households, 100 percent schools, 100 percent Anganwadis were covered under the programme'.

14. Drawing upon a field survey in Jajpur and Mayurbhanj districts of Odisha, Parida (2016) notes that participation of poor, landless and socially marginalized groups is very high in the MGNREGS, but that of women, in relation to men is not significant. Another significant finding of this study is that MGNREGS has been successful in reducing seasonal migration. Mishra (2015), based on his field survey in Nuapada, Balangir and Kalahandi districts report that MGNREGS has not been successful in controlling seasonal outmigration substantially, but a moderately dependable implementation of the scheme, does increase the bargaining power of seasonal migrants vis-à-vis labour contractors.

REFERECES

Agarwal, B., 1994a. *A field of one's own: Gender and land rights in South Asia*, Cambridge University Press.

Agarwal, B., 1994b. Gender and command over property: A critical gap in economic analysis and policy in South Asia. *World Development*, 22(10), pp. 1455–1478.

Agarwal, B., 2003. Gender and land rights revisited: exploring new prospects via the state, family and market. *Journal of Agrarian Change*, 3(1-2), pp. 184–224.

Basile, E., 2013. *Capitalist development in India's informal economy*, Routledge.

Borhade, A., 2016. Internal Labour Migration in India: Emerging Needs of Comprehensive National Migration Policy. In D.K. Mishra, ed. *Internal Migration in Contemporary India*. Sage Publications, pp. 291–336.

Das, R. and Mishra, D.K., 2015. *Uneven Development in Odisha*, Paper presented at York Centre for Asian Studies, University of York, Toronto.

Department of Women and Child Development, Government of Odisha, 2009. *Nutrition Operation Plan 2009-13*, Bhubaneswar.

Doss, C., Summerfield, G. & Tsikata, D., 2014. Land, Gender and Food Security. *Feminist Economics*, 20(1), pp. 1–23.

Government of Odisha, 2015. *Odisha Economic Survey 2014-15*, Bhubaneswar.

Gupta, A. & Mishra, D.K., 2013. Poverty and calorie deprivation across socio-economic groups in rural india: a disaggregated analysis. *Journal of Regional Development and Planning*, 2(1), pp. 15–33.

de Haan, A. & Dubey, A., 2005. Poverty, Disparities, or the Development of Underdevelopment in Orissa. *Economic and Political Weekly*, 40(22/23), pp. 2321–2329. Available at: http://www.jstor.org/stable/4416712.

Harriss, B., 1990. The intrafamily distribution of hunger in South Asia. *The Political Economy of Hunger*, 1, pp. 351–424.

Jackson, C. and Palmer-Jones, R., 1999. Rethinking gendered poverty and work. *Development and Change*, 30(3), pp. 557–583.

Krishna, S., 2005. Gendered Price of Rice in North-Eastern India. *Economic and Political Weekly*, 40(25), pp. 2555–2562.

Mishra, A. and Mishra, D.K., 2012. Deforestation and Women's Work Burden in the Eastern Himalayas, India: Insights from a Field Survey. *Gender, Technology and Development*, 16(3), pp. 299–328. Available at: http://gtd.sagepub.com/content/16/3/299.abstract [Accessed August 23, 2015].

Mishra, D.K., 2011. 'Behind Dispossession: State, Land Grabbing and Agrarian Change in Rural Orissa'. International Conference on Global Land Grabbing, IDS, Sussex. Available at: http://www.researchgate.net/profile/Deepak_Mishra18/publication/256835243_Behind_Dispossession_State_Land_Grabbing_and_Agrarian_Change_in_Rural_Orissa/links/00463524fb7d825907000000.pdf [Accessed August 23, 2015].

Mishra, D.K., 2015. *Seasonal Migration, Poverty and Livelihoods Diversification in Rural Orissa*, A Report submitted to the ICSSR, New Delhi.

Mishra, D.K., 2016. Seasonal Migration from Odisha: A Field View. In D.K. Mishra, ed. *Internal Migration in Contemporary India*. Sage

Publications, pp. 263–290.

Mishra, D.K., 2008. Structural Inequalities and Interlinked Transactions in Agrarian Markets: Results of a Field Survey. In S.K. Bhaumik, ed. *Reforming Indian Agriculture: Towards Employment Generation and Poverty Reduction Essays in Honour of G K Chadha*. New Delhi: Sage Publications, pp. 231–268. Available at: https://books.google.com/books?hl=en&lr=&id=dLOGAwAAQBAJ&pgis=1.

Mishra, S., 2009. *Poverty and Agrarian Distress in Orissa*, Mumbai. Available at: http://www.igidr.ac.in/pdf/publication/WP-2009-006.pdf [Accessed January 16, 2016].

Mohanty, M., 2014. Persisting Dominance. *Economic and Political Weekly*, pp. 39–47. Available at: http://www.epw.in/journal/2014/14/odisha-special-issues/persisting-dominance.html.

Nussbaum, M.C., 2001. *Women and Human Development: The Capabilities Approach*, Cambridge University Press.

Panda, M., 2008. *Economic Development in Orissa: Growth Without Inclusion*, Mumbai. Available at: http://www.eaber.org/sites/default/files/documents/IGIDR_Panda_2008.pdf [Accessed January 16, 2016].

Panda, P.K., 1997. Female Headship, Poverty and Child Welfare—A Study of Rural Orissa. *Economic and Political Weekly*, 32(43), pp. WS73-WS82.

Parappurathu, S. et al., 2015. Food Consumption Patterns and Dietary Diversity in Eastern India: Evidence from Village Level Studies (VLS). *Food Security*, 7(5), pp. 1031–1042.

Parida, J.K., 2016. MGNREGS, Distress Migration and Livelihood Conditions: A Study in Odisha. *Journal of Social and Economic Development*, online.

Raju, S., 2015. Women and Work in India: Simultaneous Geographies. In E. Basile, B. Harriss-White, and C. Lutringer, eds. *Mapping India's Capitalism: Old and New Regions*. Hampshire: Palgrave Macmillan, pp. 113–142.

Rao, N., 2005. 'Gender Equality, Land Rights and Household Food Security Discussion of Rice Farming Systems'. *Economic And Political Weekly*, 40(25), pp. 2513–2521. Available at: http://www.jstor.org/stable/4416780.

Ray-Bennett, N.S., 2009. The Influence of Caste, Class and Gender in Surviving Multiple Disasters: A Case Study from Orissa, India. *Environmental Hazards*, 8(1), pp. 5–22.

Sahoo, H. and Raju, S., 2007. Domestic Violence in India: Evidences and Implications for Working Women. *Social Change*, 37(4), pp. 131–152.

Shah, A., Nayak, S.K. and Das, B., 2005. *Remoteness and Chronic Poverty in a Forest Region in Southern Orissa: A Tale of Entitlement Failure and State's Apathy*, New Delhi. Available at: http://www.chronicpoverty.org/uploads/publication_files/CPRC-IIPA_34.pdf [Accessed January 16, 2016].

Thomas, D. et al., 2015. Closing the Health and Nutrition Gap in Odisha, India: A Case Study of How Transforming the Health System is Achieving Greater Equity. *Social Science and Medicine*, 145, pp. 154–162.

7

Inclusive Education: Fact or Fiction?

Supriya Pattanayak

Introduction

The theme of education of disadvantaged persons is high on the agenda of India particularly Odisha because it is related to a much wider phenomena: growing deprivation and social exclusion. While the situation is dire, the paradox is that increase in poverty and exclusion goes hand in hand with economic growth. It is in this backdrop that 'inclusive education' is being proposed so as to ensure that all members of society become part of the 'mainstream'. In a multi lingual, multi cultural, multi ethnic society like India,'mainstream' is a misnomer. To find appropriate ways of responding to 'difference' is a reality and a challenge which is only being tinkered with on the margins. It would not be inappropriate to mention that education itself is becoming 'endangered' in attempting to make 'one size fit all'.

There were several forays into experimenting with schooling, especially residential schools for disadvantaged persons both by central and state governments in India: the Kasturba Gandhi BalikaVidyalaya, Ashram Schools, Navodaya Schools and NGOs run residential schools. Government of Odisha determined that one of the ways to ensure that the needs of the disadvantaged persons are met, was to make available adequate number of residential schools. There are now over 1,000 residential schools for scheduled tribe children in the state of Odisha.

Churchill (2004) while discussing the genocidal impact of

American Indian residential schools, has alluded to 'kill(ing) the Indian, save(ing) the man' and Grant (1996) in referring to Indian residential schools in Canada says that there is 'No end to grief'. Much is written about the 'stolen generation' amongst the Australian indigenous peoples and the loss of culture amongst the Siberian Evenk. While India has for time immemorial considered residential schools as a solution to the problem of first generation learners in remote regions, the subtle difference is in assuming it, is about exercising choice. This chapter attempts to trace the education trajectory in the State of Odisha while focusing, through both primary and secondary data, as to the gendered dimension of residential schools and what they have done to tribal cultures and languages.

Inclusion and Exclusion defined

Firstly, let us understand the meaning of inclusion and exclusion. Both inclusion and exclusion are multi-dimensional and multi-layered. One could be excluded without being poor, scheduled caste, scheduled tribe or a woman, whereas belonging to one of these categories may certainly lead to exclusion. Paying attention to exclusion allows a broader view of deprivation and disadvantage than that which is allowed by other narrowly defined terms, especially 'poverty'. Inclusion, on the other hand, is often defined in terms of exclusion. Inclusion is concerned with the promotion of full participation in all aspects of community life, especially of those who are currently deprived and disadvantaged and/or, at risk of marginalization. Citizenship is significantly linked with social inclusion and incorporates issues of status, rights and duties. Therefore, in order to achieve social inclusion, there is a need for physical and social integration. Needless to say, education is a necessary condition for inclusion.

As a sub-set of social inclusion overall, inclusion in education needs to be viewed from different vantage points, from the outside (who has access to schools and of what kind, who has access to other resources meant for education, etc.) and from the inside (what happens inside the school). Clearly, what occurs in society for these marginalized persons is also important to the above two, that is, who gets access to what kind of school and what happens inside the school (who is visible and who is not). Social norms influence what happens inside the school, for example, in the attitudes and behaviours of teachers and the participation or lack thereof of parents and community leaders in schools/education of their children/ wards (Ramachandran and Naorem, 2013).

Education in India

Nobody disputes the centrality of education. The question however arises, education for whom, by whom and for what purpose? The kind of education that has come to be in India is the product of colonialism which systematically eroded and devalued what existed as traditional systems of education. Macaulay's *Minute on Indian Education* (1835 as quoted in Spivak 1988, p. 282; Marks 2002) highlights what they considered the 'civilizing project:

> We must at present do our best to form a class who may be interpreters between us and the millions whom we govern; a class of persons, Indian in blood and colour, but English in taste, in opinions, in morals and in intellect. To that class we may leave it to refine the vernacular dialects of the country, to enrich those dialects with terms of science borrowed from the western nomenclature, and to render them by degrees fit vehicles for conveying knowledge to the great mass of the population.

With this they aimed to create a 'broker class' among the colonized. In India, because of its huge population, the cost effective imperial strategy was manipulation through the broker class rather than coercion. Education of the 'colonized' became a central and conscious technique for governing a people and legitimizing 'colonization' itself.

Since then much has been written on the impact of colonisers on education of indigenous populations around the world, the stolen generations amongst the Australian aboriginals, and in many instances even extending as far as the genocide of indigenous populations.

India has since made enormous progress in education. In recent years, increasing progress has been made in the primary education attendance rate and expanding literacy to approximately three-quarters of the population in the 7-10 age group by 2011. India, with more than 1.4 million schools and more than 2.3 million enrolments is home to one of the largest and complex school education system. The Indian education system post-independence is designed along the colonial system, where teaching and learning are spoken of in the same breath. In the Indian system as well as the indigenous systems around the world, there is a fundamental difference between teaching and learning. Formal education was viewed by the then Government of India in such a manner that the barriers to inclusive education were perceived as the following: extreme poverty, diverse languages, dialects and mother tongues, high levels of child labour, girl children invisible due to involvement in domestic work and perception of lack of safety in the public domain and remote location of villages/hamlets (NCERT, 2005).

All these factors identified can be challenged on grounds of not taking into account the context in which teaching and learning happens. Behera and Nath (2012) note that different tribal[1] communities possess their own systems of informal education. The dimensions of this informal education emphasize acquisition of competence, subsistence techniques, and traditional values in order to prepare children as effective members of society. According to them, children learn to master these skills from an early age, but there are no special institutions, personnel, or rigid time frames for such instructions. Education is an informal process of learning skills and maintaining continuity with aboriginal traditions. As modern nation-states grow through absorption of smaller and weaker cultural entities, formal education is imposed, and a common language, culture, and identity severely threatens the existence of tribal people as viable collective entities. It becomes important to challenge this notion of informal education. Why should the education provided by the tribal communities from elders to youngsters be considered informal, rather than context specific, experience based, hands on and practice oriented. This divide of formal and informal education is also based on a binary either or logic that is not suited to tribal, indigenous or in fact, multi-lingual, multi-cultural and multi-ethnic communities like India.

Recent cognitive research by Howard Gardner (1991) proposes multiple intelligences and 'documents the extent to which students have different kinds of minds and therefore learn, remember, perform and understand in different ways'. According to this theory, "we are all able to know the world through language, logical mathematical analysis, spatial representation, musical thinking, use of the body to solve problems or to make things, an understanding of other individuals, and an understanding of ourselves. Where individuals differ is in the strength of these intelligences—the so-called profile of intelligences—and in the ways in which such intelligences are invoked and combined to carry out different tasks, solve diverse problems, and progress in various domains".

Gardner (1991) notes that these differences "challenge an educational system that assumes that everyone can learn the same materials in the same way and that a uniform, universal measure suffices to test student learning. Indeed, as currently constituted, our educational system is heavily biased toward linguistic modes of instruction and assessment and, to a somewhat lesser degree, toward logical quantitative modes as well". He further argues that "a contrasting set of assumptions is more likely to be educationally effective. Students learn in ways that are identifiably distinctive. The broad spectrum of students—and perhaps the society as a whole—would be better served if disciplines could be presented in a numbers of ways and learning could be assessed through a variety of means". However, in the Indian educational context the theory of multiple intelligences has not been taken into account.

In India, the Constitution now includes special educational safeguards for aboriginals (Mohanty, 2003). Aboriginal communities, commonly denoted as, 'tribal', constitute roughly 8% of the total Indian population. In 1960, the Scheduled Area and Scheduled Tribes Commission was established with the aim of integrating the aboriginal people into the mainstream. It was assumed that formal education would enable the aboriginal people to meet their needs and requirements, especially in a changing world, and that it would be instrumental in reshaping their "quality of life" by integrating them into the mainstream (Sachchidananda, 1990, p. 404).

Girls Education in India and Odisha

At the time of independence, the national female literacy rate was as low as 8.9%. Gross enrollment ratio for girls was 24.8% at primary level and 4.6% at the upper primary level in the 11-14 years age group (Census of India).

Slowly, access to schooling improved. In 1950-51, 2,09,671 primary and 13,596 upper primary schools were functional. In 2004-05, 7,67,522 schools were functional at the primary level and 2,74,731 schools at the upper primary level. In 2013-14, the provisional figures for number of primary schools was 7,90,640 and for upper primary schools was 4,01,079. Today 98% of India's rural population has access to primary schools within a kilometer of their habitation (Government of India, 2014).

In 1950-51, enrollment of boys was 13.8 million and 5.4 million girls in primary school. In 2004-05, this increased to 69.7 million boys and 61.1 million girls in primary school. At upper primary level, enrolment increased from 2.6 million boys and 0.5 million girls to 28.5 million boys and 22.7 million girls. In 2013-14, the enrolment at primary level was 67.2 million boys and 62.8 million girls and at the upper primary level 33.7 million boys and 32 million girls. At the secondary level the enrolment level is 19.4 million boys and 17.4 million girls. 48.1% boys, 46.7%, girls drop out of school by the time they reach Class X. (Government of India, 2014). Retaining children, especially girls, in school is still a challenge.

The number of teachers in 2013-14 at the primary level was 26,84,194 with a teacher pupil ratio of 28 and at upper primary level 25,12,968 with a teacher pupil ratio of 30 (Government of India, 2014).

In Odisha, during 2013-14, there were 36,399 functional primary schools in the state with 1.21 lakh teachers and 42.78 lakh students. Further, there were 21,945 upper primary schools with 62,57,000 teachers and 21.10 lakh enrolments. In 1947-48, the State had only 106 high schools with 15,000 enrolments. By the end of 2013-14, there were 9,423 high schools including 7,750 Government and aided schools, 1,595 private unaided and unrecognized high schools and the balance of 78 are run by the Ministry of Human Resource Development, Government of India with 49,997 teachers and 12.06 lakh enrolments including 5.99 lakh girls. Out of total of 9,423 high schools, 814 were girls high schools (*Economic Survey 2014-15*).

Despite all these efforts, Blum (2009) notes that a large number of these schools tend to be characterised by the need for multigrade classroom management as a result of low enrolment and/or too few teachers, and usually face significant shortages in terms of teaching and learning resources and basic infrastructure. This frequently leads to poor educational quality, student and teacher disillusionment, high rates of drop out and low rates of retention.

The frequent lack of sufficient infrastructure, resources, and support for government schools has a large impact on their functioning and on the quality of education offered to students in these areas. For example, while schools are expected to meet curriculum requirements, teachers often spend a significant amount of time on tasks other than teaching. So, in addition to the inherent difficulties of working in economically deprived areas and with scarce resources, they may also be responsible for completing all of a school's administrative tasks, arranging for the provision of mid-day meals (a nationally-mandated government policy), maintaining records for attendance and periodic medical check-ups, conducting household surveys for the national census, and administering preventative polio medication.

Balagopalan (2010) in analyzing the residential schooling scheme for girls, Kasturba Gandhi Balika Vidyalaya notes that the gender focus reveals an inordinate concern with numbers, i.e., enrolment. The instrumentalism that underlies these efforts is revealed through a double move effected by existing discourses. The first is to locate the reasons why girls are out of school strictly within a reading of cultural and familial practices and (secondly) to therefore, fail to recognize normative practices of schooling and state policies as already deeply 'gendered'. The reasons for these children not being in school or dropping out is often blamed on parents, families and the traditions of communities for why these children are not in school. There is also an increased state surveillance of girls from marginal communities.

Policy Framework

Article 15(1) of the Constitution of India, notes that the State shall not discriminate against any citizen on grounds only of religion, race, caste, sex, place of birth or any of them. In 1986, the policy of Education for All was announced by the Ministry of Human Resource Development. It was further modified in 1992. The World Bank supported Sarva Shiksha Abhiyan was started in 2001 to give shape in practice to the 'Education for All'.

The Rashtriya Madhyamik Shiksha Abhiyan (RMSA) scheme initiated in 2009, demonstrates the Government of India's ambition for a secondary education system to support India's growth and development. RMSA aims to increase the enrolment rate to 90% at secondary and 75% at higher secondary stage, by providing a secondary school within reasonable distance of every home. It also aims to improve the quality of secondary education by making all secondary schools conform to prescribed norms, removing gender, socio-economic and disability barriers, and providing universal access to secondary level education by 2017 (Government of India, www.rmsaindia.org/en/,).

At the outset, education was a State subject in the federal

structure. The 42nd Constitutional Amendment in 1976 brought education into the concurrent list, which made education then a responsibility of central government, state government and local government. This brought about a sea change to the educational management and ensured that it was more responsive to the local contexts. Education cess was also levied to raise resources.

Various policy and programme proclamations at different points in time helped advance education in India today. The Operation Blackboard, launched in 1987 in pursuance of the National Policy on Education, aimed to supply the bare minimum crucial facilities to all primary schools in the country (necessary institutional equipment and instructional material). The main goal of the Mid-Day Meal Scheme (upgraded in 2001 from the previous programme, the National Programme for Nutritional Support to Primary Education, launched in 1995) was to serve all children in Government and Government-aided primary schools a prepared mid-day meal with a minimum 300 calories of energy and 8-12 gram protein per day for a minimum of 200 days. The Scheme was extended and revised on several occasions to cover and increase cooking costs, while giving more calories per day and reaching more children.

The 86th Constitutional Amendment Act, 2002 has made elementary education a fundamental right for children in the age group of 6-14 years by providing that "the state shall provide free and compulsory education to all children of the age of six to fourteen years in such manner as the State may, by law, determine". This was amended in 2009 and The Right of Children to Free and Compulsory Education Act came into force, which was again amended in 2012. Some of the provisions of the Act are:

Every child of the age of six to fourteen years shall have a right to free and compulsory education in a neighborhood school till completion of elementary education

No child will be liable to pay any kind of fee or charges or expenses which may prevent him or her from pursuing and completing elementary education.

Special provisions have also been included for children not admitted to and who have not completed elementary education. The Right of transfer to another school has also been incorporated.

Needless to say, all these efforts made by the Government of India, the state and local governments has necessarily led to improved overall educational outcomes, and the focus on girls has meant better enrolments and retention, but critically the focus is on numbers and despite the large drop outs, not enough emphasis on the causes of drop outs and solutions to the problem is seen.

Institutionalization of Education

By institutionalization of education I mean two things: first, as Behera and Nath (2015, p. 322) identify, 'the process by which the organized routine arrangements of the school system influence children's lives and schedule their every activity throughout the day'. The second, I propose, is 'the institutionalization of children in residential schools for purposes of attaining education'. These have impacted tribal children way beyond people's expectations and imaginations. The children are imparted education by an authoritative figure and in a language alien to them. Further, tribal children in this context become associated with values and ideologies very different from their own communities', primarily a set of relationships governed by obligations and responsibilities. Behera and Nath (2015) note that some of the most criticized features of these schools are: regimentation; a rigid system of seating, grouping, grading, and marking; and the authoritarian role of the teacher.

The institutionalization of education has destroyed the very fabric of tribal communities in Odisha and India. Children are removed from their homes very early in life and have lost all touch with the families and communities from which their very identities are formed. Their relationship within the communities and the environment around themselves get eroded so much so that they have no idea of ways of living with their surroundings (In the past their survival depended primarily on abundantly available natural resources). The kinship patterns of 'obligations and responsibilities' are replaced by 'rights and entitlements'. Their world view of diversity based on multiple realities are imposed upon by unitary symbols based on a western form of education; where mono-lingual, mono-cultural, and other unitary symbols are valued over diverse symbols and lead to hierarchization rather than complementarity.

International Experience of Students in Residential Schools

The aftermath of the Indian residential Schools era has exacted a huge toll, both in the human suffering of First Nations and on Canadian society in general, but understanding the impact of residential schools can aid the healing process. One of the areas of exploration included the school policies toward language, the impact of language suppression on culture and the aftermath of language suppression. The extent of human rights abuses, physical, psychological, sexual and spiritual abuse has also been well documented (Grant 1996).

Adams (1995) examines how government boarding schools were used for acculturating American Indian youth to 'American' ways of thinking and living. He proposes that the last 'Indian War' was fought against native American children in the dormitories and classrooms of government boarding schools. The government of the time advocated the removal of Indian children from their homes for extended periods of time in order that white 'civilization' could take root while extinguishing Indian culture and any childhood memories of 'savagism'. He further analyses how educational policy was translated into institutional practice,

Miller (1996) seeks to provide a broad treatment of the motives of the three agents in residential schools history, the native peoples, governments and missionaries in addition to providing a comprehensive treatment of the boarding school experience. He examines instruction, both academic and vocational, work and recreation, care and abuse, and finally the resistance to the negative aspects of schoolings that both students and their families mounted.

Bloch (2004) found that residential schooling had both positive and negative impact on Evenk men and women. Residential schools were one of the common factors in defining indigenous Siberian people. Although there were calls to protect their subsistence way of life through the residential schooling system, the proponents of residential schools as a place to inculcate Soviet values became responsible for taking forward the residential school system. Thereby a large number of indigenous Siberians became tied to the new industrial-based Soviet cultural practices such as waged labour, biomedicine and formal education.

There are several such explorations, analyses and documentation of encounters of indigenous people with the modern schooling system, mostly imposed, rather than voluntary, which have had far reaching intergenerational impacts. Despite all these international experiences, albeit during the colonial and post-colonial periods, several nations follow the beaten track and disadvantage their indigenous populations. Should the policies in India not learn from these lessons?

Experience in Odisha

Several residential schooling strategies exist for girls in the publicly funded school system in India. The information on the performance of these schemes/programmes/initiatives remains uneven, isolated and sporadic. Major schemes funded by the union government include Jawahar Navodaya Vidyalayas (JNV) and Kasturba Gandhi Balika Vidyalaya (KGBV) funded mainly by the Ministry of Human Resource Development, and Ashram Schools (AS) and Eklavya Model Residential Schools (EMRS) funded by the Ministry of Tribal Affairs. In addition, both union and a number of state governments have grants-in-aid schemes to support exclusive schools for ST or SC children known generally as ashram schools. Several other non-fee-charging residential schools source their funding from development/philanthropic sources (Jha et al, 2015).

Following the recommendation of the Dhebar Commission, a number of Kanyashrams were opened in India during the fifth five-year plan, 1970-75. Kanyashrams are residential schools meant for tribal girls. Students and teachers live together within the school-cum-dormitory premises. Similar residential schools meant for aboriginal boys are known as 'Ashram Schools'. These schools were established to target girls and other marginalized groups in order to improve enrolment, attendance and performance in education, both at the primary and secondary levels. Children who were historically marginalized were usually scheduled tribes, scheduled castes, working children, those belonging to minorities, disabled children, and children in remote areas. Girls from these groups were even more severely marginalized.

This study was conducted in the district of Gajapati in Odisha where the total population is 5,77,817 and constitutes 1.38% of the population of the State of Odisha. The scheduled tribe population in the district is 54.3% (3,13,714) and the scheduled caste population is 6.8% (39,175) (Census of India, 2011). The proportion of girls served through residential schools at elementary level is the highest for Odisha (10.92%) (Jha, et al, 2015). Gajapati is one of the left wing extremist (LWE) affected districts in Odisha. I undertook to study all the residential high schools for girls in the district which numbered seven. Focus group discussions were conducted with girls from year 7 and 8 (the penultimate and final years in the residential schools). In some schools the focus group discussions included all the girls in year 7 and 8 whereas in other schools comprised a sample of students (this was dependent on the number of students). Further interviews were also conducted with a small number of school management committee members and a fair representative number of teachers.

Most of the students in these schools were from the Saura community and were first generation learners. They spoke the Saura language at home and learned Odia, Hindi and English at school but a bridge was never formed between the home language and the school languages. Even amongst themselves they were discouraged from conversing in the Saura language as the teachers could not understand them.

Residential Government High Schools in Gajapati District

Types of Schools	*Numbers*
Number of Higher Secondary Schools (I to XII)	02
Number of High Schools (Boys) (I to X)	06
Number of High Schools (Girls)	08
Number of Ashram Schools (I to VIII)	33
Number of Sevashrams	17
Number of Residential Sevashrams	02

Quality of Education

In all the schools visited, the school development/management committees were formed and pictures posted on the walls; albeit the photos were faded and faces unrecognisable in some instances. Parent-teachers meeting were held and the parents were appraised of the performance of their wards, but since report cards were discontinued, there was no way to inform the guardians in writing about the progress. However, the limited participation of parents in various forums or in their child's education was clearly evident, one reason being that most of these children were first generation learners. The school management committees/village education committees were not effective in ensuring the involvement of parents.

I found evidence of activity based learning—the teachers showed me some of the material developed by the students in the course of their learning. One of the biggest complaints was that there was no place to store or showcase the material so developed. Teachers claimed that they underwent training in life skills during which they were provided with teaching material, both theory and practice material. In most schools reading aloud news during the Assembly was common practice.

As indicated, the issue of resources came up time and

again. In one school only three teachers were present to teach classes I to VIII. There were no teachers for particular subjects like Hindi or Sanskrit, and the other teachers tried to just cope. Their knowledge of these subjects was limited, the teachers exclaimed, but they did not want the students to be disadvantaged, so they did their best. Eventually, they dictated the answers during the Board examinations as the students had not been taught the subjects and they would have to repeat the examinations. The advantage post RTE was that there were no exams although continuous assessment was mandated.

Most schools had adequate seating arrangements for children, but it was evident that bright students received more attention than others. The teachers (mostly from coastal region or upper caste) expressed a very poor opinion of their students, often mentioning that they just could not cope.

Experience of Residential Accommodation

The students were primarily accommodated in dormitories; cots were provided for individual students, but this was not so in all the schools and for everybody. However, they had to bring their own bedding and each morning everything was neatly folded.The government provided mosquito nets as this is a malaria prone area. Since these schools were primarily meant for scheduled tribe girls, I did not find any evidence of exclusionary practices. However, the physical infrastructure is grossly inadequate, there is overcrowding, inadequate number of fans and the lighting and ventilation is far from satisfactory as also observed by Pfeffer (2003). In some schools, "dangerous overcrowding" of students with inadequate personal space, due to lack of fixed norms on sharing rooms, was noted (GoI, 2013-14). Sanitation facilities are poor, which often meant defecating in the open and maintaining sanitation, where toilets existed, was alternated between groups of students; often students had to bathe in nearby ponds. In some instances, it was observed that the personal care products provided to the students were inferior in quality. Overall, I found that records were poorly maintained. A recent evaluation of facilities by NUEPA (2013) clearly found states wanting in following the Right to Education (RTE) 2009 infrastructure norms.

The food was good and they got non-vegetarian (chicken) food once a week and eggs twice a week (as part of the mid day meal scheme) which was more than what they would afford or expect at home. Rice had become their staple and the school did not provide minor millets which was their traditional food and nutrition source. Meeting with a member of the school management committee corroborated the above as one member visits each day to check the food, students, etc. There was no evidence either during the interviews or observation that any discrimination was made regarding who eats and who does not (first or later), who cooks, and who sits where; this may be attributed to the fact that the sample schools were all scheduled tribe schools. However, it was reiterated that district education officials were not taking any interest in the development of the school.

There was little evidence of overcrowding in the classrooms, but it was surprising to note the very small number of girls in class VII and VIII in some schools. I was informed that some teachers did not want to take the responsibility of having adolescent girls in their schools and had them transferred to other nearby schools.

Illness, if any, was reported to the health minister of the school cabinet who then informed the teachers. The immediate course of action was to see the ASHA (government health service provider) when somebody fell ill. It was the teachers who determined whether the condition was serious enough for a doctor to be consulted.

The students would visit their families and communities during school holidays. They missed their school friends during this period but also had friends in their villages. Children were extremely happy about being in hostels and claimed that they missed the school when they went home whereas they hardly reported missing their homes when they were at school. Students mainly mentioned to two reasons:

first, was because they had been placed in residential schools when they were very young and had very little contact with the family. Second, during holidays, when the children went home, they had to work—household chores, harvesting crops and cashew, etc., which was real hard work and they were exhausted at the end of the day. This meant that they had no time for study either. Clearly the disengagement from their own culture is one of the fallouts of uprooting the children from their homes at such an early age.

Students claimed that they had nothing to fear in or around the school and hostels. They mentioned that they had high walls and nobody or nothing could enter, the counter being that nobody could leave either. They could never leave the hostel premises unless accompanied by a parent or a teacher (if they were representing their school in some events). It is probably due to the RTE Act which prohibits any form of abuse, that teachers were more careful about overt forms of punishment, and on few occasions poor discipline was attributed to this. However, it was quite evident that children feared their teachers.

Language and Culture

Even though all the students were Saura speakers, they did not speak the language in school. It appeared there was a subtle pressure by the teachers and other staff to adhere to Odia as they needed to speak the Odia language in order to 'fit in with society' (as one teacher claimed). This was also because the teachers' language or the official state language was different from the mother tongue of the children. Most of the teachers were from the coastal districts and have little understanding of the different tribal languages or cultures and therefore, unable to communicate with these children.

During interactions with teachers, it was evident that teachers encouraged cultural programmes and debating in the Odia language. Teachers' attitude toward the local language was extremely problematic, with them prohibiting students from conversing in their native mother tongue. The Odia language was used as a tool to transform the language skills of the students such that their aspirations in society could be fulfilled. Teachers further perceived their role to be to address the issue of early marriages through discussions with their students and the parents.

Most of the students were Christian and there was evidence of a conflation between religion and culture. Students named only Christian festivals even though all of them were scheduled tribes. When probed further, they began to name some harvest festivals, etc.

Ashram schools are based on Gandhian principles mostly Hindu based—(Amrutlal Thakkar Bapa was a contemporary and follower of Gandhi) and therefore only Hindu festivals were celebrated in Ashram schools. Morning prayers were Sanskrit verses. The Christian children reluctantly took part in these celebrations (eg: they were engaged in decorating the pandals and would leave as soon as the idols arrived; Christian students would partake of the food only if it had no offering that was made to the Hindu Gods).

Very rarely were students able to articulate anything that they did not like about their schools which indicates how residential schools have become part of defining their identity and how young indigenous people have become alienated from their own culture and community.

Policy implications

It is important to assess whether 'one size fits all' and whether governments should be pursuing the path of residential schools. In light of the evidence provided above, it is important to consider whether one should tread the path of residential schools as being one of the main 'choices' for remotely based 'tribal' people. What are the other options that need consideration?

The Gender and Social Exclusion Assessment Framework (GSEA) developed by DFID and the World Bank (2006) analyses the relationships between people and the institutions of 'rules of the game' that shape the opportunity structure of their social, political and economic world'. The aim is to identify the domains of change—'access to assets and services' and 'voice, influence and agency' are part of the empowerment process. Needless to say, for the poor and excluded, access to assets and services is critical to progress in life and attempts to move out of poverty. The access to education whether in the form of stand alone multigrade or other schools or residential schools should be adequately provisioned and efforts should be made so that students are not subjected to any form of abuse, whether social, cultural, sexual, physical, psychological, spiritual and other forms. Instead every attempt should be made to nurture the multiple intelligences of students and every opportunity for their progress should be provided. Access to education will also then lead to sustainable improvement of livelihoods and empowerment.

The third domain of change—discriminatory and exclusionary 'rules of the game' need to change in a way that will increase the access of diverse groups to development opportunities, in this instance, to benefit from quality and appropriate education.This domain is where inclusion does or does not take place. The school management committees and parent bodies need to be strengthened such that they have voice and agency, and they should be able to use this to make a difference to the quality of educations services provided for their children. There is usually a lot of resistance to the change in the rules of the game, as it usually involves a loss of power, be it perceptual. So the barriers to change need to be removed. The rules of the game to engage, influence and hold accountable the institutions that affect the excluded must be changed in their favour and this can only be achieved if they have the capabilities or the access to resources necessary to voice their rights, to form effective representative organizations and to forge coalitions for change (DFID and World Bank 2006).

The framework thus both conceptualizes the vicious cycle in which the excluded are trapped but also identifies the specific areas or 'domains' in which this cycle can be broken through programmes or policies which both empower the excluded and change the rules of the game in their favour. The way these barriers can be overcome is through legal and constitutional entitlements and by adhering to the provisions of the Right to Education Act which gives the right to free and compulsory education to every child till the age of 16. This Rights-based approach has the potential to make a significant difference for access to educational services, in the long run ensuring social protection and livelihood security. Till they realize the provisions of this Act, it will not benefit children in remote areas such as Gajapati. The successful implementation of this Act can be put down to the administrative improvements across the board introduced by some dynamic officers, including the use of technology. The Right to Information Act is a powerful tool in the hands of the people, but its potential is not fully utilized.

The barriers to access education can also be overcome through community mechanisms. This can be through strengthening of the various governing bodies such as the school management committees, the parents committees, etc. In Odisha where there is a large network of Self Help Groups, they have never been adequately involved in education. By engaging with different groups and changing the rules of the game, it is hoped that the voice, influence of groups of both parents and children will improve and they will have greater knowledge of the provisions of the laws, also they will have greater confidence to demand their entitlements, as well as get involved in the mobilization and utilization of resources.

Clearly one needs to think outside the box. In a recent project undertaken by the Government of Odisha, the provision of safe transport for girls was offered (DFID funded Odisha Girls Incentive Programme). Anecdotally, it was found that girls dropped out of residential schools to take up the safe transport option, the following year some did not enrol at the residential school. Still another finding was that attendance of the students improved substantially. While there were challenges in the implementation of this programme, because of the mountainous terrain and poor infrastructure, the community members and girls especially found it to be a very useful approach. However, it is very resource intensive, and therefore government did not scale it up.

Conclusion

While I have taken an instrumentalist view here, I would agree with Balagopalan (2010, p. 306) that 'increasingly the figure of the child, particularly the girl child, is used as part of the disciplining and moralizing practices of the State vis-a-vis their families'. She further goes on to state that 'given this reality, a certain deliberate displacement of this liberal gaze on the indigent girl child needs to be achieved. What is urged is a questioning about the inherently 'benevolent' nature of programmes as well as an interrogation of the solutions they naturalize in order to pave the way for a more political articulation of 'gender' that does not allow the State's statistical spin-doctoring to exhaust a feminist engagement with schooling.

NOTES

1. The author has used the term 'aboriginal' which is alien to Indian anthropology. In India, the term 'tribal' is mostly used in the anthropological literature instead of the term 'indigenous', firstly, as it is not a settler colony and secondly, to differentiate between indigenous and non-indigenous would be a highly political question.

REFERENCES

Adams, D.W. 1995, *Education for Extinction: American Indians and the Boarding School Experience, 1875-1928*, Lawrence, KS: University of Kansas Press.

Balagopalan, S. 2010, Rationalizing Seclusion: A Preliminary Analysis of a Residential Schooling Scheme for Poor Girls in India, *Feminist Theory*, Vol. 11, No. 3, pp. 295-308.

Behera D.K. and Nath N., 2005, Aboriginal Female Children in Kanyashrams of Orissa, India: A Critical Assessment of the Processes of Educational Institutionalization, *Childhood Education*, Vol. 81, No. 6, pp. 321-326.

Bloch, A. 2004, *Red Ties and Residential Schools: Indigenous Siberians in a Post-Soviet State*. Philadelphia: University of Pennsylvania Press.

Blum, N. 2009, Small NGO Schools in India: Implications for Access and Innovation, *Compare*, Vol. 39, No. 2, pp. 235-248.

Churchill, W. 2004, *Kill the Indian, Save the Man: The Genocidal Impact of American Indian Residential Schools*, San Francisco: City Light Books.

DFID and World Bank, 2006, 'Unequal Citizens: Gender, Caste and Ethnic Exclusion in Nepal'. The World Bank and DFID, Nepal.

Gardner, H. 1991, *Intelligence Reframed. Multiple Intelligences for the 21st Century*, New York: Basic Books

Government of India (2013-14). Working of Ashram Schools in tribal areas: Forty-Fourth report http://164.100.47.134/lsscommittee/Social%20Justice%20&%20Empowerment/15_Social_Justice_And_Empowerment_44.pdf;Fifteenth Lok Sabha.

Government of India, 2014, *Educational Statistics at a Glance*, Ministry of Human Resource Development, Bureau of Planning, Monitoring and Statistics, New Delhi.

Government of India, website of Rashtriya Madhyamik Shiksha Abhiyan, Ministry of Human Resource Development, www.rmsaindia.org/en/, accessed on 1st June 2016.

Government of Odisha, 2014-15, *Economic Survey*, Bhubaneswar: Planning and Coordination Department, Directorate of Economics and Statistics.

Grant, A. 1996, *No End of Grief: Indian Residential Schools in Canada*, Manitoba, Canada: Pemmican Publications Inc.

Jha, J., Menon, G., Puja Minni, Shanmuga Priya, 2015, 'Residential Schooling Strategies: Impact on Girls Education and Empowerment', Bangalore: Centre for Budget and Policy Studies.

Marks, R. 2002, *The Origins of the Modern World: A Global and Ecological Narrative*, Lanham MD: Rowman & Littlefield.

Miller, J.R. 1996, *Shingwauk's Vision: A History of Native Residential Schools*, Toronto: University of Toronto Press.

Mohanty, B.B. 2003, Educational Progress of Scheduled Tribes: A Discursive Review, *Man and Development*, Vol. 25, No. 2, pp. 91-106.

National Council of Educational Research and Training (NCERT), 2005, *National Curriculum Framework*, New Delhi.

National University Educational Planning and Administration (NUEPA), 2013, India—Third Education Project (Sarva Shiksha Abhiyan—III), http://ssa.nic.in/framework-docs/LEAMF.pdf.

Ramachandran, V. and Naorem, T. 2013, What it Means to be a Dalit or Tribal Child in Our Schools: A Synthesis of a Six-State Qualitative Study, *Economic and Political Weekly*, Vol. XLVIII, No. 44, pp. 43-52.

Sachchidananda, 1990, Structural Constraints in the Education of Scheduled Tribes and Scheduled Castes, in B. Choudhuri (ed.), *Tribal Development in India*, New Delhi: Inter India Publications, pp. 403-408.

Spivak, G.C. 1988, 'Can the Subaltern Speak?' in C. Nelson and L. Grossberg (eds.), *Marxism and the Interpretation of Culture*, Chicago: University of Illinois Press, pp. 271-313.

8

Regional Disparity and Women in Local Government: Implications for Sustainable Development

Bidyut Mohanty and Sibabrata Das

Introduction

The prevailing development process has failed to arrest the continuing phenomenon of poverty, regional disparity and social inequalities in Odisha. Further, gender discrimination against women along with gender inequities in development indicators remains an important issue of concern in the State. In this paper we provide evidence for these trends. We argue that if panchyat is made the focus of planning and development, it would contribute to reducing not only poverty and underdevelopment but also gender disparity; and in it if women play the central role, then there is greater likelihood of appropriate policies being formulated and implemented from the grass-roots level onwards, which would help in reducing social inequality and achieving sustainable development. Recent evidence from panchayats in tribal areas as discussed in this paper support this line of argument.

Methods and Sources

A number of indicators are available to measure the development of the Indian population. As it is accepted that only monetary indicators do not reveal the true picture of the level of development, a set of other indicators have been selected to represent social and economic dimensions of development. The selected indicators are based on a variety of sources: demographic data from the Census of India and health indicators from the National Family Health Surveys (NFHS), Sample Registration System (SRS) and Annual Health Surveys (AHS), and poverty data from National Sample Survey Organization (NSSO). Finally, an in-depth field survey through a random sampling method among the elected women of two tribal dominated districts (Rayagada and Mayurbhanj) at two points of time (1997-2001 and 2013-14) as well as personal interviews among selected women representatives have also been conducted.[1]

Socio-economic Condition of Odisha in a Comparative Perspective

As per the 2011 Census, Odisha with a population of 41.9 million experienced a lower decadal growth rate of 13.97 during 2001-11 compared to 17.6 per cent at the all India level. In so far as female literacy rate goes, the national average rate is higher than that of Odisha. But the sex ratio and the child sex ratio of the State is better than the national figures (Table 1).

Table 1: Socio-Economic, Demographic and Health Indicators in Odisha and India

Indicators	*Odisha*	*India*
Population (in million)*	41.9	1,210.2
Share of Population (in %) *	3.0	--
Percent of Population in ages 0-6 years	12.0	13.1
Child Sex Ratio (female per thousand male in 0-6 age group)*	934	914
Sex Ratio*	978	940
Level Urbanisation (in %)*	17	27.8
Area (in sq. km)*	155,707	3,287,240
Population Density (Persons per square km)*	269	382
Scheduled Caste Population (in million) *	7.2	201.3
Scheduled Tribe Population (in million) *	9.6	104.2

Proportion of SC Population (in %)*	16.5	8.2
Proportion of ST Population (in %)*	22.1	16.2
Literacy Rate (in %)*	73.45	74.4
Female Literacy Rate (in %)*	64.4	74.0
Total Fertility Rate**	2.1	2.2
Percentage of People Living Below Poverty Line (BPL)***	32.0	21.9
Crude Birth Rate (CBR) ****	20.5	20.4
Crude Death Rate (CDR) ****	7.8	6.4
Infant Mortality Rate**	39. 6	40.7
Under Five Mortality Rate**	48.1	49.7
Maternal Mortality Ratio (MMR) Per 100,000 Live Births*****	180	130
Underweight (children of age below five years)**	34.4	42.5
Stunting (children of age below five years)**	34.1	48.0
Wasting (children of age below five years)**	20.4	19.8

Sources: * Census, 2011: India, Registrar General (2011) ** NFHS-4: International Institute of Population Sciences and ICF (2017), *** NSSO, 2011-12: Government of India (2013), and **** SRS, 2016: India, Registrar General (2016), ***** SRS, 2014-16: India, Registrar General (2018).

Maternal Mortality Ratio (MMR) during 2014-16 was 180 in Odisha compared to the national figure of 130 (India, Registrar General, 2011) which is very high. The NFHS-4 estimates 61.2 per cent of the ever-married women in the age group of 15-49 as anaemic. Similarly, 41.4 per cent of the women in the 15-49 age groups are suffering from Chronic Energy Deficiency (CED). Child health status in the State is also equally disturbing. 34.4, 34.1 and 20.4 per cent of the children below five years were underweight, stunted and wasted respectively in 2015-16 (Table 1). Besides, 44.6 per cent of the children in the age group of 6-59 months are anaemic. Childhood mortality rates for the state of Odisha are higher than that of national figures. Therefore, Odisha has been grouped with other backward states in National Population Policy 2000 as the goal is not only to achieve TFR of 2.1 but also to take care of reduction in IMR, MMR, and malnutrition. The sex ratio particularly the child sex ratio, though better than that of India, has started declining. In other words in terms of socio-economic conditions women and children, the State is lagging behind.

Gender Dimensions of Development in Odisha: What Do Figures Reveal

Gender equality is one of the pre-conditions for social and economic prosperity. In post-independent India, a great stride has been made to raise the status of women in the country. The Constitution of India too provides equal rights and privileges for women and men. The five year plans have time and again placed special emphasis on providing health, education and employment services for women. The status of women is determined by levels of health, nutrition, education, standard of living, and participation in decision-making. Table 2 provides an overview of status of women in Odisha based on the last two rounds of National Family Health Survey (NFHS)- 3 and 4 those which were conducted in 2005-06 and 2015-16 respectively. Aggregate figures however, do not reflect a favourable situation for women in Odisha.

No significant achievement has been made with regard to the women's decision-making and spousal violence against women even in the twenty-first century. As per the recent round of NFHS data, even during pregnancy, 3.2 per cent of ever-married women have experienced violence in 2015-16[2]. When people are talking about digital revolution, only 39.2 per cent of women have mobiles for their own use. However, a substantial improvement has been made with regard to bank account holders—the percentage of women having a bank or savings account for their use has increased from 9.8 per cent in 2005-06 to 56.2 per cent in 2015-16. A comparison of NFHS 3 and NFHS 4 reveals a substantial improvement in the indicators of women's well-being in all social groups during 2005-06 and 2015-16. The impact of state-sponsored Self-Help-

Table 2: Status of Women in Odisha: A Comparative View of Scheduled Tribes and Non-tribal Populations

Indicators	*Scheduled Tribes*		*Scheduled Castes*		*Other Backward Classes*		*Non-SC/ ST/OBC Population*		*All*	
	NFHS 3	*NFHS 4*	*NFHS 3*	*NFHS 4*	*NFHS 3*	*NFHS 4*	*NFHS 3*	*NFHS 4*	*NFHS 3*	*NFHS 4*
Percentage of women participating in household decision making+	43.8	63.3	45.8	60.6	39.2	59.1	40.2	58.5	41.8	60.3
Percentage of women who have money that they can decide how to use	35.4	31.8	38.1	32.5	33.3	28.9	37.9	32.7	36.2	31.1
Percentage of women who have a bank or savings account that they themselves use	5.4	51.4	8.7	54.4	8.1	57.0	14.6	662.0 ??	9.8	56.2
Percentage of ever-married women age 15-49 who have ever experienced Emotional, physical, or sexual violence	48.8	41.4	47.6	39.3	34.1	35.2	37.3	30.6	41.2	36.6
Ever-married women who have experienced violence during any pregnancy (%)	N.A	3.9	N.A	4.6	N.A	3.0	N.A	1.3	N.A	3.2
Women age 15-24 years who use hygienic methods of protection during their menstrual period– (%)	N.A	31.4	N.A	41.0	N.A	51.4	N.A	68.9	N.A	47.4
Women having a mobile phone that they themselves use (%)	N.A	24.1	N.A	34.6	N.A	42.3	N.A	55.6	N.A	39.2
Percentage of women aged 15-49 years with Chronic Energy Deficiency (BMI below 18.5 Kg/M2)4	51.3	36.5	50.8	30.4	39.3	23.5	31.7	16.3	41.4	26.4
Percentage of women aged 15-49 years with anaemia	73.8	63.3	64.2	55.0	58.6	46.7	53.4	40.4	61.2	51

Notes: +Percentage of women who usually participate in decision making with respect to own health care, making major household purchases, making purchases for daily household needs and visits to her family or relatives. – Locally prepared napkins, sanitary napkins and tampons are considered as hygienic methods of protection. NA-Data not available

Sources: NFHS 4: IIPS and ICF (2017) National Family Health Survey (2015-16), India, 2015-16, Odisha, Mumbai.

NFHS 3: IIPS and Macro International (2007) National Family Health Survey (2005-06), India, 2015-16, Odisha, Mumbai.

Group Schemes as well as other schemes involving women, perhaps is instrumental in bringing in a positive impact on gender empowerment but the caveat is that women should have control over it. One should investigate if the women having bank accounts also have power to spend that money or not.

Status of ST and SC Women

Scheduled caste and scheduled tribe women take part in decision-making in higher percentages compared to women from other categories. However, this power never gets translated into the decision-making power at the political level.Highest percentage of ST women experience emotional, physical and mental violence followed by the SCs and OBCs. Further less than 47.4 per cent of women aged 15-24 years, who use hygienic methods of protection during their menstrual period. Around 26 per cent of women aged 15-49 years suffer from chronic energy deficiency as measured by Body Mass Index (BMI). The figure is higher among tribal women as compared to women belonging to other social groups. Further, highest percentage of ST women in the age groups of 15 to 49 are anaemic compared to SC and other social groups. Lowest literacy rate among ST women followed by SC

Table 3: Literacy Rate and Sex Ratio in Odisha: A Comparative View of Scheduled Tribes and Non-tribal populations

Indicators	*Scheduled Tribes*	*Scheduled Castes*	*Others*	*ALL*
Effective Literacy Rate	41.2	58.8	74.0	64.0
Overall Sex Ratio	1029	987	958	979
Child Sex Ratio	980	951	917	941

– Census of India does not provide data on socio economic indicators for OBCs separately. Hence, literacy rate and sex ratio figures for OBC and general caste populations are combined together.

Sources: India, Registrar General (2013), Primary Census Abstract, CD-ROM, Census of India, 2011.

women remains a matter of concern (Table 3). For example, the female literacy rate among tribes is only 41.2 per cent, while the figures stand at 58.8 per cent and 74 per cent for SC and non-SC/ST population respectively. Similarly, ST women are not found to have better decision-making power and access to financial resources than non-ST women though in terms of social decision-making such as marriage, separation etc., they are relatively more autonomous. Thus in all respects except in sex ratio, ST women are found to have been adversely placed as compared to non-ST women.

Table 4: Gender Inequality by Social Categories

Social Categories	*Gender*	*Percentage of men and women in the age group of 15-49 years with Chronic Energy Deficiency (BMI below 18.5 Kg/M²)*		*Percentage of men and women aged 15-49 with anaemia*	
		NFHS 3	*NFHS 4*	*NFHS 3*	*NFHS 4*
Scheduled Tribes	Male	38.9	23.7	51.6	40.1
	Female	51.3	36.5	73.8	63.3
Scheduled Castes	Male	44.8	22.8	35.6	30.4
	Female	50.8	30.4	64.2	55.0
Other Backward Classes	Male	33.9	18.1	25.4	24.8
	Female	39.3	23.5	58.6	46.7
Non-SC/ST/OBC populations	Male	28.6	13.6	23.2	18.0
	Female	31.7	26.0	53.4	40.4
ALL	Male	35.7	19.5	33.9	28.4
	Female	41	26.4	61.2	51.0

Sources: NFHS 4: IIPS and ICF (2017) National Family Health Survey (2015-16), India, 2015-16, Odisha, Mumbai. NFHS 3: IIPS and Macro International (2007) National Family Health Survey (2005-06), India, 2015-16, Odisha, Mumbai.

Data on nutritional status reveals that substantially higher percentage of tribal women suffer from chronic energy deficiency and anaemia than their male counterparts (Table

4). It is generally believed that female education has profound effect on economic, demographic and health conditions of populations. Several empirical studies also show that illiterate women are likely to have high rates of fertility, mortality and under-nutrition, low earning potential, and little autonomy within the household. It also has a negative impact on the health and well-being of her children. Apart from these variables, tradition, poverty and body assimilation of various inputs also have an impact at the nutrition deficiency.

Spatial Patterns

In Odisha, regional disparity on social development indicators remains conspicuous despite some improvement. Female literacy rate is 64 per cent with significant variations across regions/districts (Table 5 and Table 5a). The southern districts, having concentration of tribal population, form the belt of low female literacy rate (43 per cent). The corresponding figures for coastal and northern region are 73.3 per cent and 62 per cent respectively. Male-female difference in literacy rate in the southern region is the highest followed by the northern and coastal region (Table 5). However, the prevalence of gender inequality in literacy achievement is evident in all the districts of the state (Table 5a). A substantial variation in female literacy rate is also observed across social groups with a very low figure for tribal women (41.2%). The gap in female literacy

Table 5: Regional Variations in Gender Inequality in Literacy Rate, 2011

Region	*Total*	*Male*	*Female*	*Gap*
Southern	54.4	66.1	43.0	23.2
Northern	71.4	80.7	62.0	18.6
Coastal	80.6	87.7	73.3	14.4
All	72.9	81.6	64.0	17.6

Note: Figures are computed from the Census of India, 2011 CD-ROM.

Source: India, Registrar General (2013), Primary Census Abstract, CD-ROM, Census of India, 2011.

rate between scheduled tribes and general caste population is around 33 percentage points (Table 5b). Social category-specific figures show that female literacy is the lowest among ST population, followed by the SCs followed by general population in almost all regions.

Table 5a: District Level Variations in Gender Inequality in Literacy Rate, 2011

District/State	*Male*	*Female*	*Gender Gap*
ODISHA	81.59	64.01	17.58
Bargarh	83.68	65.38	18.30
Jharsuguda	86.61	70.73	15.88
Sambalpur	84.35	67.93	16.43
Debagarh	81.92	63.05	18.87
Sundargarh	81.01	65.48	15.53
Kendujhar	78.12	58.28	19.84
Mayurbhanj	73.76	52.71	21.05
Baleshwar	87.00	72.28	14.72
Bhadrak	89.64	75.83	13.81
Kendrapara	91.45	78.96	12.50
Jagatsinghapur	92.38	80.63	11.76
Cuttack	91.11	79.55	11.55
Jajapur	86.84	73.29	13.55
Dhenkanal	86.18	71.00	15.18
Anugul	85.98	68.64	17.34
Nayagarh	88.16	68.64	19.52
Khordha	91.78	81.61	10.17
Puri	90.85	78.28	12.56
Ganjam	80.99	61.13	19.86
Gajapati	64.38	43.18	21.21
Kandhamal	76.93	51.94	24.99
Baudh	83.34	59.79	23.55
Subarnapur	84.40	64.04	20.36

Balangir	75.85	53.50	22.35
Nuapada	70.29	44.76	25.53
Kalahandi	71.90	46.68	25.22
Rayagada	61.04	39.19	21.86
Nabarangapur	57.31	35.80	21.51
Koraput	60.32	38.55	21.77
Malkangiri	59.07	38.28	20.79

Note: Figures are computed from the Census of India, 2011 CD-ROM.

Source: India, Registrar General (2013), Primary Census Abstract, CD-ROM, Census of India, 2011.

Table 5b: Gender Gap in Literacy Rate by Social Groups, 2011

Category	*Total*	*Male*	*Female*	*Male-Female Gap in Literacy Rate*
All	72.9	81.6	64.00	17.6
NON-SCST	81.4	88.5	74.0	14.4
SC	69.00	79.2	58.8	20.4
ST	52.2	63.7	41.2	22.5

Note: Figures are computed from the Census of India, 2011 CD-ROM.

Source: India, Registrar General (2013), Primary Census Abstract, CD-ROM, Census of India, 2011.

As far as gender gap in the literacy rate is concerned, it is observed that gender gap is the highest among tribes followed by the scheduled caste and the general caste population. Male-female gap in literacy rate among STs is 22.5 percentage points while the figures for SCs and the general caste population are 20.4 and 14.4 percentage points respectively. As a whole there is a gender gap of 17.6 percentage points in literacy rate in Odisha. It is important to note that the extent of gender gap in the literacy rate is higher in the southern districts of the State inhabited by substantial percentage of tribal population.

How far adult females fared as compared to their male counterparts (Table 6)? According to NFHS 4 data 28.4 per cent adult male are anaemic while the figures for adult female is 51 per cent. Around 26. 4 per cent of adult women are suffering from chronic energy deficiency (CED) as compared to 19.5 per cent among adult males. There are considerable variations in degree of disparity by districts; the level of gender gap in nutritional status is higher in southern districts. (District level estimates for nutritional status for earlier years are not available).

Table 6: Gender Gap in Nutritional Status Among Adults, 2015-16

	Anaemia		*CED*	
District/State	*Male*	*Female*	*Male*	*Female*
ODISHA	28.4	51.0	19.5	26.4
Bargarh	35.0	68.5	31.1	13.8
Jharsuguda	34.1	69.2	27.9	27.3
Sambalpur	45.0	73.0	28.1	21.4
Debagarh	28.4	42.6	31.4	20.3
Sundargarh	39.6	71.4	27.2	15.2
Kendujhar	18.8	40.5	28.9	19.9
Mayurbhanj	23.4	42.4	31.6	16.4
Baleshwar	21.4	41.1	25.4	15.4
Bhadrak	22.0	43.5	30.3	19.7
Kendrapara	35.2	42.3	24.3	28.4
Jagatsinghapur	10.4	35.8	17.3	17.4
Cuttack	18.4	37.8	19.2	15.3
Jajapur	18.8	43.3	28.4	21.0
Dhenkanal	31.3	39.4	25.6	23.3
Anugul	27.0	44.0	21.8	22.1
Nayagarh	19.2	39.8	16.4	17.5
Khordha	13.6	45.3	15.4	9.8
Puri	16.1	44.3	15.5	14.5
Ganjam	34.5	41.3	21.5	17.7
Gajapati	33.6	58.5	11.2	13.7
Kandhamal	27.9	52.7	28.1	23.8

Baudh	27.3	49.9	31.0	23.4
Subarnapur	34.4	69.2	32.3	18.0
Balangir	37.1	61.1	31.8	20.6
Nuapada	43.8	64.0	34.0	27.4
Kalahandi	36.4	68.7	34.2	30.4
Rayagada	29.3	55.4	33.1	30.4
Nabarangapur	41.4	71.5	36.1	26.4
Koraput	40.0	63.3	34.5	24.7
Malkangiri	47.2	71.3	45.9	26.0

Source: IIPS and ICF (2017), National Family Health Survey-4 Factsheets, Odisha, 2015-16

In 27 out of 30 districts of Odisha, IMR was higher among females than that of males. In Anugul, IMR for both boys and girls were equal while IMR was higher among males as compared to females in the districts of Bargarh and Nabarangpur (Table 7). This also reflects how the patriarchal values pervaded the tribal areas.

Table 7: Gender Divide in Infant Mortality in Odisha by Districts, 2010-11

State/Districts	*Total*	*Male*	*Female*	*Gender Gap (Female-Male)*
ODISHA	62	59	66	-7
Nayagarh	67	55	82	-27
Kandhamal^	88	76	101	-25
Jagatsinghapur	56	46	67	-21
Baudh	64	54	75	-21
Gajapati	65	57	74	-17
Sonapur	54	48	62	-14
Puri	80	74	87	-13
Debagarh	58	53	65	-12
Kalahandi	59	53	65	-12
Rayagada	65	60	71	-11

Ganjam	61	56	66	-10
Sambalpur	56	52	61	-9
Khordha	76	72	80	-8
Nuapada	56	53	59	-6
Koraput	56	53	59	-6
Malkangiri	55	52	58	-6
Cuttack	63	61	66	-5
Kendrapara	64	61	66	-5
Mayurbhanj	53	51	56	-5
Jajapur	53	51	55	-4
Kendujhar	58	56	60	-4
Dhenkanal	76	75	78	-3
Bhadrak	55	54	57	-3
Sundargarh	55	53	56	-3
Balangir	100	99	101	-2
Jharsuguda	51	50	52	-2
Baleshwar	49	49	50	-1
Anugul	50	50	50	0
Bargarh	66	68	63	5
Nabarangapur	54	58	51	7

Source: India, Registrar General (2012). Annual Health Survey, 2010-11 Estimates

Notes: ^the district Kandhamal was earlier known as Phulbani

HDI and GDI values for the year 2004 are provided in Table 8. It shows that districts located in the southern part of the State occupy the bottom positions as far as GDI value is concerned and the districts in the coastal region form the belt of higher GDI. It is to be noted that the southern part of the State is inhabited by substantial proportion of tribal population. These values were not computed for the later years.

Table 8 : HDI Values and GDI Values in Odisha, 2004

District	*HDI Value*	*GDI Value*	*HDI Rank*	*GDI Rank*
Khurda	0.736	0.632	1	5
Jharsuguda	0.722	0.687	2	1
Cuttack	0.695	0.618	3	7
Sundargarh	0.683	0.659	4	2
Deogarh	0.669	0.647	5	3
Anugul	0.663	0.637	6	4
Puri	0.657	0.516	7	17
Bhadrak	0.646	0.497	8	21
Mayurbhanj	0.639	0.621	9	6
Kendrapara	0.626	0.516	10	18
Kalahandi	0.606	0.579	11	8
Dhenkanal	0.591	0.531	12	12
Sambalpur	0.589	0.56	13	10
Nuapada	0.581	0.561	14	9
Nayagarh	0.571	0.452	15	23
Sonepur	0.566	0.543	16	11
Bargarh	0.565	0.528	17	13
Balasore	0.559	0.519	18	14
Jagatsinghpur	0.557	0.491	19	22
Ganjam	0.551	0.518	20	15
Balangir	0.546	0.518	21	16
Jajpur	0.54	0.386	22	28
Boudh	0.536	0.509	23	19
Keonjhar	0.53	0.504	24	20
Rayagada	0.443	0.428	25	24
Nabarangpur	0.436	0.422	26	25
Koraput	0.431	0.415	27	26
Gajapati	0.431	0.401	28	27

Kandhamal	0.389	0.372	29	29
Malkangiri	0.37	0.362	30	30

Source: Government of Odisha (2004), *Odisha Human Development Report*. Bhubaneswar: Planning and Coordination Department.

Women in Local Government System

Looking at the analysis of data in the sections on status of women and imbalanced regional development, it is quite evident that women of the tribal communities are most excluded and did not gain much from the growth process. In the measures given by Raghuram Rajan (2013)[3] Odisha comes almost first in terms of poverty level. Those indicators include: monthly per capita consumption expenditure, education, health, household amenities, poverty rate, female literacy rate, per cent of ST and SC population, urbanization rate, financial inclusion, and connectivity. Precisely because of that reason, formation of local government system was initiated after 1988 and recommendation of giving 30 per cent seats for women was accepted for the first time, though it was earlier rejected in 1975. The formation of local bodies in 1994 under the 73rd Constitution Amendment Act[4] had twin objectives namely, to give clean, transparent and participatory governance at the doorstep of the marginalized villagers in which they have a say, and secondly to make women effective partners in decision-making to engender the growth process and minimize the social discriminations in the family and society by changing the image of women being only home makers. The women were elected not only to one third of the seats but sometimes exceeded the quota. Besides, in order to augment the income and provide sustainable livelihood, micro-credit groups were formed under TRIPTI and National Rural Livelihood Mission (Odisha Livelihood Mission). In addition, a number of rights based flagship programmes were initiated such as Mahatma Gandhi National Rural Employment Guarantee Act (scheme) (MGNREGA), National Food Security Act (NFSA-2013) and National Rural Health Mission (NRHM) in which women in general and that of panchayats had a stake. In all these schemes, the panchayat have a role in monitoring, selecting the labourers, or keeping the job cards intact, and last but not the least disbursing the wages immediately.

Interestingly the Fourteenth Finance Commission has paid more attention to the local government system and allocated 42 per cent of the total tax receipts of the central government. According to the Central Minister for Urban Development about 10 lakhs of engineers and technicians are being trained to help the panchayat members to plan for their development. Because of this enhancement, each panchayat will be entitled to get Rs. 2,404 per capita and 17 lakhs per year for five years that will be used for basic services, sanitation, drinking water and maintenance of the community assets (Naidu, 2016). In other words, more and more attention is supposedly being given to the local bodies but both the Centre and the State are unable to devolve real power to panchayats. At the same time however, it is to be noted that all the schemes are being executed by different departments or under the bureaucratic control leaving out the true spirit of the decentralized participatory governance at the grassroots level. Further, in multi-ethnic villages, the high caste and patriarchal communities try to be manipulative and deprive the marginalized sections of the people especially women, to benefit out of participatory governance. Further, the local government system lacks financial power and don't have any power to raise their own resources, and thus depend only on the central and state grants which are meant for different straight-jacket plans. In other words, the systemic problems prove to be a real deterrent in effective functioning of the panchayats. Nonetheless the village people are trying to gain by the use of Right to Information Act, (RTI) 'Jan Sunwai' and other legal means.

In so far as the women leaders are concerned, there is a presence of large number of women in the public—out of three million elected leaders more than a million are women. In Odisha alone 53,000 women or 53 per cent of women got elected in 2012 (Election Commission of Odisha, 2012).

The share of women members in PRIs in Odisha was close to 60 per cent in 2017. If we add the number of micro-credit groups the number increases considerably. In other words, the democratic space has already become more participatory than before. But as to what extent they have engendered the development process, that is the matter of enquiry; given the constraints of political participation, inter-caste/class and intra-caste/class and communities domination, as well as the societal and patriarchal obstacles.

Our scope is limited to an empirical survey of two districts to find out if even after 23 years of being assimilated with the local government system, women of tribal areas have been integrated in the development process to some extent or not.

To focus on only one district namely, Rayagada may be hazardous since it may not be a representative one. But our experience in working with the other tribal areas convinces us that a similar process is taking place everywhere[5]. Along with Rayagada we had interviewed some women sarpanches in Mayurbhanj. The reason for taking Rayagada are many, namely, we have a kind of time series data: one set was collected in 1997-2001 and the other set was collected in 2013-14.

The limitations were also many and should be kept in mind. First of all the first project was to monitor and evaluate the performance of the elected women representatives to build their capacity. They were the first set of elected women representatives and were novices in politics. At that time the socio-economic data was collected to know the background of the newly-elected women. A number of training programmes, creation of awareness, involving the society and families were also taken up. Besides, mock 'gram sabha', awareness of various government schemes were highlighted[6]. Second time, we, on behalf of the Institute of Social Sciences (ISS), New Delhi surveyed a group of 62 elected women leaders in all the three tiers of panchayats in two blocks of Rayagada namely, Rayagada and Bissam Cuttack. In Mayurbhanj district, the blocks of Udala and Baripada were taken up. The blocks and panchayats were selected using random sampling method.

A detailed questionnaire was filled up; various focus group discussions as well as in-depth case studies were documented[7].

The findings are based on these field studies. First of all we found that female education has made a tremendous stride. Most of the sarpanches at present have studied up to intermediate level. In the first round on the other hand most of the sarpanches were barely literate or just primary pass.In terms of age groups in both the cases, 87 per cent of women leaders belonged to the age group of 18-35. Further, access to drinking water in terms of tubewells had reached 80 to 90 per cent in 2013-14, though the villagers started demanding piped water. In terms of housing compared with the result of 1997-2002, in 2013 it was noticed that only 24 per cent of the houses were *kuchha*houses, rest were either 'semi-pucca' or complete 'pucca'. Eighty seven per cent have access to electricity and most of the households have a scooter which is under the control of the husbands.

In terms of awareness unlike the first generation, this time, the elected women were exposed to various training programmes including that of the government at the block level. Even though, they complained of not gaining much because of the use of the standard Odia language, most of them knew about PESA, functioning of gram sabha and almost all the welfare schemes. However, in terms of making the budget they still depended on their CEOs or husbands if he was educated. This was the case in the earlier period also.

The in-depth case studies showed that the husbands still overshadowed them, though in many cases they were visible in attending the panchayat meetings and going to the block and conducting *pallisabha* unlike during the period of 1997-2000. During the earlier study, we really had problems in getting the women alone. In all the meetings the husbands accompanied them. This time however, women were free to attend alone. Most of the women leaders were a part of women's self help groups though some of the groups were not functional. The formation of groups has been recent development which was absent in the first term. However, the synergy which was expected from the collective was almost absent except for one or two cases. In many places, the women lamented that just after the elections, the members of self help groups became alienated even though they encouraged them to contest the elections.

Case studies in Mayurbhanj and Rayagada conducted during 2013-14 by the Institute of Social Sciences, New Delhi team showed that women sarpanches were making a difference by using various welfare schemes to augment the productivity of the land, prevent distress migration, ensure girls' education and protect the environment etc.

For example, Suni Singh, the Sarpanch of Bahubandh panchayat, has been engaged in horticulture cultivation, and has facilitated to build a resevoir to increase the productivity of the land by using the MGNREGS' money. She identified twenty beneficiaries to build 20 goat sheds with the help of above money. She took her ward members into confidence to allocate the Indira Awaas Yojana. She encouraged women to meet the ASHA workers to know about health issues. A group of social workers advise her about development issues to execute in the panchayat. Initially she worked as a factory worker and formed a self-help group in her village. The group was engaged in augmenting the income generating activities by producing useful products with locally available resources. Since she helped the village women, they requested her to contest the election. She won the elections twice. But in 2017 she lost because of intra-party rivalry. However, her spirit to work for the panchayat is still burning. She plans to contest the election again. In yet another case, Tapaswini Nayak, of Bhagbatchandrapur was able to add 200 pension holders to the existing list and also mobilized seven million work days under MGNREGS for her people. By using the above money she facilitated renovation of a big pond to do pisciculture. Her panchayat got the best award for the MGNREGA work in 2013. It is heartening to note that she has been re-elected. Her aim is to create a swacch panchayat.Of course she takes the help of her husband.

Nandini Nayak of Parulia panchayat encouraged large number of women to attend the gram sabha. She has been able to help in renovating 13 farm ponds for fishery and small irrigation. Further, she has been able to add 130 pension holders to the list and new 21 low cost shelters under the Indira Awaas Yojana. The most important achievement of Nandini is to allot 22 forest land pattas to the most needy persons of her village. Under her leadership, a self help group monitors the PDS.

Lakshmipriya Nayak of Bagabanpur GP, on the other hand has been able to form a synergy with the self help group to work effectively in her panchayat. So far she has been able to complete a number of development work like construction of panchayat roads and ponds for raising fishery by using MGNREGS' money. She has been able to allot 300 pension holders and 30 Indira Awaas shelters. Because of her leadership more and more women have started to come to attend the palli sabha and gram sabha making them more participatory. Unfortunately she has not been able to build a panchayat office because of the apathy of the lower level officials. However, she was defeated in 2017 due to intra-party rivraly.

On the other hand, Pramila Marandi, sarpanch of Badajode panchayat could not deliver any substantial benefits in her panchayat because she is always busy in managing a grocery store while her husband looks after the panchayat work. It can be pointed out that if she could manage the grocery store she would also manage the panchayat work very well[8]. Dinja Jakasika, the first woman sarpanch from the most vulnerable tribe, Dongria Kandh, Kurli panchayat has made a considerable difference.She herself is illiterate but wanted to send all the girl children to the school. Apparently in her community it is considered that if a girl child goes to school, then all the ancestral persons would go to hell. She defied that and encouraged the children to go to school. Besides, she also monitors the ration shops to find out if the women are getting the correct amount of ration. Of course, her brother helps her in conducting the panchayat work. It is encouraging to know that she has been re-elected in 2017. Her ambition is to set up a fruit processing factory to give employment to the women and youth.

Sansa Huika, sarpanch of Tadama panchayat, however, in spite of her enthusiasm and after getting all the support from her mother-in-law and other family members could not work as an effective sarpanch because of her husband. She has taken up various trainings and very much wanted to work for the development of the panchayats, but she is not allowed to work at all by her husband. She has been elected twice but the same story gets repeated every time. This time however, she was defeated. Being interviewed, her husband picked up the phone and said that he was defeated this time. He snapped the phone connection the moment I insisted on knowing the cause!

Similarly Puspabati Timaka, of Jemadeipentho is unable to work at all inspite of her willingness because the CEO never takes her into confidence. Of course it is interesting to note that all these women have a desire to work for the panchayats but because of the domination of patriarchy in different forms, they are unable to do so.

The most significant positive result which keeps us optimistic is the fact that most women monitor the ration shops and see to it that women get right amount of ration. They also encourage pregnant women to go to the hospital for delivery. As a result institutional delivery has increased significantly. The functioning of the Standing Committee on Health and Sanitation has become quite active where both sarpanchs and women ward members take interest to convene the monthly meeting. Women members come regularly to attend the same and discuss various issues[9]. Yet in another development, the local SHG members belonging to SC community of Rayagada are collecting cess of electricity and women are engaged in processing organic turmeric and oranges. But still other locally produced grains, oilseeds, fruits are sold at a very low rate which could contribute to their income if proper price could be ensured.

In fact, Reetika Khera (2015) has pointed out that the Integrated Child Development Scheme (ICDS) is working well in the tribal areas because of the decentralized participation of the village women and that of the panchayat members. Secondly, development to them means increasing the productivity of land, access to drinking water, and access to education[10]. In fact, the same story was revealed when the correspondent of *Indian Express* which has adopted the poorest district of Odisha namely, Nabarangpur asked the local people about their dreams. The children and old felt that education is development for them[11]. The *Indian Express* chose the poorest district Nabarangpur to find out the ground reality starting the journey on Independence day 2015. It was evident that the children and old alike are becoming aware of their deprivation and trying to find the solution to the same as the reporter observed. It was a matter of hope and not despair. Similarly the health scheme for women under NRHM has created an interest among them and many tribal young women do come to the ICDS centre to listen to the ASHA workers about vaccination and nutrition along with panchayat members. They also avail the monetary gain of the MAMTA scheme[12]. Objectively speaking, recently the institutional deliveries have increased significantly. Hopefully, the availability of additional grant from the Fourteenth Finance Commission and availability of the skill of local level engineers would help the panchayat members and other women to take stock of the locally available natural resources apart from the minerals to help to diversify the agricultural base through agri-industries to pave towards sustainable development without creating environment degradation. In other words one does not have to adopt 'one size fits all' development model for all over Odisha. Depending on the availability of the local resources and women power, suitable economic models can be developed in which women talent could be harnessed as an entrepreneur to utilize the resources for the common welfare. Women in general and those of panchayat in particular can take lead to be managers as well as partners of the growth process.

But before that, the panchayat elected women have to overcome certain obstacles which are still prevalent namely, absence of democratic husbands[13], insensitive bureaucracy and lack of acceptance from the communities. The women leaders are still saddled with domestic work in terms of taking care of children, cooking for the elderly and looking after other chores. So they get less time to do panchayat's work. Their domestic burden is yet to be reduced except perhaps availability of drinking water nearby. For fuel however, they have to travel a long distance since deforestation is rampant. In the public space, indirect violence in the form of ignoring the women leaders by the husbands, male community members, the panchayat CEO, BDO, *rojgarsahayak* etc, are quite widely prevalent. The training modules do not focus on the utilization of locally available resources to develop the area. Alcoholism by men is partly responsible for their underdevelopment. Finally women's collectives which has been working as a support group in Maharashtra (Menon, 2015) is yet to develop in the tribal areas partly because the SHGs formed by the tribals are mostly defunct though that of *dalits* are working well[14].

Conclusion

Odisha has seen an impressive rate in economic growth in the last two decades. However, achievement in the economic front does not robustly correspond to the levels of social development. Worse, Odisha is persistently suffering from multi dimensional intra-state regional and social disparities. Gendered divide in development outcomes is appalling. Though there is some evidence to indicate a movement towards convergence on development indicators, the performance in this regard is not satisfactory. The southern districts with substantial percentage of tribal population continue to form the less developed belt in the State while coastal districts are a bit ahead. Besides, the 'KBK region' is still underdeveloped after many years of planning.

Even though the poverty ratio estimates by gender are not

available, the GDI at the district level showed that the tribal areas are languishing. Women in this region are critically deprived of basic rights, including that of education and health. The analysis of the socio-economic data has made it amply clear that the tribal areas in general and the tribal women in particular have not gained much. Starting from health, education and livelihood, tribal women are not faring at par with other women. Keeping all these developments in mind one may argue that given a sense of ownership and more freedom, women leaders in the tribal areas will be able to take up the leadership mantle of the local area. Only some miniscule steps have been initiated towards developing the locally suitable development model which is not only demanding MGNREGS money for employment but also for increasing the productivity of the land in order to minimize the distress migration which has remained a disturbing phenomenon in those areas. Locally produced food items for mid day meals in schools and anganwadis has helped women in many ways. It helps the local economy where women play an important role. Besides women leaders have promoted demand driven services such as vaccinations and safe drinking water. Further women strongly feel that only education can lead to the development of the tribal people[15]. However, it is to be remembered that the education has to be culturally sensitive.

A focus on the locally suitable and sustainable development model with the involvement of local people, more particularly, women, will have far-reaching positive effects in the backward regions, and thereby, will reduce regional as well as gender divide in development outcomes in the State. To this effect, Government has an important role in promoting space-based development model and encouraging women to participate in local government systems. Women's local knowledge and social interaction should be integrated in regional development strategies to achieve sustainable development. Their self-esteem as productive actors in development has to be accepted. The equal entitlement of women in all spheres of production and reproduction, resource control, knowledge and decision-making needs to be realized. This will require reformulation of policy goals, redesign of programme components, and reorganization of administrative structures, with due attention to the women at each stage. Thus, it can be concluded that given the enabling conditions, women in general and those of the tribal areas in particular can effectively exercise decision-making power in the local areas and materialize their broader citizenship claims.

NOTES

1. We should add that the data set might have a sampling error since the size is small. Besides, the oral interview may have reporting bias as well. We have tried to overcome that bias by asking similar questions to different stake holders ranging from the state officials, leaders and the beneficiaries at the village level.
2. Of course we don't know how have the experts collected the data. Because one notices that nowadays women are beaten up if the men are drunkards. The incidence of liquor drinking has gone up considerably. As a result, women are agitating in many places.
3. www.finmin.nicin/reports/Reports_CompDevState.pdf
4. Finance Commission and Election Commission were established as well as 29 development subjects were to be devolved to panchayats in true letter and spirit involving finance, functionaries and functions.
5. Institute of Social Sciences, New Delhi (1997-2002) " Monitoring and Evaluating the Performance of elected women representatives of panchayats in three districts of Odisha in coastal, inland and tribal belt". A five year project . Unpublished report. Supported by Swedish International Development Agency (SIDA) Later on we conducted an intensive impact study of women's leadership in 2013-14 in Rayagada and Mayurbhanj , the tribal area. The objective was to find out what kinds of changes have taken place between then and now. We also tried to find out if the first generation of women candidates are also contesting in the 2012 panchayat election or not. As expected only a couple of women out of 44 have come forward. Unlike the first tenure, women along with the women's collective were campaigning

for themselves. They were also more focused regarding the development issues. Further we also visited the same Block of Jagatsinghpur in 2014-5. One noticed that women do take the support of the male family members but for the welfare of the villagers. They were not completely overshadowed by the men.

6. During the first study awareness generation was taken up.
7. The Institute of Social Sciences, New Delhi 2013-14 'Functioning of Grassroots Democracy in India: A study of Tribal women leaders in select districts of Odisha'.
8. Unfortunately we could not know if she won the recent election because she does not have a phone.
9. As per a survey report conducted among around five hundred elected women representatives, the same story was repeated. The survey was conducted by the ISS team in 2012 and the report was published. "Report of a Survey on National Rural Health Mission and Panchayats: To what extent are the panchayats participating in Health Policy" https://www.mainstreamweekly.net/article4000.html
10. Oral interview of a vulnerable tribal woman sarpanch.
11. http://indianexpress.com/article/india/india-others/district-zero-she-folds-the-indian-flag-and-unfolds-her-dream/
12. Conditional cash transfer scheme for pregnant women who get four installments on the fulfillment of certain conditions of the mother as well as the child.
13. By democratic husbands we mean that one can't categorize all patriarchies as homogenous. Some of them believe in Sen's 'Gender and cooperative in conflict' in WP18, 1987 https://www.wider.unu.edu/sites/default/files/WP18.pdf. In that case, the husbands also give space to women leaders to be visible. So the entire concept of 'Proxy women' has to be revisited. (Mohanty, 2014) http://geographyandyou.com/life/women-studies/women-prepared-to-lead/
14. As per the UNDP report the Kerala model of Kudumbshree and PRI synergy under NRLM has started working in Odisha also. Let us hope it takes root in the tribal areas as well (http://keralanro.org/).
15. Oral interview.

REFERENCES

Government of India. 2013. *Report of the Committee for Evolving a*

Composite Development Index for States. New Delhi: Ministry of Finance.

Government of India. 2013. Press Notes on Poverty Estimates, 2011-12. Planning Commission, New Delhi: Press Information Bureau.

Government of India. 2013. *Economic Survey, 2012-13*. New Delhi: Ministry of Finance.

Government of Odisha. 2004. *Orissa Development Report 2004*, Bhubaneswar: Planning and Coordination Department.

Government of Odisha. 2013. *Economic Survey, 2012-13*. Bhubaneswar: Planning and Coordination Department.

IIPS and ICF. 2017. National Family Health Survey (NHFS-4) Fact Sheets, 2015-16.

IIPS and ICF. 2017. National Family Health Survey (2015-16), India, Odisha, Mumbai.

IIPS and Macro International (2007) National Family Health Survey (2005-06), India, 2015-16, Odisha, Mumbai.

India, Registrar General. 2012. Sample Registration System (SRS) Report 2010, Report No. 1 of 2012. New Delhi: Government of India.

India, Registrar General. 2016. Sample Registration System (SRS) Report 2016. New Delhi: Government of India.

India, Registrar General. 2013. Primary Census Abstract, CD-ROM, Census of India, 2011.

India, Registrar General. 2012. Annual Health Survey, 2010-11 Estimates. New Delhi: Registrar General of India.

India, Registrar General. 2018. Special Bulletin on Maternal Mortality in India 2014-16, New Delhi: Government of India.

Khera, Reetika. 2015 'Baby Steps in Odisha,: Children's Development of Children', *Economic and Political Weekly,* Vol. 15, No. 40, pp. 44-49 (October, 3).

Menon, Gayatri, 2015 'Interrogating the Promise of Microcredit' in Mohanty, Bidyut and Victor Faessel (eds.), *Our Money Our Lives: Women and Microcredit in a Cross-Cultural Perspective,* Delhi: Aakar Books.

Mohanty, Bidyut (ed.) 2014. *Panchayats, Women and Health for All.* New Delhi, Concept.

Naidu, M. Venkaiah 2016, 'True Panchayati Raj', *The Hindu* April, 26 Delhi Edition, p. 13.

IV. On the Margins

9

Skills for Employment Programme in Apparel Industries and Trends in Female Migration: A Study on SEAM of Odisha

Manasi Mohanty

Introduction

In the global apparel sector, there has been a dramatic shift from the permanent and regular employment to temporary and contract based labour practice. Such a process has often driven vulnerable groups of workers like migrant workers who constitute an important part of the global textile workforce. Significantly, women represent an overwhelming majority of migrant working class in the apparel manufacturing industries (Kate and Theuws, 2016). While entering into the sector, women workers face added risks of gender discrimination and inequality in both the recruitment process and employment conditions. In many cases, the women themselves may not have selected to participate in migration towards distant cities for work in manufacturing industries but have been forced to do so due to their vulnerable conditions at home. In such cases, their family members also play an important role pushing them to migrate outside the State for work.

In India, around 60 per cent of the garment workforce is feminized in nature (UN Women 2015). The country has high proportion of informal and home based work, especially among women workers which often do not come with formal employment contracts. In recent years, the Government of India has launched "National Skill Development Mission" under which various skill development agencies provide skill training to rural youth in backward regions and states like Odisha, Jharkhand, Chhattisgarh, Assam, West Bengal, Uttar Pradesh, Andhra Pradesh, etc. It brings trainees from rural areas to urban centres of developed states to enable employment in various manufacturing sectors like apparel industries which mainly operate from the southern parts of India such as Karnataka, Tamil Nadu and Kerala. These trainees are often the first unmarried women of villages who migrate to the city in search of work, which is to be considered as their first formal employment opportunities (BSR 2017). However, there is high degree of informalization in the garment manufacturing industries operating within Special Economic Zones (SEZs) and Export Processing Zones (EPZs) of formal sector. The tendency towards subcontracting to meet the fast fashion demands results in a greater extent of informality in the formal based apparel sector. In actual practice, workers are often absorbed as contract workers in a highly informalized manner in these industries at the end of a supply chain, without any definite form of social protection and unionization.

In this context, the present paper explores the process of female migration in Odisha at its source location. It analyses the growth and organizational structure of the skill training centres of Odisha at the supply side which imports women trainees into the southern parts of India for placement in the garment manufacturing units. The state of Kerala is a stark example where vast numbers of women migrant workers are absorbed as contract workers in the KINFRA apparel park. While collecting information from the skill training centre and qualitative interviews with its women trainees and also returned migrants from KINFRA apparel industries, such trends of recruitment and migration of female trainees came to be noticed in the present study.

The current paper is based on two studies in two different phases of research work. In the first, the field investigation in the source area (i.e Hinjlicut block and its surrounding villages) of Ganjam district explores the movement of Odia young men and largely women to the garment industry of Texport Private Ltd which is active within the premise of KINFRA Apparel Park.[1] In the course of field work during PhD, the researcher examined the Vikas Apparel Training Centre under the project 'SEAM' (Skills for Employment in Apparel Manufacturing) which worked under the supervision of Hinjlicut block and District Rural Development Agency (DRDA) of Ganjam district. The second part of the field work has covers the destination site during the post doctoral field investigation in 2015 when the researcher came to know about the KINFRA Apparel Park where M/s. Texport Industries Pvt Ltd has been working as one of the leading garment exporters. The garment industry is located in the Special Economic and Export Processing Zones at Thiruvantapuram which functions under the scheme 'Apparel Parks for Export' (APE) of the Government of India.

SEAM Training Centre of Odisha

The District Rural Development Agency (DRDA) has emerged as a labour market institution mediating the recruitment and migration of girls and young women for a whole range of new spinning and textile factories located in the rural areas of southern India (Agnihortri et. al 2012: 57). A similar DRDA arranged migration is also found in Ganjam district of Odisha which is known as project 'SEAM' (Skills for Employment in Apparel Manufacturing) (Mahanty 2012: 269). Under the project, hundreds of young women and girls are being sent to work in garment factories such as Texport Industries Private Limited in the State of Kerala. In the course of field work, the researcher met several young women and girls of some villages under Hinjlicut block of Ganjam district who worked in such garment manufacturing factories.

Skills for Employment in Apparel Manufacturing (SEAM)

Realizing that the majority of workers at the shop floor level are with low level education, the Infrastructure Leasing & Financial Services Cluster Development Initiative Ltd (IL&FS CDI)[2] has launched the project 'SEAM' (Skills for Employment in Apparel Manufacturing)[3]. The project supported by the Ministry of Rural Development, is targeted at the rural poor for enabling them to benefit from the growing economy while also meeting the skills required by this industry. This initiative has developed as a Special Project in 2005-06 under Swarnajayanti Gram Swarozgar Yojana (SGSY: a scheme for self-employment of rural poor) and National Rural Livelihood Mission (NRLM) in private partnership with Dr. Reddy's Foundation (Asha 2015, p. 78). The main purpose for launching this programme is essentially two fold. Today, there is a large number of unemployed rural youth in the country, but with no employable skills even though there is labour shortage in employment-intensive manufacturing industry, especially in the garment and leather sectors. Hence, this programme has been launched with two objectives for: (i) meeting the requirement of shortage of skilled human resources for the apparel industry and (ii) assisting the government in terms of its poverty alleviation mission.

The project 'SEAM' is a unique initiative which trains rural youth living below the poverty line to work in the garment industry. There are three main factors which make this initiative unique. Firstly, as a business model, it is conceived as a public-private partnership where the Government of India, industry partners, and IL&FS cluster-based training institutions are stakeholders, for catering to the skill deficit of the apparel industry and in the process uplifting the 'below poverty line' (BPL) youth[4]. Thus, the programme draws on the skills and expertise of all three stakeholders. Secondly, under the scale of the project, it is perhaps the flagship skill development programme focused on training of 5 lakh rural 'below poverty line' (BPL) youth in the age group of 18 to 35 years over a period of 5 years and provided them with jobs in the apparel industry. Thirdly, the project does not only train young people (with low levels of education) and enhances their skills but also guarantees placement with some of the leading garment industries in India.

Vikas Apparel Training Centre: A Study on Source Location

In Ganjam district of Odisha, the SEAM training centre named 'Vikas Apparel Training Centre' has been working over the last ten years. It was inaugurated by the Chief Minister of Odisha on 27th July 2008. It is the first centre of Odisha supported by the Ministry of Rural Development, Government of India; Government of Odisha and State Employment Mission. The training centre was set up with the management of IL&FS Cluster Development Infrastructure Limited. The Vikas Apparel Training Centre has received ISO 9001: 2008 certificate in September 2011. It is situated within the premises of the Hinjlicut block office. The training centre simulates the exact industry shop floor with industrial sewing machines. Besides Ganjam, the other six SEAM centres have been working in districts like Bolangir, Sundergarh, Gajapati, Kandhamal and Malkangiri. Hinjlicut is the oldest among all centres, followed by Phulbani of Kandhamal district, Tangarpalli and Rourkela under Sundergarh district and Raigarh of Gajapati district which started in 2010 and later Bolangir and Malkangiri in 2011. The Table 1.1 gives information on the number of SEAM trainee beneficiaries under the Aajeevika–SGSY project in Odisha. As per the tracking record, since April 1st, 2012, a total of 11,053 workers have been trained in Odisha under this scheme. In Ganjam district alone a total of 3,526 workers have been trained beneficiaries under SEAM.

An impact study of trainees of IL&FS clusters across Odisha was undertaken by IL&FS Cluster Development Initiative Ltd under the supervision of Xavier Institute of Management (XIMB), Bhubaneswar. An impact assessment of the skill development initiatives was conducted in areas surrounding eight training centres such as Phulbani, Hinjlicut, Raigarh, Malkangiri, Bolangir, Sundergarh, Tangarpalli and Rourkela

(Das n.d)[5]. Some findings of the impact study are presented in tables from 1.2 to 1.9. The table 1.2 reflects that the enrolment of trainees in the SEAM centre of Hinjilicut per year has been highest i.e. 59.5 followed by Phulbani (58.1), Tangarpalli (54.3) and Raigarh (50.1). The table shows below 50% enrolment in Rourkela, Bolangir and Malkangiri. The data from table 1.3 to 1.9 shows the majority of female trainees being trained at these centres and placed in textile industries of Karnataka, Tamil Nadu and Kerala under the Skills Development Programme.

While interviewing the coordinator of Vikas IL&FS Skills School at Hinjilicut during field investigation, the coordinator stated that most of the young people of Ganjam district have migrated to places like Surat, Mumbai, Hyderabad, Bengaluru, Chennai and other parts of the country, as there is no job security in their native areas. He claimed that the skills schools have put efforts to start Apparel Training for the BPL unemployed young rural labour in order to deal with the problem of increasing migration. It helps in placement and also meeting industry skills standards with the support of IL&FS while reaping benefits from the growing economy. Most of the trainees are recruited in Texport Pvt Ltd at Thiruvantapuram in Kerala. Here, the researcher argues that the SEAM training project has initiated such skill development programme to facilitate and to extend further migration of rural young men and women without taking concrete measures to enable employment at their native villages and to stop the current migration process.

In Ganjam district, independent labour migration has always been largely a male phenomenon. Women of this district do not generally migrate independently in a group or even associational. A very small number of women migrate with their families in order to accompany their husbands to destinations for the purpose of family unity. The cultural sanctions impose restrictions on women mobility in villages. Women are not allowed to move on their own for economic opportunities. However, the SEAM scheme under SGSY programme took initiative to facilitate the movement of low educated unmarried girls to other states for jobs. But, the purpose of IL&FS Skill School has not been properly served without creating an employment based industry in the source areas and the State. During field investigation, such kind of arguments have been raised by many male and female trainees and their family members in the surrounding villages of Hinjilicut.

As per the ISO certificate guidelines, the IL&FS Skill School can select and screen candidates for apparel training; impart expertise knowledge in apparel making and enable placement in the private industry. The following norms are essential for the selection of apparel training. The candidate should belong to the background of BPL family; the age of the candidate should be between 18 to 35 years and should be prepared to serve outside the State. The preference for apparel training will be given to the candidates of socially and economically backward castes viz., the scheduled caste/scheduled tribe. The qualification of trainees ought to be fifth standard pass and a rural unemployed person. The minimum weight and height required to become a trainee in the centre is 35 kg and 137 cm respectively for operating the sewing machine. Every trainee taking admission under the SEAM project is informed about the placement details before commencement of the training programme.

The coordinator is in charge for the selection of candidates on every Wednesday and Friday of the week. After receiving the applications from candidates, he verifies certificates and other documents and tests the hand-eye-coordination, colour blindness etc. The coordinator however furnished certain problems in selecting candidates. In certain times, candidates were disqualified for not meeting the height and eye-test requirements for operating the sewing machine. During the selection of trainees under the SEAM project, village meetings, inclusive job fairs, task force, recommendation of PRIs and district administration are the main procedures followed in identifying suitable candidates for the training centre.

During a personal interview with the coordinator of

Hinjilicut, the researcher asked many questions regarding the employment prospects and placements for the candidates being trained at their centre, which is discussed here. He said that the share of retention of labour in the garment and apparel factories has gone up to 80 per cent. The SEAM centre officers stay in the respective factories for a week where the trainees are employed with a purpose to find out the problems of the workers. As per the placement conditions, the trainees have to work a minimum of six months in the factories where they are recruited. It includes the period of two months training provided by the company. They are entitled for ten days leave to visit their villages every six months. The remuneration they receive differs depending on the companies and type of work. The monthly minimum payments start from Rs 3,800 and going up to 5,000. Many companies provide social security benefits such as provident fund and health insurance. Along with, the workers are paid premium benefits and bonus for working overtime and attaining the production targets in terms of quality and quantity.

Apart from the coordinator in charge of Vikas training centre[6], the respective panchayat and *Sarpanch* (the elected head of the village panchayat), ward members, ruling political party workers etc. play a crucial role in such process of labour mobilization in convincing the prospective trainees' parents about sending their girls to the skill school (Asha 2015: 87). For this purpose, the quarterly meetings of the PRI representatives, the company representatives, IL&FS officials and parents of trainees are organized to encourage the poor unemployed youth to acquire skills in the apparel training centres. In certain cases, financial assistance for trainees is provided under the project to meet the travel cost, food expenses etc.

In the initial years of the training programme, very few number of girls joined the center.[7] Earlier, the parents were not willing to send their young and unmarried daughters outside the State. In order to avoid such problems, panchayat meetings are conducted to develop the confidence level of the parents of the beneficiaries. In this direction, PRI representatives have had to convince the families of female trainees and give an assurance about their safety and security in the garment units. Besides these, Anganwadi teachers, ASHA health workers and even some NGOs play an important role in mobilizing workers to the centre. During the field investigation in Ralaba, Sikiri and Burupada villages, the researcher, at the same time, observed that some of the families of the trainees are not fully aware about the details of apparel industries where their daughters are placed for work even though they have been informed by IL&FS and SEAM officials through meetings.

The skill school fixes the intake capacity of 64 numbers of trainees for the SEAM programme. The duration of residential skill training is one month. There have been two instructors appointed by IL&FS to impart training. The training runs in two shifts per day having 32 sewing machines. The first shift starts from 7 am to 1 pm and second shift from 2 pm to 8 pm for each batch per day to stimulate the exact industry working culture. Not only did the technical skills, but soft skills helped them to adjust to the new environment. Apart from sewing training of 6 hours a day, the trainees are also provided with soft skills, life skills and also two hours of English and Hindi languages proficiency classes. These have been imparted to aquire knowledge on motivation and leadership skill, HIV AIDS, yoga, health checkup, company law, etc. These placements in states like Kerala, Tamil Nadu, and Karnataka come in handy in.

The old Food Corporation of India godown situated at the block campus has been selected as the training hall. The building has been re-modeled as per requirement. As such the T.P. Centre, Hinjilicut (block campus) and hostel building of Brundaban High School are also being used as ladies and gents hostels respectively for free accommodation of trainees. There is provision of Rs 60 per day per trainee for lunch & dinner including breakfast. In this connection, the District Rural Development Agency (DRDA) of Ganjam provides Rs 1,15,200 towards food charges and other related expenses each month out of the Employment Mission Grant of Ganjam district. The total per head cost of trainees for one month reaches upto Rs 10,000 with accommodation and food expenses in the skill school. As per instructions of the DRDA, one woman Self Help Group (SHG) named Madan Mohan of Gandala has been chosen for catering. The same SHG provides breakfast, lunch and dinner as per menu provided by Block Development Officer (BDO) of Hinjilicut[8].

There is a signboard on the wall of the SEAM skill centre which endorses the large development impact on the BPL families of Ganjam district (Mahanty 2012, Asha 2015). It was projected that 1,125 females were trained and placed whereas 1,066 number of male trainees were covered by the SEAM project. It is also claimed that after employment, female trainees remit Rs 2,000-2,500 per month to their families. In case of male trainees, they remit Rs 1,500-2,000 per month. The average remittance by a worker to his/her family is stated to be around Rs 2,000. As per SEAM's official figure, 2191 youth were trained and placed from Ganjam district alone by the year 2008. The centre has claimed that Rs 43,82,000 was sent to their families in Ganjam district per month under this programme. Hence, the total amount sent by the youth during the entire year is more than Rs 5 crores and more than 60 youth gained employment every month after training.

In the course of fieldwork, the researcher had interaction with some female returnees. Most of the girls returned from Kerela because of poor salary. The study indicates that the assurances given by Hijilicut block office, SEAM centre and private industries seem to be quite false. Some of the young girls who had returned from KINFRA textile factories narrated their experiences regarding the working conditions in the garment units. They were not paid by their employers during the first six months. They have revealed that it was an apprenticeship-cum-training programme in the industry. It was in fact exploitative as their labour remained unwaged. After such a so-called six-month 'apprenticeship programme', they received Rs 2,000-2,500 only per month in Kerela's Texport industry. Out of this amount, Rs 500 was deducted towards provident fund account. It was extremely difficult for them to manage with Rs 1,500-2,000 at their destinations. In the first year, workers could hardly remit Rs 5,000 to their families per year. The official claim of monthly average remittance of Rs 2,000 is not substantiated by the findings collected through the interactive session with female returnees. The official projection of total remittance amounting to more than Rs 5 crores per annum is grossly exaggerated.

The current paper reveals that the SEAM scheme has not given employment but trained these girls under the apprenticeship programme. It is in fact a premeditated approach of the garment factories to deny legal entitlements and to increase the profit margins by giving placement to theses adolescent workforce for lower remuneration. In actual practice, these young girls are recruited as "apprentices" for labour, under the SEAM project. These recruitment and employment practices are quite similar to 'Sumangali scheme' of Tamil Nadu[9].

After their training from SEAM centre, these women were sent to Kerela, Karnataka and Tamil Nadu in a contract for employment in apparel manufacturing industries. After few months and years, they return to their villages and become unemployed in their own areas. Very few girls become employed after returning to their villages. The researcher met three female returnees who worked in one local non-governmental organization (NGO) at Hinjilicut for Rs 700 per month. Most of them are unable to open up their own business like say a tailoring shop. The basic problem lies in the fact that their remittance and saving amount are inadequate for buying a sewing machine and investing money in business. So it is very hard to accept the projection of the SEAM programme about reaching the targets for empowering women and alleviating poverty and creating self-employment in rural areas. In reality, these young women and girls work under a contract scheme, have to stay in an almost curtailed environment through various forms of restrictions on their mobility. Even parents and family members are hardly allowed to visit their daughters and sisters in the industrial premises.

In General, the workforce of the garment industry is highly feminized. The strength of female trainees in the centre has exceeded compared to male trainees. Table 1.10 shows that the centre had trained a total 3,577 workers until May 2013. There were eight batches of workers trained from the skill school from August 2008 to March 2009, in which the share of female trainees was 38 per cent and the share of males 62 per cent. From the ninth to the twentieth batch during April 2009–March 2010, out of the total 711 trainees, 50 per cent were female. During April 2010 to March 2013, out of the 734 total trainees, the share of female reached upto 79 per cent from 21st batch to 56th batch. From 57th-58th batch during April 2013-May 2013, out of the 106 total trainees, 85.5 per cent were female. It shows that even the number of male applicants was higher than women during the early years as the families of the young girls were not interested to send their daughters to other states for work. But the strength of female trainees in the training centre has outweighed the number of male trainees since 2010 batches. Such trend coincides with the increasing feminization of the garment and apparel industries even at the global level.

As discussed previously, the SEAM project emphasizes imparting skill training to the rural unemployed BPL families who come from scheduled caste (SC) and scheduled tribe (ST) background. Table 1.11 provides an account of the social category of the trainees in Vikas Skills School. During the session 2008-09, out of the total trainees, 32 per cent belonged to SC, 28 per cent to other backward castes (OBC), 17 per cent to socially and educationally backward castes (SEBC) and 23 per cent were other category (OC). In the year 2009-10, the highest number of trainees were from OBC with 60 per cent, and SC trainees about 26 per cent. The same trend was also seen in the session 2010-11, that is around 63 per cent from OBC and 24 per cent from SC. By 2011-12, 35 per cent were SC, 9 per cent were ST, 55.5 per cent were OBC and only 1.3 per cent was OC. In 2012-13, out of the total trainees 34 per cent were from SC, 11 per cent were ST, 54 per cent were from OBC (the highest), and 3 per cent from OC. During 2013-14, in two batches, the highest number of trainees belonged to OBC with 64 per cent and SC belonged to 36 per cent. The Table 1.11 clearly indicates that the OBC, SC and ST trainees have hugely benefitted from the training school.

Table 1.12 shows the ratio of female and male trainees among different caste categories. As the researcher has already mentioned, the higher percentage in the admission of female trainees compared to males from 2010 onwards, the table 1.12 also gives similar findings regarding the higher share of female beneficiary trainees in different caste categories. In case of SC, the share of female trainees has increased since 2011-12 from 33rd batch. During this period, its proportion has risen up to 25 per cent. In the ST category, the proportion of women trainees has also increased from 2011 onwards but its share is lower compared to other caste categories of women trainees such as OBC and SC. In case of OBC, the share of female trainees has exceeded the proportion of males from 2009 onwards (from 9th to 55th batch). The share of female trainees is more than 30 per cent from 9th to 32nd batch, while it is more than 40 per cent from 33rd to 55th batch. The most beneficiary female trainees belong to OBC categories compared to other vulnerable castes like SC and ST.

Table 1.13 clearly signifies the fact that the largest number of trainees from Ganjam district is from Hinjilicut, Beguniapada, Jaganathprasad and Digapahandi. The share of female trainees in most of the blocks is higher compared to males. Out of 3,252 trainees, young women and girls represented highest numbers with 60 per cent compared to males with 38 per cent.

Most of the apparel manufacturing industries are mostly based in southern parts of India. Table 1.14 indicates that highest percentages of trainees from Vikas Apparel Training Centre were placed in Tamil Nadu with 45 per cent. Kerala has emerged as the second highest placement State with 28.4 per cent. In Karnataka, the share of placement was 24.2 per cent. The highest percentage of trainees was female in states of

Tamil Nadu (52.3) and Uttar Pradesh (2.13 per cent). In Kerala, the share of female placement was 24.5 per cent whereas male was 34.5 per cent. Table 1.15 gives a list of name of garment companies which employed the trainess from Vikas Apparel School. Training displays the fact that Texport Industries Pvt Ltd of Kerala employed highest number of trainees (447 in number) of Vikas Apparel Training Centre. The largest number of female trainees (205) were placed in Kerala's Texport garment units compared to all other placement companies.

As per the data collected from the Vikas IL&FS training centres, it is clear that the majority of the workers employed at KINFRA belong to BPL families and socially and economically backward castes such as SC, ST and OBC. Most of the migrant workers come from poor families where their families mainly depend on agriculture as a source of subsistence. Thus, the study observes that migrant workforce of Odisha belongs to poor and the economically backward. The migration of youth and largely female trainees from the villages of Odisha to the garment industries of other states including Kerala shows that the relative deprivation and lack of economic opportunities in their respective villages have pushed them to work outside for the betterment of their livelihoods.

KINFRA International Apparel Park of Kerala

KINFRA International Apparel Park Ltd (KIAP) is located at Thumba, on the outskirts of Thiruvananthapuram, the capital city of Kerala. It provides basic infrastructure facilities exclusively for the establishment of the garment manufacturing units. The park is operated by Kerala Industrial Infrastructure Development Corporation (KINFRA), a public sector agency in the State. It is a fully owned subsidiary of KINFRA, a statutory body under the Government of Kerala which was formed in 1993. The park works under a centrally sponsored scheme of Government of India named "Apparel Parks for Exports" (APE) which has been formulated with a view to involve state governments in promoting investment in the apparel sector; and to impart focused thrust to setting up of apparel manufacturing units of international standards at potential growth centres[10].

KIAP is built on 50 acres of land with allotted area of 36 acres and has been particularly developed for the textile industry[11]. The entrepreneurs, who seek to start their apparel manufacturing units, can avail developed land inside the park. The infrastructure facilities also include working women's hostel for 500 people, Apparel Training and Design Centre (ATDC) by Government of India for Training and also training centres for new operators. The Government of Kerala has declared minimum wages for the readymade garment manufacturers, which is well comparable to the neighbouring states.

The KINFRA Apparel Park is one of the largest government recognized garment manufacturing and export zone. Its branches are strategically located in cities like Mumbai, Bangalore and Tirupur. It has certified ISO 9001: 2000 by Underwriters Laboratories which guarantees safe, reliable and good quality products and services[12]. This certification gives a boost to apparel companies in accessing their new markets and facilitating their free and fair international trade. M/s. Texport Industries Pvt Ltd, M/s. Bombay Rayon Fashion Ltd and M/s. Pooja Garments are the leading garment exporters in the Apparel Park. The major suppliers of the company belong to Tirupur textile centre.

Despite the advantages of the strategic location and infrastructure setup, the Kinfra apparel manufacturing park faces its inherent problems. One of the major problems is the limited availability of workforce in the garment units. The HR representative stated that the garment industry is facing a serious labour shortage in Kerala as the Malayali workers prefer to go to UAE for better wages and employment prospects. The HR also claimed that as the Malayali natives are better educated and more skilled compared to migrant workers, they are in a better position to bargain for higher wages. The local companies cannot afford to match the wage standard paid in UAE to the locals. So the companies consider ending up hiring migrant workers to fill the void. The garment sector provides just the minimum wages. However, the prospect of increasing the remuneration package over a period seems to be very low. It is important to note that the central government facilitates women trainees from rural villages under the skill sponsored programme and recruits them in KINFRA in order to enhance the competitiveness of the garment industries and also to reduce the competitive pressure on the industries to mitigate mainly by reducing labour costs.

The current paper attempts to find out the conditions of female labour, particularly the female migrant workers while working in the KINFRA textile factories. After collecting information from the skill training centres and gathering findings through interviews with trainees and returned migrants at Hinjilicut (source location), the destination study was conducted in KINFRA apprael park to explore the increasing casualty and flexibility of labour in the garment manufacturing units where the trend of women migrants are much likely to be in the informal economy. Three focus group discussions among Odia women migrants and three in-depth interviews were conducted among the management personnel in KINFRA garment industry and also with trade union leaders.

The garment industry basically targets the younger workforce for employment. The HR personnel of one of the apparel manufacturing units in KINFRA stated that most of the girls employed in these industries were very young. More than half of the women migrant workers in the KINFRA industrial sites are under the age of 25 years. They prefer only unmarried young girls for their garment units although they quit jobs once their marriage is fixed. He further said that it is difficult for them to recruit married women and provide accommodation in working women's hostel. In most occasions, husband and in-law families of married women deny them to work outside the State after their marriage. It becomes difficult to accommodate married girls in hostel if they get pregnant or accompanied by children. Apart from this, if the married workers come with their husbands and start living outside industrial premises, it would lead to more absent worker, as they have to balance family life and their work. This kind of situation would hamper the productivity of textile industries. It is noticed in several cases that the women workers do not turn up to claim their provident fund and gratuities. The number of incidences in case of migrant workers are higher compared to native workers as the migrants do not want to visit a long distant state for collecting their gratuities etc., following their marriage or quitting the job after expiration of the contract period or for other reasons.

During one focus group discussion at KINFRA, the researcher met three young girls who worked in Texport Pvt Ltd since the last seven months. They belonged to Hinjilicut block of Ganjam district. They revealed certain facts about the problems of married women not rejoining the garment factory.

Respondent I, II and III (Current Employees) stated that many of them from their native village were trained in Vikas apparel training centre, Hinjilicut and placed in Texport Pvt Company for operating sewing machines. These respondents further said that they knew some of their village girls who have not come to the company after they got married as their husband and in-laws did not allow them to work in factories and that too in a distant place. They mentioned that in one of the cases, they had come across a girl of their neighboring village whose marriage did not work out after the groom's family came to know about her working in another State. There was another incident of one of her co-worker Bihari girl, who was asked to under take a virginity-test after marriage as she had worked in a different State.

While interviewing both workers and HR personnel of the apparel manufacturing units, the researcher came to know that there is no wage difference among the local and migrant women workers. The textile companies give payment (an average amount) which lies between Rs 4,000-4,500 per month. They receive the same monthly wages for the same work excluding overtime payments. The workers who are eager to do overtime work in the factory are likely to get extra payment. In general, the garment manufacturing industries require overtime work to reach their production targets. Therefore, the industries mostly consider migrant workers over local workers.

As the migrant workers live in the hostel dormitories provided by KINFRA Park, they are available doing overtime whenever the industries need them. There are a very few local workers who belong to other districts of Kerala, stay in the hostel. While the majority of the local workers are usually daily commuters, it is not feasible for them to do overtime work at the worksite. Most of the daily commuting local workers face problems in working overtime in the factory as they have to manage their household chores. Therefore, it is mostly migrant workers who work overtime compared to their local counterparts. Here, the researcher presents two different viewpoints from HR personnel and working employees of the industry on overtime work.

During an in-depth interview with one HR staff of KINFRA Park, the management personnel expresse certain facts like the availability of migrant workers in the factory sites and their contribution to the production process of the industry. The HR officer stated that migrant workers are willing to do overtime not the local workers, as they are mostly young and unmarried. The HR further added their sincerity and hardworking nature. They reside in hostels following strict rules and regulations prescribed by the company as they are restricted to live outside and are compelled to live in a hostel for security reasons. They are unable to do other jobs besides the current employment, as they cannot go outside without prior permission of the warden. This creates an opportunity and availability for overtime job in the factory. On the other hand, many Malayali workers are daily travellers and are engaged with many other jobs including the one in the factory for earning more income. They are in a hurry to go back home after working hours. On many occasions, they remain absent for celebrating local festivals, social gatherings like marriage, and supplementary domestic work. So the management prefers migrant workers over locals to avoid labour shortage problems to enable meet their production targets.

At the same time, a different kind of opinion from migrant workers points out their distress for doing overtime work in the industry. A migrant worker from Digapahandi reveals certain interesting facts. A respondent VII claimed that most of them were unmarried with no previous work experience. She has also stated that their entry in to the industry is the first migratory experience in their lives; she disputes the statements that they are new and young and have zeal to do overtime work over the locals. Furthermore, she adds that they have family burdens and come from poor conditions with no available jobs in their villages. They are concerned about their marriage and future life and do overtime work to earn more and save money.

While asking questions about health and safety issues, many workers complained about musculoskeletal problems like vision, skin, muscular pain, etc. It affects the body muscles, joints, bones and nerves. The monotonous nature of working conditions in the assembly line of the garment sector has turned into increased worker fatigueness because of continuous handling of loads, awkward postures, prolonged standing and also repetitive movements of both hands and wrists. They said that they had back problems, stiffness in the neck, shoulders and other parts of the body as they continue to sit in unnatural posture throughout the day without back seats and with their necks bent. They further claimed that the cases of needle injuries are common and on injury they are immediately sent to hospital for treatment by the company supervisors and wardens.

In the working hostel of the company, the separate dormitories are arranged for both migrant and local workers for their accommodation. It also has a warden and security personnel patrolling the premises to provide safety to the boarders. Each hostel room provides accommodation for five to ten workers. The outsiders or visitors are restricted to enter the hostel premises without the prior permission of the security officers. The hostel residents also have to take prior permission for visits outside hostel during the weekend from the warden for a few hours or from the HR personnel of the respective apparel industry for the whole weekend. It is being said that these restrictions are imposed to ensure the protection of the female workers.

The hostel warden gives authorization to the resident workers to go out for buying items and for entertainment purposes. The security guards in the entrance have to register their name and allow them to visit outside till the time mentioned in the authorization letter. The workers are allowed to leave the hostel before 6 pm. While interviewing the hostel warden, she said that most of the hostel residents are young migrant workers who do not know the Malayali language. She further said that the company has to take responsibility if anything goes wrong with them. If such unfortunate news spreads among the working personnel, they would be in fear to stay in the hostel and feel insecure to work. She also claimed that the parents would be hesitant to send their daughters to the company. In one incident, one of the migrant worker's father was critically ill and later died in her village. The migrant girl wanted to go back home but the management denied giving permission to let her go alone. They called her brother and then the warden gave permission to go with her brother. In another case, one of the migrant employees got ill with dehydration and fever and was admitted to the hospital. She also wanted to go back to her village but even in that case, the management was not ready to send the girl with some fellow workers who belonged to her native village. The company called her parents to come and take their daughter home.

During the field investigation, majority of migrant workers expressed their satisfaction with the services provided by the hostel. They did not face any problems in the hostel. They mentioned that the hostel had better amenities than their homes at Odisha. Therefore, their parents allowed them to work outside the State. Five migrant workers from Jaganathprasad block of Ganjam district who worked in Texport Pvt Ltd expressed these feelings.

Respondent IV, V and VI (Odia migrant employees): Few of the respondents said that they were quite happy and satisfied with the hostel accommodation and the kind of security maintained in the industrial campus. They further claimed that they understood that the restrictions imposed on them in the hostel is for their safety and security, and families back home also are relaxed as they were staying inside the company premises which is safe. They said that they had no complaints about accommodation apart from food.

Respondents VII, VIII and IX (During interactions with them at market): Some of the workers narrated some problems which they encountered while living in the hostel. These were food, language barriers, freedom of movement, infrequent contact with their families, etc. While interviewing migrant workers, the researcher came to know that choice of food was a major problem for Odia workers. Most of them wanted Odia food, in the absence of which they wanted to shift their jobs. A supervisor of the Bombay Rayon Fashion industry claimed that Best Corporation Company had appointed a cook from Odisha to cook Odia food for Odia workers on the request of SEAM centre officials in order to reduce the drop out of workers.

There is no union activism inside the KINFRA apparel park. There is tight security system at the entrance gate with security guards. Outsiders are not allowed inside the factory premises without prior permission of security personnel and HR officers. The workers have never organized any activity either for demanding other social security measures or bargaining more remuneration package before the management. While visiting the KINFRA apparel park, the researcher had seen one poster which was put up on the office's wall. It projected the celebration of International Women's Day in four languages like Odia, Malayali, Hindi and English.

While interviewing migrant workers in the focus group

discussions, the researcher asked questions about organization and mobilization of trade unionism in the campus. Some migrant workers from Ganjam district said that they were literally busy with work in garment production and even doing overtime work, which hardly gave them any leisure time to discuss about work conditions with their fellow workers.

Respondents VII, VIII, IX and X (Local employees at the factory): During interaction with few local workers, the researcher came to know that local workers wait for company vehicles and are in a hurry to go home and prepare food for their family members after the working hours. They had to bear their own transport expenses.

In the course of focus discussions with both local and migrant workers, the study found that there has been no activity of organizing and mobilizing of either local or migrant workers in the factory premises. There has not been any situation that workers would assemble for wage bargaining. Being with locals, they have been in an advantage situation to demand more wages and other measures for their betterment but still they had not dared to put any sort of demands with the help of their local unions. The migrants felt that they could not make any demands or do union activity before the management as they were outsiders.

There have been efforts to organize workers in the EPZs, and unions have complained that such attempts were suppressed in Kerala (Roy 2001). The organizers are barred from the zone which helps to prevent unions from organizing workers. While interviewing trade union leaders in their offices, they stated that workers are provided with accommodation in hostels by the company, under strict surveillance system by employers even during non-working hours. As the workers are not familiar with the location, the management has exploited them in the pretext of providing boarding and lodging facilities. Management has been successful to get them to do overtime work to meet their production targets whenever required and control all aspects of the lives of workers.

Conclusion

The present case study on SEAM based training centres and its network with International Apparel Park shows the exploitative dimension of acquiring cheap and flexible labour. The SEAM project under SGSY programme has established a channel in the migration process of young rural women not for empowering them but basically strengthening their own informal economy and getting profits. As shown in the field survey, an increasing proportion of women migrant workers are being concentrated in the larger and more consolidated garment export factories. At the same time, casualization and contractualization of employment through the increased in-contracting has accompanied the process of consolidation of manufacturing base. It has also led to harsher conditions of labour including regularization of overtime work mostly without full compensation with extended hours of work becoming a condition of service.

The SEAM centre and its associated private industries generally prefer unmarried young girls and women for the jobs in apparel manufacturing. There are four strategic and deliberate reasons in preferring these people for jobs. First, the employers take the benefit from the disadvantageous situations like poverty and low level education of these girls. The selected girls have no choice but to accept the adverse conditions of work and low wages working in such industries in exchange for employment. Moreover, families of these girls allow them to work outside of the State to meet the marriage expenses and dowry. Most private garment industries look at this as an opportunity to attract young girls in the age group of 18-25 years from the rural areas. Second, the employers of industries hired mostly unmarried women who can wholeheartedly dedicate their work and life to the shop floor activities of apparel manufacturing units. Since working conditions are undesirable, they often look forward to recruiting these submissive types of persons who would not resist the work burden, the long working hours and poor irregular wages.

Third, married women's recruitment in these apparel

industries is costing more to employers. For married women and those who have children, the basic social safety measures such as maternity leave, child care, creche facilities, breast-feeding breaks have to be ensured. The employer of industries deliberately tries to avoid these demanding conditions. The management also complained that there would be absenteeism that is more frequent if they employ married women and mothers. Thus the conditions undoubtedly restrict the women's access to jobs and unmarried girls are preferentially recruited to the garment manufacturing factories. As Ghosh (2002) points out, the life cycle changes of women such as marriage and childbirth are significant reasons for dismissing these persons from their jobs. The paper, however, observes more diverse reason in the employment process of women. From the beginning itself, the employer refrains from recruiting of married women in the garment sector.

Fourth, the employers prefer such type of female workforce who could be periodically replaced and appoint a new batch of female workers in order to establish temporary type of employment and maintain casualization and contractualization of labour relations. Accordingly, they avoid standard employment relationships and strengthen informalization of work and contribute to be able to garner greater profit margins for private garment manufacturing industries operating within the Special Economic Zone (SEZ). Moreover, the average age of women working in these industries is between 18-25 years and they are fired when they get married or cross 30 years of age. Such a type of employment strategy is considered to be best option for the employers of private industries.

LIST OF TABLES

Table 1.1: AJEEVIKA-SGSY Special Projects in Odisha for Apparel Training

Districts	*SEAM I*	*SEAM II*	*SEAM III*	*SEAM VI*	*SEAM IX*	*Total*
Ganjam	664	548	359	705	1250	3526
Khordha	387	440	64			891
Kandhamal		241	288	504	450	1483
Sonepur		17				17
Sundergarh		186	307	506	1000	1999
Gajapati			168	341	350	859
Rourkela				318	750	1068
Bolangir					460	460
Malkangiri					750	750
	1051	1432	1186	2374	5010	11053

Source: http://skillschools.com/ilfs/index.php?r=status/ (Total Track since 01/04/2012)

Table 1.2: Batch-wise Average Across SEAM Training Centres of Odisha

Sl No	*District wise Training Centre*	*Year of Establishment*	*Total no of SEAM Batches*	*Yearly Passed Out Trainees*					*Batch wise average*
				2008	*2009*	*2010*	*2011*	*2012*	
1.	Hinjilicut, Ganjam	2008	44						59.5
2.	Raigarh Gajapati	2010	16				272	530	50.1
3.	Tangiripali Sundargarh	2010	25			677	550	131	54.3
4.	Rourkela Sundergarh	2010	16				501	249	46.8
5.	Phulbani	2010	23			689	584	64	58.1
6.	Bolangir	2011	07				204	74	39.7
7.	Malkangiri	2011	06				218	66	47.3

NB: Each batch is for each month. Therefore, the number of traines per month is as per the batch average. The above mentioned figures summarized from an impact assessment report from IL&FS Skills website. Source: http://www.ilfsskills.com/IMPACT/FILES/5XIMB_V1

Table 1.3: Summary of Trainees at Vikas Apparel Training Centre, Hinjilicut, Ganjam

	Summary of SEAM Trainees	*Male*	*Female*	*Total*	*Percentage*		
					Male	*Female*	*Overall*
1.	Enrolment for training	1209	1463	2672	45.25	54.75	100.00
2.	Dropout during the session	60	41	101	4.96	2.80	3.78
3.	Completion of training successfully	1142	1461	2558	94.46	96.79	95.73
4.	Placement offered	1142	1461	2558	100.00	100.00	100.00
5.	Not joining the job	130	127	257	11.38	8.97	10.05
6.	Joining job after training	1025	1296	2321	89.75	91.53	90.73

Source: http://www.ilfsskills.com/IMPACT/FILES/5XIMB_V1

Table 1.4: Summary of Trainees at Vikas Apparel Training Centre, Raigarh, Gajapati

	Summary of SEAM Trainees	*Male*	*Female*	*Total*	*Percentage*		
					Male	*Female*	*Overall*
1.	Enrolment for training	490	412	902	54.32	45.68	100.00
2.	Dropout during the session	67	35	102	13.67	8.50	11.31
3.	Completion of training successfully	423	377	800	86.33	91.50	88.69
4.	Placement offered	423	377	800	100.00	100.00	100.00
5.	Not joining the job	93	106	199	21.99	28.12	24.48
6.	Joining job after training	322	259	581	76.12	68.70	72.63

Source: http://www.ilfsskills.com/IMPACT/FILES/5XIMB_V1

Table 1.5: Summary of Trainees at Vikas Apparel Training Centre, Tangiripali, Sundergarh

	Summary of SEAM Trainees	*Male*	*Female*	*Total*	*Percentage*		
					Male	*Female*	*Overall*
1.	Enrolment for training	271	1161	1432	18.92	81.08	100.00
2.	Dropout during the session	17	57	74	6.27	4.91	5.17
3.	Completion of training successfully	254	1104	1358	93.73	95.09	94.83
4.	Placement offered	254	1104	1358	100.00	100.00	100.00
5.	Not joining the job	41	400	441	16.14	36.23	32.47
6.	Joining job after training	223	666	889	87.80	60.33	65.46

Source: http://www.ilfsskills.com/IMPACT/FILES/5XIMB_V1

Table 1.6: Summary of Trainees at Vikas Apparel Training Centre, Rourkela, Sundergarh

	Summary of SEAM Trainees	*Male*	*Female*	*Total*	*Percentage*		
					Male	*Female*	*Overall*
1.	Enrolment for training	84	609	693	12.12	87.88	100.00
2.	Dropout during the session	1	29	30	1.19	4.76	4.33
3.	Completion of training successfully	82	550	632	97.62	90.31	91.20
4.	Placement offered	82	550	632	100.00	100.00	100.00
5.	Not joining the job	09	284	293	10.98	51.64	46.36
6.	Joining job after training	56	276	332	68.29	50.18	52.53

Source: http://www.ilfsskills.com/IMPACT/FILES/5XIMB_V1

Table 1.7: Summary of Trainees at Vikas Apparel Training Centre, Phulbani, Kandhamal

	Summary of SEAM Trainees	*Male*	*Female*	*Total*	*Percentage*		
					Male	*Female*	*Overall*
1.	Enrolment for training	358	649	1007	35.55	64.75	100.00
2.	Dropout during the session	30	51	81	8.38	7.86	8.04
3.	Completion of training successfully	319	539	858	89.11	83.05	85.20
4.	Placement offered	319	539	858	100.00	100.00	100.00
5.	Not joining the job	50	94	144	15.67	17.44	16.78
6.	Joining job after training	263	446	709	82.45	82.75	82.63

Source: http://www.ilfsskills.com/IMPACT/FILES/5XIMB_V1

Table 1.8: Summary of Trainees at Vikas Apparel Training Centre, Bolangir

	Summary of SEAM Trainees	*Male*	*Female*	*Total*	*Percentage*		
					Male	*Female*	*Overall*
1.	Enrolment for training	78	245	323	24.15	75.85	100.00
2.	Dropout during the session	7	30	37	8.97	12.24	11.46
3.	Completion of training successfully	64	174	238	82.05	71.02	73.68
4.	Placement offered	64	174	238	100.00	100.00	100.00
5.	Not joining the job	16	48	64	25.0	27.59	26.89
6.	Joining job after training	49	125	174	76.56	71.84	73.11

Source: http://www.ilfsskills.com/IMPACT/FILES/5XIMB_V1

Table 1.9: Summary of Trainees at Vikas Apparel Training Centre, Malkangiri

	Summary of SEAM Trainees	*Male*	*Female*	*Total*	*Percentage*		
					Male	*Female*	*Overall*
1.	Enrolment for training	129	155	284	45.52	54.58	100.00
2.	Dropout during the session	8	8	16	6.20	5.16	5.63
3.	Completion of training successfully	99	137	236	76.74	88.39	83.10
4.	Placement offered	99	137	236	100.00	100.00	100.00
5.	Not joining the job	21	55	76	21.21	40.15	32.20
6.	Joining job after training	78	82	160	78.79	59.85	67.80

Source: http://www.ilfsskills.com/IMPACT/FILES/5XIMB_V1

Table 1.10: Admission of Trainees in Vikas Apparel Training Centre/IL&FS Skills School up to May 2013

Sl No.	*Year*	*Batch No.*	*Month*	*Fe-male*	*Female share in per-cent-age*	*Males*	*Male Share in Per-cent-age*	*Total*
1.	2008-09	1st - 8th	Aug. 08 to March 09	193	38.5	309	61.5	502
2.	2009-10	9th—20th	Apr 09 to March 10	352	49.5	359	50.5	711
3.	2010-11	21st-32nd	Apr 10 to March 11	405	53.6	351	46.4	756
4.	2011-12	33rd-44th	Apr 11 to March 12	562	73.2	206	26.8	768
5.	2012-13	45th-56th	April 12-March 13	581	79.2	153	20.8	734
6.	2013-14	57th-58th	April 13-May 13	91	85.8	15	14.2	106
Total				2184	61.1	1393	38.9	3577 (100.0)

Source: Vikas Apparel Training Centre, Hinjilicut

Table: 1.11: Caste-wise Trainees

Sl No.	*Year*	*Batch No.*	*SC*	*ST*	*OBC*	*S.E.B.C*	*O.C*	*Total*
1.	2008-09	1st to 8th	162 (32.2%)	0 (0.0%)	140 (27.8%)	87 (17.3%)	113 (22.5%)	502
2.	2009-10	9th to 20th	184 (25.8%)	40 (5.6%)	430 (60.4%)	1 (0.14%)	56 (7.8%)	711
3.	2010-11	21st 32nd	185 (24.4%)	60 (7.9%)	475 (62.8%)	4 (0.5%)	32 (4.2%)	756
4.	2011-12	33rd to 44th	263 (34.2%)	68 (8.8%)	427 (55.5%)	0 (0.0%)	10 (1.3%)	768
5.	2012-13	45th to 56th	260 (34.0%)	78 (11.0%)	372 (51.0%)	0 (0.0%)	24 (3.2%)	734
6.	2013-14	57th to 58th	38 (35.8%)	4 (3.8%)	64 (60.3%)	0 (0.0%)	0 (0.0%)	106

Source: Vikas Apparel Training Centre, Hinjilicut

Table 1.12 Gender-wise Trainees Among Different Castes upto February 2013

Sl. No.	*Year*	*Batch No.*	*SC*			*ST*			*OBC*			*SEBC*			*OC*			*Total*		
			F	*M*	*T*	*F*	*M*	*T*	*F*	*M*	*T*	*F*	*M*	*T*	*F*	*M*	*T*	*F*	*M*	*T*
1	2008-09	1st to 8th	29 5.8	133 26.4	162 32.2	0 0	0 0	0 0	70 13.9	70 13.9	140 27.8	33 6.5	54 10.8	87 17.3	63 12.5	50 42.2	113 22.5	193 38.4	309 61.5	502 99.9
2	2009-10	9th to 20th	62 8.7	122 17.1	184 25.8	16 2.2	24 3.4	40 5.6	244 34.3	186 26.1	430 60.4	1 0.14	0 0	1 0.14	29 4.0	27 3.8	56 7.8	352 49.5	359 50.4	711 99.9
3	2010-11	21st to 32nd	89 11.8	96 12.6	185 24.4	19 2.5	41 5.4	60 7.9	277 36.7	198 26.1	475 62.8	4 0.5	0 0	4 0.5	16 2.1	16 2.1	32 4.2	405 53.5	351 46.4	756 99.9
4.	2011-12	33rd to 44th	189 24.6	74 9.6	263 34.2	31 4.0	37 4.8	68 8.8	337 43.8	90 11.7	427 55.5	0 0	0 0	0 0	5 0.65	5 0.65	10 1.3	562 73.1	206 26.8	768 99.9
5.	2012-13	45 to 55th	169 25.1	58 8.6	227 33.7	46 6.8	28 4.1	74 10.9	300 44.6	54 8.0	354 52.6	0 0	0 0	0 0	0 0	0 0	0 0	532 79.0	141 20.9	673 99.9
Total			538 15.8	483 14.1	1021 29.9	112 3.2	130 3.8	242 7.0	1228 36.0	598 17.5	1826 53.5	38 1.1	54 1.58	92 2.69	113 3.31	98 2.87	211 6.18	2044 59.9	1366 40.0	3410 99.9

Source: Vikas Apparel Training Centre, Hinjilicut

Table 1.13: Block-wise Trainees of Ganjam District upto February 2013

Sl.No.	*Name of the Block*	*Female*	*Male*	*Total*
1.	Hinjilicut	241 (43.5)	312 (56.4)	553
2.	Sheragada	91 (45.9)	107(54.1)	198
3.	Kukudakhandi	55(63.2)	32(36.8)	87
4.	Purushotampur	129(73.2)	47(26.7)	176
5.	Chatrapur	45(86.5)	7(13.4)	52
6.	Surada	93 (39.2)	144(60.7)	237
7.	Sanakhemundi	105(48.3)	112(51.6)	217
8.	Beguniapada	165(64.7)	90(35.2)	255
9.	Chikiti	15(28.3)	38(71.6)	53
10.	Aska	90 (81.0)	21(18.9)	111
11.	Rangelilunda	120(75.4)	39(24.5)	159
12.	Dharakote	60(63.8)	34(36.1)	94
13.	Kabisuryanagar	104(67.9)	49(32.0)	153
14.	Polasara	93(70.9)	38(29.0)	131
15.	Digapahandi	140 (68.6)	64(31.3)	204
16.	Ganjam	14(60.8)	9(39.1)	23
17.	Bhanjanagar	62(82.6)	13(17.3)	75
18.	Buguda	79(78.2)	22(21.7)	101
19.	Belaguntha	35(72.9)	13(27.1)	48
20.	Jagannathprasad	160(64.2)	49(19.6)	249
21.	Khalikote	27(61.3)	17(38.6)	44
22.	Patapur	22(68.7)	10(31.2)	32
	Total	1945(60.1)	1267(38.9)	3252

Source: Vikas Apparel Training Centre, Hinjilicut (2013 upto February)

Table 1.14: Placement Position of Trainees upto January 2013

State	*Female*	*Male*	*Total*
Tamil Nadu	908 (52.3)	397(34.8)	1305 (45.39)
Karnataka	368 (21.1)	328 (28.7)	696 (24.2)
Kerala	426 (24.5)	393 (34.5)	819 (28.4)
Uttar Pradesh	37 (2.13)	21 (1.84)	58 (2.01)
Total	1736 (100.03)	1139 (99.84)	2875 (100.0)

Source: Vikas Apparel Training Centre, Hinjilicut

Table 1.15: Company-wise Placement Position upto January, 2013

Sl. No.	*Name of the Company*	*Ladies*	*Gents*	*Total*
1.	Texport Pvt Ltd, Thiruvananthapuram, Kerala	205	272	477
2.	KITEX Ltd, Alluva, Earnakulam, Kerala	34	7	44
3.	K. Mohan, Cochin, Kerala	137	98	235
4.	Bombay Rayon Fashions Ltd, Thiruvananthapuram, Kerala	47	16	63
5.	Arvind Ltd, Bengaluru, Karnataka	66	96	162
6.	K. Mohan, Bengaluru, Karnataka	104	77	181
7.	INTEGRA, Bengaluru, Karnataka	83	23	106
8.	Unitex Apparels Pvt Ltd, Bengaluru, Karnataka	45	18	63
9.	Sahi Exports Pvt Ltd, Bengaluru, Karnataka	0	12	12
10.	Texpro, Bengluru, Karnataka	70	102	172
11.	Imperial Readymade, Chennai,Tamil Nadu	28	1	29
12.	Meenakshi (I) Ltd, Salem, Tamil Nadu	84	29	113
13.	Evolve Clothing Co., Alandur, Chennai, Tamil Nadu	82	13	95
14.	White House, Kanchipuram, Tamil Nadu	45	0	45
15.	Mahameru Fashions, Apparel, Kanchipuram, Tamil Nadu	30	27	57
16.	S.K.L Exports, Tirupur, Tamil Nadu	47	14	61
17.	Sharadha Terry Products, Coimbatore, Tamil Nadu	50	11	61
18.	Cotton Blossom, Tirpur, Tamil Nadu	32	22	54
19.	Sahi Exports Pvt Ltd, Bengaluru, Karnataka	0	12	12
20.	Sri Renga Creatives Apparels, Coimbatore, Tamil Nadu	26	6	32
21.	S.P. Apparels, Avinashi, Tirupur, Tamil Nadu	49	7	56

22.	Unitex Apparels Pvt Ltd, Bengaluru, Karnataka	45	18	63
23.	Anugraha Fashion Mills Pvt Ltd, Tirupur, Tamil Nadu	45	0	45
24.	Subbarow Apparels, Chennai, Tamil Nadu	45	14	59
25.	Penguin Apparels, Madurai, Tamil Nadu	43	0	43
26.	Stanfali Apparels Ltd, Chennai, Tamil Nadu	0	5	5
27.	Best Corporation Ltd, Tirupur, Tamil Nadu	119	61	180
28	SABS Export, Noida, Uttar Pradesh	37	21	58
	Total	1736	1139	2875

Source: Vikas Apparel Training Centre, Hinjilicut

NOTES

1. During the PhD study, the present researcher has conducted field investigation in villages of Ganjam district and came to know about the migration of young women from villages of Ganjam in garment and textile industries of Kerala (Mahanty 2012, pp. 267-274).
2. http://www.ilfsindia.com/projects.aspx?prid=5&catid=1&slnk=109&cid=5 (accessed 9-10-2015)
3. http://www.ilfs-spring.com/index.php?val=SEAM (accessed 9-10-2015)
4. https://www.changemakers.com/socialbusiness/entries/skills-employment-apparel-manufacturing-seam-programme
5. Das, S.P. (n.d) Some of the figures are collected and summarized from an impact assessment report from IL&FS Skill's website. http://www.ilfsskills.com/IMPACT/FILES/5XIMB_V1.pdf
6. These findings came to be noticed during the field investigation in SEAM and KINFRA. The retuned migrants, trainees at Vikas Apparel Training Centre, working female employees at Kerala garment factories and all of their families revealed certain facts relating to the training and recruitment process under such skill development mission programme. While interacting with one ex-Sarapanch from Sikiri village, and other SEAM staff members, the researcher came to know about their role in mobilization of rural youth in the entire process. They have taken credit in

the training and recruitment process of young girls from rural villages in the apparel training centre and private industries. The researcher collected this information from villages namely Burupada, Sikiri, Ralaba, Nandika and also Hinjilicut town. In the course of the field study, SEAM staff was not available in the training centre twice as they had gone to villages of neighbouring blocks to meet some families of the trained girls to convince them for allowing their daughters for jobs in garment factory in Kerala. According to one staff member, they frequently visited villages of Ganjam district and even other districts to create awareness of the SEAM scheme for the admission of young girls in the Vikas training centre

7. See the table 1.10. It shows the admission of trainees in Vikas IL&FS Skill School/SEAM Training centre.
8. As the SEAM project is working under Swarnajayanti Gram Swarozgar Yojana (SGSY: a scheme for self-employment of rural poor) and National Rural Livelihood Mission, the DRDA has arranged the involvement of Self Help Groups (SHGs) for facilitating meals to these apparel trainees.
9. The spinning mill workers are recruited migrants, generally young and unmarried girls. Documentation at the instance of the Madras High Court, has established the prevalence of such a system in Tamil Nadu, where girls have been recruited from rural areas of the southern districts of the State for production work in spinning mills in the districts of Erode, Dindigul, Tirupur/ Coimbatore. For some years such labour recruitment operated under the guise of an apprenticeship cum marriage assistance scheme, known as 'Sumangali Marriage Scheme', whereby girls worked on a 2-3 year contract with a spinning mill, at the end of which a lumpsum was given to them purportedly for use in their marriage. Since the girls were confined to residential camps run by the mill managements, it became known as a 'camp coolie system' and following a court order in 2007, decreeing it as bonded labour, the scheme as such has gone underground, although the pattern of migration it initiated, does not appear to have changed (Agnihotri et. al. 2012: 57)
10. Guidelines for the establishment of apparel parks for exports. http://dcimanipur.gov.in/documents/Guidelines_of_Apparel_Parks.pdf
11. http://www.apparelpark.com/
12. http://www.iso.org/iso/catalogue_detail?csnumber=21823

REFERENCES

Asha K G (2015) *Dynamics of labour relations across different circuits of globalisation: Evidence from garment making and cashew nut processing circuits in Kerala.* Doctoral dissertation, National Institute of Advanced Studies, Bangalore.

BSR (Business for Social Responsibility) (2017) Three Areas for Business Action Empowering Female Workers in the Apparel Industry. https://www.bsr.org/reports/BSR_Empowering_Female_Workers_in_the_Apparel_Industry.pdfAccessed on 6 June 2017.

Das S P (n.d) Final Report on Impact Study of trainees of IL&FS Centres from Odisha Implemented by IL&FS Clusters in Association with Ministry of Rural Development (MORD, Government of India. Xavier Institue of Management, Bhubaneswar and IL&FS Cluster BDevelopment Initiative Limited Bhubaneswar. http://www.ilfsskills.com/IMPACT/FILES/5XIMB_V1.pdf

Kate Gisela ten and Martje Theuws (2016) Fact Sheet Migrant labour in the textile and garment industry A focus on the role of buying companies. https://www.somo.nl/wp-content/uploads/2016/02/FactsheetMigantLabour.pdf Accessed on 1 Feb 2016

Ghosh J (2002) Globalization, Export-Oriented Employment for Women and Social Policy: A Case Study of India. *Social Scientist* (30) 11/12 : 17-60

Mahanty M (2012) *Gender, Migration and Women's Rights in Orissa: A Case Study of Ralaba Grama Panchayat in Ganjam Districts.* Unpublished doctoral dissertation, F.M. University, Balasore, Odisha.

Roy M (2001) Restrictions on trade union freedoms in State: U.S. report. *The Hindu*, March 11. http://www.thehindu.com/2001/03/11/stories/0411211q.htm. Accessed on March 11 2001.

UN Women (2015) Progress of the World's Women. http://progress.unwomen.org/en/2015 Accessed on 2015.

10

Caste Narratives: Odia Dalit Women in Literature and Society

Raj Kumar

Although Indian society has for centuries been the most hierarchical among the known civilizations with a clear gradation in the exercise of power and privilege, Indian literature barring few poets and writers has hardly focused on the problem of caste inequality for very long time. That is because the pen has by and large been in the hands of those who wielded power through their caste locations, and those outside the grid of authority and agency have generally been rendered invisible in the canonized literary texts of India. Though in the medieval times bhakti saint-poets like Kabir, Chokamela, Namdev and many others raised questions on caste oppressions and inequalities through their poems, it is only towards the end of the nineteenth century that a few unusual novels take up the theme of social oppression as their major concern. In the twentieth century there is gradually a growing awareness in literature of those who have so far remained outside the threshold of mainstream Indian society: the outcastes, the landless, the dispossessed, the tribals, and of course, women across caste, class and ethnic boundaries.

It is a strange paradox that often in Indian literature, the body of the lower caste or the tribal women has been romanticized, perceived as possessing a primal energy, vitality and spontaneity that the privileged women in seclusion have lost due to patriarchal social order. The focus of my paper is to study the literary representation of dalit Odia women in the writings of some Odia writers. Out of several texts, I will give examples and instances from Gopinath Mohanty's *Harijan* (1948), and Akhila Naik's *Bheda* (2010) to see how these two writers have given treatment to gendered subjects differently. Gopinath Mohanty is an upper caste Odia writer whose concern for dalits and adivasis is well known throughout the world. Akhila Naik, on the other hand, is a young Odia dalit writer who is known as the author of *Bheda*, the first Odia dalit novel. While the primary focus of my paper is to deal with how the theme of 'untouchable body' has been perceived and described by these two male writers in their writings, it will be equally interesting to see how some of the contemporary Odia dalit women writers like Supriya Mallik have treated the same theme with different perspectives. Before we look into the gendered positions of dalit Odia women, it is important to see how caste and gender operated in Odia society over the years, so that we properly understand the contexts of the texts.

Dalits and Caste Questions in Odisha

Dalits in Odisha, as elsewhere in India, have been victims of caste oppression for centuries. Predominantly rural and illiterate, they have become one of society's most exploited peripheral groups. Over the years, they have been living in sub-human conditions and suffering economic exploitation, cultural subjugation and political powerlessness. Even after seventy years of India's Independence many civic and other amenities are not available to them so easily. They often have to fight to get what is their due, but due to stringent caste practices they mostly live a compromised life accepting their fate. A study undertaken by the National Institute of Social Work and Social Sciences, Bhubaneswar in 1994, on the implementation of the Protection of Civil Rights Act (PCR) in Odisha, reveals that untouchability practices are rampant. According to it, "As revealed in our study, some of the types of untouchability still practiced in Orissa are: denial of access to the Scheduled castes to village pond, public well, bathing ghats, etc, denial of entry into the village temples and access to places of worship, burial ground, denial of entry into shops, hotels and tea-stalls, refusal of service by barbers and washer men etc. this list is suggestive but not exhaustive. What was even more painful for us to notice was that the ill-treatment by the upper castes of the Scheduled castes does not end with the imposition of these disabilities on them. It goes beyond that and the caste dynamics in the empirical situation is usually accompanied by and/or develops with physical violence and atrocities." (Dash and Kumar 1994: 91-2)

Living in such a hostile environment where insecurity reigns, Odia dalits always have to work hard and lead a life of compromise, alienation and resignation. According to the 2011 Census, Odisha has more than 75 dalit communities, constituting 18 per cent of the State's population. Following the Hindu caste structure, dalit communities too have rigid internal hierarchies among themselves, and inter-caste dining and inter-caste marriages are still not allowed between any two dalit communities. Dalit politics in the State is fragmented as dalits are divided into too many groups and sub-groups. They also follow different religious practices. Because of these problems dalits cannot come together to voice their grievances. Dalit groups are split and fragmented, each carrying the tag of being a dalit.

It is sad that today when people are talking about human rights and social justice, Odia dalits continue to suffer due to inhuman caste practices. Odia society, being feudal in many aspects, does not allow people from the lower castes to exercise many civil and democratic rights enshrined in the Indian Constitution. The brahmins, karanas and khandayats and other upper caste communities still wield what might be called historical power and continue to exploit and oppress the dalits. As a result, the condition of dalits is miserable. Though they can move freely in towns and cities, there are several restrictions on them in villages where they are still confined to the outskirts. For example, they cannot walk on certain roads nor may they ride a cycle or a motorbike. They are not allowed to enter temple premises. Even though they can go to schools, they are not allowed to sit along with the upper caste children. They have separate wells and in the ponds, there are separate *ghats* where they take a bath. There are separate burial grounds as well. Angina P. Chatterji from her fieldwork in Odisha makes a list of incidents pertaining to caste discriminations: "...Among a list of incidents, I recall a Dalit community member being beaten for entering a Hindu temple in Bargarh district in April 2001, and fined Rs 4,000. In Kendrapara district, also in Orissa, Dalits have been disallowed entry into the two hundred year-old Jagannath temple in Keradagada village. In 2005, four Dalit girls who attempted to enter the temple were physically assaulted and fined. In October 2006, faced with the denial of their right of entry into temple, 1,200 Dalits instituted a 'Dalit Manch' in the village, resolving to renounce Hinduism if the ban continued. In December 2006, led by the Orissa Mukti Morcha (Orissa Liberation Front, also battlefront), about 3,000 Dalits resolved to convert to Buddhism, in dissent to being refused entry to the temple by upper caste groups and Hindu priests." (Chatterji 2010: 69-70)

The caste discriminations mentioned above are clear instances of how dalits are systematically denied their civil rights in Odisha. Such discriminations only strengthen the walls and barriers of social differences in society and unnecessarily bring communal tensions. Education, in such a scenario, should help both the perpetrators of caste violence as well as the victims to come out with some sort of solutions to the caste problem. But education was not available to dalits in Odisha for very long due to typical structural problems. Many sociologists and anthropologists have studied the social structures that exist in Odisha. For example, American anthropologist James M. Freeman (1979) in a study of untouchability in Kapileswar village (now a part of Bhubaneswar, the capital of Odisha) in 1979 reveals how high caste people force the lower castes away from educational institutions. Freeman interviewed Muli, an untouchable narrator, who said, "The villagers never forgot, nor did they let us forget that we were untouchables. High-caste children sat inside the school; the Bauri children about twenty of us, sat outside on the veranda and listened. The two teachers, a Brahman outsider, and temple servant refused to touch us, even with a stick. To beat us, they threw bamboo canes. The higher caste children threw mud at us. Fearing severe beatings we dared not fight back." (Freeman 1979: 90)

Thirty seven years have already passed but dalits in Odisha have hardly got equal opportunities in education. As a result the literacy percentage of dalits is quite low, just 55 per cent as compared to the total literacy rate of the State which is 72 per cent as per the Census 2011. This has led to serious problems. Apart from not getting any secure jobs due to illiteracy, the dalits in Odisha cannot avail of many of the constitutional provisions that guarantee them a life of dignity and self-respect. For example, there is a general lack of awareness among the rural illiterate dalits about the various provisions mentioned in the PCR Act or the Scheduled Caste Atrocities Act. So they fail to regard the practice of untouchability or caste atrocities as a serious violation of the fundamental law of the land, an offence punishable under the law. Illiteracy combined with poverty play a major role in the day to day life of dalits. Struggling to meet their daily livelihood, Odia dalits, therefore, continue to accept caste violence as a cultural fact in conformity with a long established tradition. Thus, rather than reporting to the police and other law-enforcing agencies, the victims of caste violence hold back to the karma theory, live within and take care not to cross the cultural boundaries traditionally demarcated for their 'low' caste.

That no militant movement or rebellion on the part of dalits has taken place against their upper-caste Hindu counterparts in the State does not indicate the absence of socio-economic inequalities. It only underlines the fact that Odia dalits have endured caste oppression mostly silently. One reason for this could be that the socio-economic life of dalits in Odisha, has not undergone the same level of change as that of dalits elsewhere. For example, dalits in Maharashtra had witnessed non-Brahmin movements led by Jotiba Phuley in the nineteenth century and B.R. Ambedkar in the twentieth century. Odia dalits never organized such dalit movements. History testifies that a few cases of unorganized sporadic resistance did take place but they were swiftly suppressed by the upper castes. It may be necessary to mention here that whenever there is any protest against caste oppression, the upper castes always succeeded in appropriating the dissenting voices. As a result, the voices of the oppressed gradually faded away. It is only after the centenary celebration of Ambedkar in 1991-92 that Odia dalits have started coming together to demand their political and constitutional rights in a bigger way. But not many changes have in fact happened. In fact social scientists like Manoranjan Mohanty have already warned us the way Odia society is going through a crisis in the post-liberal phase. To quote Mohanty, "Odisha presents a crisis of democracy with upper caste, patriarchal domination that has been consolidated through the formation and expansion of a middle class, which provides services to the capitalist extractive economy, while vast sections of the population, especially adivasis, dalits, and agricultural workers, remained marginalized. This process has been accentuated during the recent decades of neo-liberal policies, during which the scale and magnitude of mining-based industries and their implementation through a massive deployment of security forces have hugely grown. The strategy has done little to reduce regional disparity between the coastal districts and inland regions. This system of dominance and governance has been legitimized through the electoral process, welfare support, and the media." (Mohanty 2014: 46) In such a background what will be the positions of Odia dalit women? To find out the answer let's travel through the pages of Odisha's socio-cultural and literary history.

The Existential Situations of Dalit Women in Odisha

The existential situations of dalit women, as elsewhere in India, seem to be grim in Odisha. Generally speaking, they are the most under-privileged group left out at the bottom of the hierarchical caste society for centuries. Compared to dalit men they suffer more due to their dual disadvantages: being dalit and being women. Being dalit they suffer due to caste discrimination. Being women they become the victims of the patriarchal social order in their families and outside. The scholars studying the conditions of dalit women believe that they are thrice alienated due to their caste, class and gender positions. Ruth Manorama, for example writes, "Dalit women are referred to as "Dalits among the Dalits" or "downtrodden among the downtrodden" because they are thrice alienated on the basis of their class (poor), caste (outcaste), and gender. Women of Dalit communities may be the biggest examples of marginalization. They are the ones who are most vulnerable victims of repression and discrimination." (Manorama 2013: 258)

While the upper caste men sexually exploit them in their workplaces, at home they are beaten up by their own men. Thus, violence against dalit women in Odisha is rampant. How does one understand the systemic use of violence on the dalit women's body? Experts who have worked on the subject have offered the following opinions, "Violence perpetrated against Dalit women must (also) be analysed in a wider context; that is, how this violence is compounded and facilitated by, as well as an outcome of, systemic discrimination denying women substantive socio-economic and political rights. This is because Dalit women's socio-economic vulnerability and lack of political voice, when combined with the dominant risk factors being Dalit and female, increase their exposure to potentially violent situations, while simultaneously reducing their ability to escape. Violence against Dalit women, in turn, has a serious impact on their socio-economic rights, especially their right to health, besides constraining their ability to bring out positive social change for themselves, their children, and their communities." (Irudayam et al 2014: 14)

In Odisha a majority of dalit women live in rural areas amidst poverty, illiteracy and backwardness. Several decades of Government sponsored rural development programmes such as, the Jawahar Rozgar Yojana (JRY), Integrated Rural Development Programme (IRDP), Training for Rural Youth for Self-Employment (TRYSEM), Public Distribution System (PDS) and National Rural Employment Guarantee Scheme (NREGS) among others have not been able to help them to get out of poverty and underdevelopment. Therefore, they have to heavily rely on the traditional sources of employment for their livelihoods. Majority of dalit women are daily wage labourers, agricultural workers, maidservants and unskilled workers in industrial units. They even work in hazardous worksites such as mines and quarries. Even though the labour they put in their work is no less than their male counterparts they are always paid lower wages. In a survey conducted to understand untouchability in rural India, Ghanshyam Shah and his team find that dalit women workers are paid low. They write, "In south Orissa, Dalit women who work as agricultural labourers are paid as little as Rs 15 a day. Dalit women from Orissa report that they prefer to migrate to towns in search of work. Not only are the wages higher, they do not have to face caste-based discrimination. In rural Orissa, Dalits are made to wait for several hours before being paid, and non-Dalits place the money on the ground instead of directly handing it to the Dalit worker." (Shah 2006: 118)

Dalit women also land up doing extra duties at home as compared to their male counterparts. When their men run away from shouldering family responsibilities, it is they who are responsible to run their families with meager incomes. It has been observed that dalit women travel long distances spending lots of their time and energy to collect water and fuel for their daily use and becoming caste victims in the process. In this context Anupama Rao (2003) in her Introduction to *Gender and Caste* writes, "Caste relations are embedded in dalit women's profoundly unequal access to resources of basic survival such as water and sanitation facilities, as well as educational institutions, public places, and sites of religious worship. On the other hand, the material impoverishment of dalits and their political disenfranchisement perpetuate the symbolic structures of untouchability, which legitimates upper-caste sexual access to dalit women." (Rao 2003: 11)

With the change times dalit women are also facing new challenges. With more and more rural areas coming under the spell of modernization projects, technology is replacing human labour. Dalit women are the immediate victims of this process. It is in this context Ruth Manorama writes, "The life of Dalit women is one of misery and agony. Dalit women were displaced from productive activity in the guise of development manifested in modernization and its technologies, computerization, option for various nuclear power plants and dam construction in the name of energy and power and urbanization. These development projects appropriated or destroyed the natural resources base. It decried women's productivity by removing land, water and forests from their management and control. While gender subordination and patriarchy are the oldest forms of oppression, they have taken a new and more violent form." (Manorama 2013: 259) Thus, dalit women have no respite from caste repression.

In recent years many non-governmental organizations (NGOs) have started working with dalit women for their upliftment. Literacy, health, sanitation, legal aids, self-help economy etc. are some areas in which they are receiving training and getting benefits. The recently made constitutional provisions of not less than one-third of seats reserved for women in the panchayat bodies have also helped many dalit women to exercise their political power and be part of the decision-making process. Though these changes are small in measures in the long run they are sure to bring some changes in the lives of Dalit women. But much more needs to be done so that dalit women everywhere feel that they are equal citizens of India. Aloysius Irudayam et al, the authors of the book, *Dalit Women Speak Out* offer the following suggestions in this regard, "By fulfilling its national and international obligations to protect Dalit women from violence, complemented by an adequate focus on improving their socio-economic conditions, the Indian state could contribute to enlarging the choices and actions of Dalit women. Increased Dalit women's action would, in turn, contribute to social change not only for their families and their communities, but also for the wider Indian society. It is only when support is extended to Dalit women across India that these women will become empowered and enjoy the fundamental rights that are enjoyed by the rest of Indian citizenry." (Irudayam et al 2014: 3)

With literacy and some sorts of empowerment dalit women have started speaking out. While going through dalit women's writings in Odisha the readers have come to know of the painful experiences they have gone through because of their caste and gender positions. Before we look into few select Odia dalit women's writings it may be relevant here to talk about how dalit women have been portrayed in Odia literature.

Representation of Dalit Women in Odia Literature

Even though Odia language is considered to be a people's language, Odia literature has been the monopoly of few Odia upper caste male writers till very recently. It is true that the origin of Odia literature began with the idea of social protests during the period from the eighth to eleventh century when *Boudha Gan O Doha* otherwise known as *Charyapadas* were written by the Buddhist Sidhas. It is believed that *Charyacharya Binischaya* or *Acharya Charyachaya*, an anthology of poems was written by some twenty three Buddhist Siddhas. Hadi Pa, Kanhu Pa, Tanti Pa, Chourangi Nath, Gorakh Nath, Maschendra Nath and Lui Pa were supposed to be the authors of the charyas. Scholars have mentioned that many of these saints belonged to Odisha and their writings can be read as examples of early Odia literary tradition. The language and the themes of the texts are important because they reflect the day to day perceptions of ordinary and common people including dalit women. The most quoted charyas are Charya 10 and 18 where there has been reference to Dombi, a dalit woman. Both of which are attributed to Kanhu Pa. The following is the few lines of the English translation of Charya 10:

On the outskirt of the city lies your shelter, O Dombi
You play coquettish with the shaven-headed Brahmans.
I want to make love to you, O Dombi
I am the chaste ardent Kanhu Kapalik yogi …
I ask of your loyalty, O Dombi …
Do not sell bamboo baskets any more
For you I have left the dancer's box …

In the poem Dombi is a woman from the Domb community who lives in a hut at the outskirts of the town (Nagar bahire) whose family profession is weaving baskets. Interestingly the Dombs, one of the dalit communities of Odisha continue to weave baskets till date and earn their livelihood by selling them. The poet is in love with Dombi and wants to make love to her. In the same stanza the poet also complains that instead of paying attention to him she indulges in selfish pleasure which makes her character a suspect. This is a stereotypical image of a dalit woman who is always suspected as a 'whore' ready to offer her sex to everyone. In Charya 18 also the poet describes Dombi as clever (Chaturi), goddess of sex (Kama Chandali) and coquettish (Chhinali):

… How do you intent, O curly haired Dombi
To put the nobles out and allow the Kapali in?
O Dombi, you destroy everything …
Some describe you as formless
But the wise ones never forget you
Kanhu sings of you as Kamachandali
O Dombi, none more coquettish than you.

Charyapadas can be read in the backdrop of how tantric cult had an influence on Buddhism which Odisha had to witness during the seventh and eighth centuries AD. But the portrayal of Dombi and other common men and women suggests that Odia literature had concern for the common and ordinary people from the very beginning. This is what Mayadhar Mansinha (2005), the famous Odia poet and critic writes in his book, *A History of Oriya Literature*, "The most outstanding characteristic of the Oriya literature, when one surveys its entire panorama, appears to be very gratifying fact that essentially it is a literature of the common people. In all other modern Indian languages literature was ushered into existence by persons who were seasoned scholars in Sanskrit, India's great sacrosanct classical tongue. But poor Oriya cannot boast of either royal patronage or a scholastic foundation. Oriya literature was born and has developed and thrived because of the unseen but powerful urge of an isolated and neglected people who earnestly wished to see their own humble and homely thoughts, dreams, aspirations and experiences given expression to in the speech of their day-to-day life. No Maharaja ever helped his poets on the scale or with the enthusiasm that was the case with other Indian languages ...Oriya literature, more than any other literature, is really democratic, created by the people and for the people." (Mansinha 2005: 9)

Mansinha is partially right because taking common people into account many voices particularly in literary forms, during the fifteenth and sixteenth century, have been raised against inequality and injustice. To begin with Sudramuni Sarala Dasa in the fifteenth century and Panchasakhas, the five saint-poets, named Balarama Dasa, Jagannatha Dasa, Achyutanda Dasa, Jasobanta Dasa, and Ananta Dasa throughout the sixteenth century, dominated Odia literature by rejecting the dominance of Sanskrit in literature and espousing the cause of the vernacular as the medium of expression, thus, contributing towards the use of everyday Odia in the literature of their region. Together the poets also protested against the rigidities of life in temples and monasteries and sought to rise above the prejudices and debates that had reduced religion to the level of an intellectual polemic. Out of several writings by the Panchasakhas, Balaram Dasa's *Lakshmi Purana* needs our closer attention because it raises issues relating to the religious rights of dalit women in Odisha. The story revolves around Sriya Chandaluni, a Dalit woman who keeps fast and worships Lakshmi, the Goddess of wealth and the reining deity of Puri Jagannath temple on a *dasami,* the tenth day in the month of *Margashira.* Seeing her true devotion Lakshmi pays a visit to her untouchable hut and blesses her. But when Lakshmi returns and wants to enter the temple she is being prevented by Jagannath and Balabhadra, her husband and elder brother-in-law, respectively. They accuse her of being 'polluted' because of her visit to a dalit household. Having evicted Lakshmi from her home in the course of the story both the brothers suffer untold miseries till they get realization that nobody to be treated as 'untouchable'. Balaram Dasa by bringing a dalit woman into the centre of the debate not only raises caste questions in the narrative, he also underlines the significance of reading a gender issue along with caste. This is, perhaps, the reason why Satya P. Mohanty, a critic considers *Lakshmi Purana* as a feminist text. Mohanty, for example, writes, "Balaram Das(a)'s *Lakshmi Purana* is a feminist text primarily because it shows a female goddess using her personal power to challenge the way society defines identities and rewards virtue, and the way tradition—even when sanctioned by the Lord himself—understands our ascribed *jati*-identity and its implications for how we are to be treated." (Mohanty 2008: 9)

The story of Sriya Chandaluni suggests that Hinduism as a religion is quite liberal in its principles because it can allow the untouchables to have their fare share of it. But, we all also know that Hinduism is a bundle of contradictions. What it preaches in principles, the Hindus never practice in their daily lives. The caste system which is a discriminatory provision to exploit the common people is heavily backed by religion. It is, therefore, difficult to break the monopoly of caste. Keeping this background in mind, let's go further deep down the history of Odia literature to understand how the positions of dalit women have been depicted.

Dalit Women and Odia Nationalism

After the Panchasakhas, the tradition of writing protest literature focusing on and depicting people's lives and language came to an abrupt end because the kings and princes now took over as writers and poets of Odia literature. A remarkable change in the approach of literature both in theme as well as in style is clearly discernible. The lead was taken by the princes of the royal family, for example, Dhananjaya Bhanja and Upendra Bhanja of eighteenth century who were acquainted with the themes and discussions of old Sanskrit works, their forms, their ornate style and articulations. Following the old Sanskrit works, poems are written in ornate style depicting women's bodies and celebrating 'beauty' in nature and life. This continues till the nineteenth century when Bhim Bhoi arrives in the literary scene.

Born into a Kondh, adivasi family, Bhoi was the follower of Mahima Dharma, an autochthonous religious movement which made its presence felt in Odisha in the nineteenth century and drafted most of its followers from the oppressed classes of society, the dalits and the adivasis, both men and women. Bhima Bhoi was also a poet of distinction who composed several poems and also wrote philosophical treatises. His most widely known works are the *Stuti Chintamani,* the *Srutinisedha Gita* and the *Nirbeda Sadhana*. Apart from these there are scores of his 'Mahima' bhajans whose language is so simple that even an illiterate person can memorize them. Bhoi attacked orthodox rituals and customs of Odia society. His literary works sought to redefine and redesign societal norms, manners and behaviour promising the poor a better world. Bhoi in his religious as well as literary practices gave equal status to both men and women, sometime valourizing women as mother-goddesses. He, however, does not make any specific reference to Odia dalit women.

During India's independent movement, Odia women from all castes and communities joined in the struggle. Since the movement was mostly led by the upper caste men—Madhusudan Das, Gopabandhu Das, and Harekrushna Mahatab to name only few—the history of Odisha that we read during this period mentions only about the upper caste men. It does not mention the name of many upper caste women, except names of Ramadebi Choudhury, Malati Choudhury and Sarala Devi. The names of dalit men and women never get mentioned. Thus, dalits in Odisha look like history-less people.

It was only after India's independence that a sizeable number of dalits after availing literacy and education started writing about caste inequalities and injustices. Dalit writers and activists like Govind Chandra Seth, Santanu Kumar Das, Jagannath Malik, Kanhu Malik and Kanduri Malik came together to set up the Dalit Jati Sangha (Dalit League) in 1953. Ambedkar, who was alive then, was a great source of inspiration. These writers through their writings tried to bring awareness among dalits. For example, Govind Chandra Seth wrote a biography of Ambedkar that instantly became famous. Santanu Kumar Das seems to have written four novels on caste inequalities and social injustices. Many other dalit writers also wrote literature dealing with caste issues. But they hardly wrote about the conditions of dalit women in their writing.

However, during the same period we find some amount of writings on dalit life-situations by upper caste writers mainly within the over-arching ideology of nationalism. Few of them have written also about dalit women. But they are biased towards them. In their writings dalit women have invariably been shown as the victims of the lust of the higher caste men and never as rebels to fight against injustice perpetrated upon them. They have completely ignored the fact that even dalit women can fight back like any other victims of social oppression, to guard their dignity and self-respect. Thus, in Odia literature whenever there is a portrayal of a dalit woman she is never a fighter but always a victim. This makes it imperative to look into Gopinath Mohanty's novel *Harijan* (1948) in detail.

Gopinath Mohanty's *Harijan*

Written just one year after India's independence, Mohanty's novel can be read along with several other Indian novels on the lives and works of dalit communities in the day to day functioning of Indian caste society. Mohanty in the novel takes up the plights of the Mehentars, a dalit community whose traditional occupations include sweeping roads and streets and also cleaning kuttcha toilets of the rich. Puni and her old widowed mother Jema are the central characters in the novel. They live in a basti called Nakdharapur, probably a part of Cuttack city. Like in a jajmani system Jema is privately attached to Abinashbabu's household to clean their toilets. As the novel progresses the reader comes to realize that Puni was born out of an illicit relationship between Abinashbabu and Jema. That's perhaps the reason why Jema hesitates to send Puni to Abinashbabu's house even when she becomes ill and cannot manage to do her day to day work properly. But during the course of the event Puni has no other choice but to inherit her mother's painful job of cleaning dirty latrines. Later Puni gets molested by Aghor, Abinash's son. Instead of reacting to the act negatively Mohanty writes that it was a sheer chance for an untouchable girl like Puni to surrender her body to a rich upper caste man. It is almost as if Puni is favoured by this act of Aghor. Refusing to look at it as caste and gender exploitation, Mohanty invests the act with naturalness and spontaneity. Puni thinks of the spontaneous union among birds, animals and insects and tries not to put too much importance to whatever happened to her. I quote below Mohanty's justification of the act in my translation: "Nothing has happened to Puni. What really has happened? Puni passes her days as usual laughing at her little worries and gets consolation. She thinks this primitive desire has been the rule of law throughout the world. Everyone does it: from the insects of the gutter to the big people of the glittering palatial buildings. Therefore, she was not wrong. Such philosophical thoughts console Puni and she learns to reconcile her troubling mind. Her once soft skin, which has already turned to become rough like bricks due to her daily dirty work of scavenging, is surely entitled for a sensuous touch." (Mohanty 1994: 196) This is certainly a biased view by an upper caste Hindu male writer. But Mohanty is not alone in justifying such acts. Indian literature is full of such instances. Let's go through few famous Indian novels written by some of the best known progressive writers of this country to understand their treatment of caste and gender relationship.

Untouchable Body, Labour and History

Paula Rabinowitz in her book, *Labor and Desire: Women's Revolutionary Fiction in Depression America* refers to two different strands of radical fiction written by men and women. She suggests that while radical fiction by men deals with body, labour and history, radical women writers engage desire and language in their writings. (Rabinowitz 1991: 35) True to Rabinowitz's above observation, Mulk Raj Anand in his novel *Untouchable* (1935) deals with body, labour and history of the untouchable community. The novel is a statement against Indian caste society as it talks about modernity as the only alternative to bring down several heinous caste practices. He portrays an untouchable family in the novel, comprising of Lakha, Bakha and Sohini, who has been inhumanly deprived of all the basic social necessities of life. While the novel examines the nature of the degradation imposed on the lower castes by the caste Hindus, it also expresses the upper caste's hypocrisy and double standards.

For example, there is an instance in the novel when Pandit Kali Nath, a brahmin priest takes advantage of his caste and tries to molest Sohini, Bakha's sister in the temple yard. And when she screams, he comes out shouting that he has been defiled. This is not just a caricature of a lecherous brahmin priest taking advantage of his upper caste status, it raises questions about the logic of "pollution" also. In this connection C.D. Narasimhaiah in his book, *The Swan and the Eagle* comments: "We are now shown brother and sister suffering ignominy and shame, with the lie not in their hearts but in those who pretended to keep the truth of God, His abode and themselves in pristine purity. The untouchables, Anand's art has made us to see, are not Bakha and his sister, but those others who called them so." (Narasimhaiah 1969: 115) It may be mentioned here that enjoyment of carnal desires flouts the norm of so called caste purity. Anand rightly brings this utter hypocrisy of Indian upper caste men through this novel. More importantly, his physical descriptions of Sohini has subtle inference: they are nothing more than a reflection of male hunger for sex.

Sohini is not the only untouchable girl in Indian literature to be shown as a victim of the lust of the upper castes. There are similar examples in many other Indian novels. The immediate case in point is Premchand's *Godan* (1936). *Godan* occupies a special place in Indian fiction because it is the most incisive and moving human document about the different kinds of oppression the poor peasant in India is subjected to, and it also captures the paradoxes inherent in the transition from the agrarian to industrial way of life in India. The presence of two brahmin characters—Datadin and Matadin gives a caste dimension to the cycle of oppressions in the novel. In a transitional society where capitalism is replacing feudalism and allowing sufficient social space to a money-lending class, the brahmin is also adopting a new profession to better his material position. That is why Datadin is a money lender in the novel. Having sufficient financial resources in his hands in addition to the existing caste privileges, he is now in a better position to exploit poor peasants like Hori. Like the zamindar Rai Saheb and the capitalist Mr. Khanna in the novel, Datadin tries to make an estate of his own where Hori works at first as his share-farmer. Finally Hori loses his plot of land and becomes a daily wage labourer and ends up by dying of overwork and exhaustion. This kind of brahmanic exploitation is not new in the traditional Hindu society. Since the brahmin is the law maker and the law giver in social rituals, the rules are generally in his favour. As the priestly class the brahmins have always enjoyed special privileges and powers in caste Hindu society. That is why Matadin, Datadin's son who is a sensual character in the novel repeatedly molests a low caste Chamar girl, Siliya who, due to her poor socio-economic conditions, is vulnerable. Even though Siliya gives birth to a child fathered by Matadin she is never accepted as wife but treated like a domestic servant. She works hard day and night in order to get nothing but two meals a day and sometimes a sari. She works like a machine to improve the economic standards of the brahmin family at the same time satisfying the sexual needs of a brahmin's son. Premchand perceives a certain permanency about the power of the brahmins in the caste Hindu society, at least in rural India which we can see even today.

Premchand, like Anand, is also a realistic novelist who does not hesitate to describe the physical features of the lower caste and tribal women as something which must be appreciated. His description of Siliya runs like this: "Siliya was a dark, provocative, lively young thing, attractive though perhaps not beautiful. There was joyful abandon in her laugh, in her glances and in her sensuous limbs, as though every part of her were dancing." (Premchand 1936: 303) Premchand also describes a tribal woman briefly in Chapter 7 to highlight her health and vigour and to contrast her with the wilted and wan city-bred Malati. He writes: "The girl was dark—very dark, in fact. Her clothes were extremely dirty and coarse, her hair was tangled, and her only ornaments were the two bangles on each arm. None of her features could have been called beautiful; but the fresh and pure surroundings had given her dark complexion such lustre, and being raised in the lap of nature had made her body so trim and shapely, that an artist seeking model of ideal youth could have found no greater beauty. Her robust health seemed to radiate strength and energy to Mehta." (Premchand 1936: 103)

There is no doubt that here the bodies of the lower caste and the tribal women have been romanticized, perceived as possessing certain primal energy, vitality and spontaneity that the privileged women in seclusion have lost. Obviously Premchand is not alone in doing so. We can draw parallel examples from several other authors. Evidently most of these writers are male, and belong to the upper caste. Take, for example, the stand taken by Anantha Murthy on the question of an untouchable body. In his famous novel *Samskara* (1976) the author depicts Chandri and Belli, two untouchable women as essentially sensual characters. He implicitly contrasts the lower caste women with the brahmin women who are depicted as frigid with dwarfish braids and withered bodies. Anantha Murthy even goes to the extent of comparing the physical beauty of Belli with Kalidas's most famous heroine Shakuntala: "Which Brahmin girl, -- cheek sunken, breast withered, mouth stinking of lentil soup, -- which Brahmin girl was equal to Belli? Her thighs are full ...Not utterly black-skinned, nor pale white, her body is the colour of the earth, fertile, ready for seed, warmed by an early sun." (Murthy 1976: 37) Although Shripati is not a particularly positive character in the novel, his sexual exploitation of Belli is almost condoned by the author because Shripati's own wife is unappetizing, and Belli is irresistible in her eroticism: "her hair washed in warm water, wearing only a piece below her waist, naked above, waves of hair pouring over her back and face ..." (Murthy 1976: 40)

Compared to all the novels cited above Mohanty's *Harijan* is somewhat different. Mohanty, for example, does not describe Puni as a sexual object. She becomes a victim of the caste society. Mohanty also brings a tragic end to the novel by writing about dalit atrocities. In the novel Abinash wants to drive the Mehentars from their basti so that he can construct a big hotel there. The Mehentars, on the other hand, continue to fight for their rights to live there under the leadership of Dhanibudha. Unable to drive them out even through the Municipalty's bulldozers, the basti is finally burnt down. Finding no other ways the Mehentars set on their journey to look for a new place. Mohanty's *Harijan* thus is a national narrative on dalit atrocities perpetuated by the upper castes/ classes for their private goals. The fruit of development, Mohanty seems to be suggesting, is the displacement of dalit community. Contrary to Mohanty's understanding of caste atrocities in Odisha, Akhila Naik's novel *Bheda* (2010) captures the relationship between caste and gender in a complex form. Let's look into the novel closely.

Gender Issue in Akhila Naik's *Bheda*

The central focus of *Bheda* is the caste atrocity. The plot of the novel is a remote rural village of Kalahandi district situated in the western part of Odisha. It may be recalled that Kalahandi is dubiously known for poverty, drought, famine, child-selling, malnutrition, etc. Several social scientists have investigated the true story of Kalahandi. Out of several, Jagdish Pradhan (1993), Kishore Samal (1994), Gail Omvedt (1996), Biswamoy Pati (1999), Bob Curie (2000), Fanindam Deo (2003), and Manoranjan Mohanty (2012) need to be mentioned here. The novel, on the other hand, is both a creative as well as critical attempt to rewrite social history of the Kalahandi region with special focus on dalits.

Naik raises the gender issue in *Bheda* through Mastrani, Dinamastre's wife and Laltu's mother. As a dalit woman she represents her class in the novel. But compared to many poor dalit women of her neighbourhood who work hard for their survival, Mastrani does not have to work for a living. Being financially secure, she commands both power and social position for which the other members of the community respect her. Even though she takes pride in dalit culture, she imitates upper caste lifestyles by observing religious fasts and visiting Hindu temple. A charitable woman, she gives alms to beggars and mendicants and helps the poor and the destitute.

Naik points out how dalit patriarchy works to the advantage of dalit men. Even though Mastrani is literate she sacrifices her career by prioritizing her family. She shares Dinamastre's dream of seeing Laltu in a respected position. Laltu's inability to complete his education and his failure to get a good job makes Mastrani very unhappy. But throughout his activism she supports him whole heartedly. When he comes home late at night he finds her waiting for him. If he is unable to come back home she stays up all night worrying. Thus when Laltu sacrifices his career for his community and society, it is Mastrani who sustains his dream by sacrificing her time and energy just to see a new society without caste discriminations.

It is through Mastrani that the author throws light on the social as well as cultural life of the dalit community in Kalahandi district of Odisha. Dalit communities across Kalahandi district have been worshipping their own gods and goddesses such as,

Budharaja, Dokribudhi, Thutimaili, Kalisundri etc. since time immemorial. But with the hinduization and brahminization the area has been flooded with Hindu gods and goddesses. Local people are often seen worshipping these new gods and goddesses leaving their folk deities aside. This is precisely what happens in the novel. After availing education, a government job and economic security Dinamastre's family starts worshipping Hindu deities—Mahadev in particular—which the illiterate villagers never like. There is a debate in the novel between Majhibaba, an adivasi who is also the village priest and Dinamastre as to which gods and goddesses the villagers should worship. While Majhibaba argues for sticking to tradition by worshipping only folk deities, Dinamastre offers justification to worship Hindu gods and goddesses along with folk deities. Since women are custodians of culture, it is through Mastrani that we get to know about Hinduization of dalit culture. Mastrani in her day to day life imitates the lives of the upper castes. She takes bath early in the morning, puts on good clothes and regularly keeps fasts. She also visits the Hindu temples, though she is not allowed to go near the sanctum sanctorum, and worship the gods and goddesses herself. The temple priests always worship for on her behalf. It is an irony that Mastrani by imitating the everyday life of the upper castes, perhaps, thinks that she will be accepted as one among them. Instead, she is discriminated and told to mind her business as a dalit woman. It takes time for Mastrani to discover her mistake. She later condemns the hypocrisies of the caste Hindus.

Mastrani's son Laltu, on the other hand, is an agnostic from the beginning. Even as a child he criticizes his mother when she drags him to the temple. When he grows up he challenges the existence of God when Mastrani tries to convince him of the significance of visiting the temple. He cites many instances from the *puranas, sashtras* and everyday life to tell her how hinduism as a religion discriminates against dalits. This she finally realizes when she visits the Mahadeva temple in her neighbouring village. She cannot offer worship to the deity like others from the upper castes. She can offer her *puja* only through the brahmin temple priest. Being disturbed she questions herself: is a dalit not a human being? Though she realizes that the caste system is a discriminatory provision made by the upper-caste Hindus against dalits, she points no accusatory fingers at upper caste Hindus to correct their behaviour. Of course she is not an activist like her son. Naik, thus, portrays Mastrani not as a revolutionary dalit woman but a devoted wife and a loving mother who places her family before anything else.

Supriya Mallik's Fictional Accounts of Dalit Women

Akhila Naik by virtue of being a dalit male writer takes up dalit women's issue somehow uncritically. Thus compared to dalit men dalit women writers portray dalit women characters differently. Among Odia Dalit women poets and writers I would like to take up Supriya Mallik's fictional accounts of dalit women particularly in her two short stories, 'Papa' and 'Prabahman' for illustration. In the first story 'Papa' (Sin) the central character is named Motidei. Unlike the upper caste male writers' portrayal of dalit women who are invariably depicted as weak, meek and docile, Motidei is a courageous dalit woman who confronts the upper castes for asserting her dalit rights. When the upper castes deny her to collect water from a well situated at the temple premises for the fear of pollution she defies their dictum and quarrels with them. She also uses crude language to curse them, which signifies a symbolic act of her defiance. Finally with a strong push of an upper caste she falls down and gets wounded. When she gets up, blood oozes out from her bruised lips but she continues her curses in an act of bravery. Mallik thus portrays her woman character as an angry dalit woman who can bravely fight for her basic rights as well as her community's right even at the time of adversity.

In another story 'Prabahman' (The Flowing Dreams) Mallik documents the predicament of an educated dalit woman. Ashmita Dalai is a highly ambitious dalit woman.

Having realized that it is only through entering into electoral politics that she can bring changes in the caste ridden society, she becomes a political activist. She becomes a cabinet minister by dint of her hard work. She makes plans and initiates different programmes for the improvement of the exploited communities. But before bringing any change she is forced to resign from her post because the upper caste politicians see danger in her action plans. With her resignation the dream of a community also comes to an end thereby hinting, 'there is no respite to dalit sufferings'.

Conclusion

This article is an attempt to understand Odia dalit women's subjectivity in society and literature. Since caste and patriarchy go hand in hand in Indian society, at the beginning we tried to make a review of how Indian literature in general has dealt with issues pertaining to the relationship between caste and gender. Most of the Indian writers are caste and gender-biased. Even progressive writers like Mulk Raj Anand, Premchand, Anantha Murthy have portrayed a dalit women's body wrongly in their novels. Such a depiction of dalit women characters is due to the caste positions of the authors. Coming to Odisha society in particular we felt that dalit subjegation in general particularly dalit women in particular has not been properly depicted in literature by the male writers, whether non-dalit or dalits. Justice towards subject of dalit women is done only when Odia dalit women writers write about them.

Denise Riley in her book *'Am I That Name?': Feminism and the Category of 'Women' in History* while discussing about the subjectivities of women's bodies thus writes: "That women's bodies become women's bodies only as they are caught up in the tyrannies, the overwhelming incursions of both nature and man—or, more optimistically, that there are also vehement pleasures and delights to offset a history of unbridled and violent subjection. But to be faithful to the suggestion that 'the body' is really constantly altering as a concept, means that we must back off from the supposition that women's bodies are systematically and exhaustively different, that they are unified in an integral otherness. Instead we would need to maintain that women only sometimes live in the flesh distinctively of women, as it were, and this is a function of historical categorizations as well as of an individual daily phenomenology. To say that is by no means to deny that because of the cyclical aspects of female physiology, there may be a greater overall degree of slipping in and out of the consciousness of the body for many women. But even this will always be subject to different interpretations, and nothing more radical than the facts of intermittent physiology really holds the bodies of women together." (Riley 1988: 105)

View-points will be always different from one writer to another. But the challenge is how to stick to the idea of justice, dignity and self-respect in one's writing. Odia dalit women writers like Supriya Mallik by raising these issues in their writings have not only challenged the way Odia male writers have treated dalit women's subjectivity quite casually, but by writing differently they have tried to rehabilitate such subjectivity in a proper perspective. Finally, it will not be an exaggeration to say that Odia dalit women's writings could be interpreted as an alternative way to understand Odia history, language, culture and literature.

REFERENCES

Anand, Mulk Raj. 1981. *Untouchable* (1935). New Delhi: Arnold Associates.

Currie, Bob. 2000. *The Politics of Hunger in India: A Study of Democracy, Governance and Kalahandi's Poverty*. London: Macmillan Press Ltd.

Channa, Subhadra Mitra and Mencher, Joan P. 2013. *Life as a Dalit: Views from the Bottom on Caste in India*. New Delhi: Sage.

Chatterji, Angana P. 2009. *Violent Gods: Hindu Nationalism in India's Present. Narratives from Orissa*. New Delhi: Three Essays Collective.

Dash, Anup Kumar and Raj Kumar. 1994. *A Study on the Implementation of the PCR Act in Orissa*. Bhubaneswar: National Institute of Social Work and Social Sciences.

Deo, Fanindam. 2009. *Roots of Poverty: A Social History*. Bhubaneswar: Amadeus Press.

Editorial. 2009. 'Epic Shame.' *Combat Law: The Human Rights and Law Bimonthly*. 20 December.

Freeman, James M. 1979. *Untouchable: An Indian Life History*. London: Allen and Unwin.

Gopal, Priyamvada. 2005. *Literary Radicalism in India: Gender, Nation and the Transition to Independence*. London: Routledge.

Irudayam, Aloysius et al. 2014. *Dalit Women Speak Out: Caste, Class and Gender Violence in India*. New Delhi: Zubaan.

Kumar, Raj. 2010. *Dalit Personal Narratives: Reading Caste, Nation and Identity*. New Delhi: Orient BlackSwan.

Mallik, Basant Kumar. 2004. *Paradigms of Dissent and Protest: Social Movements in Eastern India*. New Delhi: Manohar.

Mallik, Supriya. 2004. *Nidagha*. Cuttack: Grantha Mandir.

Mallik, Supriya. 2010. *Baridanka Hasa*. Bhubaneswar: Kitab Bhavan.

Manorama, Ruth. 2013. 'Dalit Women in Struggle: Transforming Pain into Power' in Channa, Subhadra Mitra and Mencher, Joan (eds.), *Life as a Dalit: Views from the Bottom on Caste in India*, pp. 255-60, New Delhi: Sage.

Mansinha, Mayadhar. 1962. *A History of Oriya Literature*. New Delhi: Sahitya Akademi.

Mohanty, Gopinath. 1994. *Harijan* (1948). Cuttack: Vidyapuri.

Mohanty, Janaki Ballabha. 1988. *An Approach to Oriya Literature*. Bhubaneswar: Panchashila.

Mohanty, Jatindra Mohan. 2006. *History of Oriya Literature*. Bhubaneswar: Vidya.

Mohanty, Manoranjan. 2014. 'Persisting Dominance: Crisis of Democracy in a Resource-rich Region'. *Economic and Political Weekley*. XLIX(14): 39-47.

Mohanty, Nivedita. 1982. *Oriya Nationalism: Quest for a United Orissa*. Delhi: Manohar.

Mohanty, Satya P. 2008. *Alternative Modernities and Medieval Indian Literature: The Oriya Lakshmi Purana as a Radical Pedagogy*. Bhubaneswar: Utkal University.

Murthy, U.R. Anantha. 1990. *Samskara* (1965). Translated by A.K. Ramanujan. Delhi: Oxford University Press.

Narasimhaiah, C.D. 1969. *The Swan and the Eagle*. Simla: Indian Institute of Advanced Study.

Nayak, Akhila. 2010. *Bheda*. Bhubaneswar: Duduly Prakashani.

Nayak, R.K. 1984. *A Study on the Problems of Untouchability with Emphasis on the Incidents of the Atrocities on Harijans in Orissa*. Bhubaneswar: National Institute of Social Work and Social Sciences.

Omvedt, Gail. 1996. 'Worst in a Hundred Years: The Kalahandi Drought'. *Manushi*. 97. November-December.

Pati, Biswamoy. 1999. 'Environment and Social History: Kalahandi, 1800-1950'. *Environment and History*. 5.

Pradhan, Jagdish. 1993. 'The Distorted Kalahandi and a Strategy for its Development'. *Social Action*. 43. July-September.

Premchand. 2007. *Godaan* (1936). Translated as *The Gift of a Cow* by Gordon C. Roadarmel. New Delhi: Permanent Black.

Rabinowitz, Paula. 1991. *Labor and Desire: Women's Revolutionary Fiction in Depression America*. Chapel Hill: University of North Carolina Press.

Rao, Anupama. 2003. *Gender and Caste*. (Ed.) New Delhi: Kali for Women.

Riley, Denise. 1988. *'Am I That Name?': Feminism and the Category of 'Women' in History*. London: Macmillan Press.

Samal, Kishor C. 1994. 'Drought and its toll in Kalahandi.' *Mainstream*. XXXII: 14. 19 February.

Satpathy, Sumanyu. 2009. *Reading Literary Culture: Perspectives from Orissa*. New Delhi: Rawat.

Saxena, K.B. et al. 2012. *A Fistful of Dry Rice: Land, Equity and Democracy*. Delhi: Aakar.

Shah, Ghanshyam et al. 2006. *Untouchability in Rural India*. New Delhi: Sage.

Tripathy, Rebati Ballav. 1994. *Dalits: A Sub-human Society*. New Delhi: Ashish Publishing House.

11

Social Security and Unorganized Sector: An Overview of the Women Construction Workers in Odisha

Amrita Patel and Swarnamayee Tripathy

Introduction

Globally, women's participation in the labour force has remained relatively constant in the two decades from 1990 to 2010, at approximately 52 per cent (Choudhury and Verick, 2014). At a more disaggregated level, the participation of women in the labour market varies greatly across countries with some of the lowest rates witnessed in South Asia. In terms of the female labour force participation rates across South Asia, most notable is the falling participation of women in the Indian labour force, especially in rural areas, which occurred despite strong economic growth and rising wages/incomes. Out of 131 countries with available data, India ranks 11th from the bottom in female labour force participation, according to the International Labour Organization (ILO) *Global Employment Trends 2013 Report*.[1] One of the most intense debates in recent years has centred on the declining labour force participation rate of women in India, which dropped from 42.7 per cent in 2004-05 to 31.2 in 2011-12. The latest data from the Labour Bureau indicates a similar participation rate of women in 2013-14 (31.1 per cent).[2]

The Indian labour market is characterized by the predominance of informal employment and within it, the large presence of women. Women as workers are most vulnerable due to their ignorance and gender. They work in poor conditions and are bereft of many social security provisions and statutory benefits like the maternity benefit.[3] In recent times, there has been a focus of workers' welfare boards to provide the necessary social security entitlements. As the unorganized sector suffers from cycles of excessive seasonality of employment, the majority of the unorganized women workers do not have stable durable avenues of employment. Their workplace is scattered and fragmented. There is no formal employer-employee relationship. In addition to this, in rural areas, the unorganized women labour force is highly stratified on caste and community considerations. In urban areas, while such considerations are much less, it cannot be said that it is altogether absent as the bulk of the unorganized workers in urban areas are basically migrant workers from rural areas. The unorganized women workers do not receive sufficient attention from the trade unions. Inadequate and ineffective labour laws and standards relating to the unorganized sector often fail to provide 'social protection' to these women workers.[4]

Unorganized Sector and Women Workers

The informal economy provides a major source of livelihood for women in the countries of South Asia. This work of women is however concentrated in a narrow range of sectors resulting in occupational segregation in the labour market. These sectors are essentially vulnerable and insecure. There exists a high incidence of informality which is pervasive in these sectors, such as construction, wholesale and retail trade, and accommodation and food service industries (ILO, 2018).[5]

The informal economy in India is otherwise known as the 'unorganized sector'. The first National Commission on Labour (NCL)[6] was set up in 1966 which defined unorganized sector in India as that part of the workforce "who have not been able to organize in pursuit of a common objective because of constraints such as casual nature of employment, ignorance and illiteracy, small and scattered size of establishments and superior strength of the employer operating singly or in combination". The Commission listed illustrative categories of unorganized labour consisting of construction workers, labourers employed in small scale industry, casual labour, handloom/power loom workers, beedi and cigar workers, employees in shops and commercial establishments, sweepers and scavengers, workers in tanneries and tribal labour and other unprotected labour.[7] The term unorganized in the country refers to a vast number of men and women engaged in home-based work (beedi, papad etc), household enterprises, small units, agriculture, construction, domestic work, self-employment and a myriad other forms of casual and temporary employment.

National Commission for Enterprises in Unorganized Sector (NCEUS) defines unorganized sector as "all unincorporated private enterprises owned by individuals or households engaged in the sale or production of goods and services operated on a proprietary or partnership basis and with less than ten total workers." Amongst the characteristic features of this sector are ease of entry, the smaller scale of operation, local ownership, uncertain legal status, flexible wage, unequal payment of wages and lower protection against employers indulging in unfair or illegal practices. As per the report of NCEUS, India had 4.89 million informal workers in 2006 (NCEUS Report, 2007).[8]

The Ministry of Labour, Government of India[9] in its 2008 report, has categorized the unorganized labour force under four groups depending on occupation, nature of employment, especially distressed categories and service categories. As per the occupation, the unorganized workers comprise of small and marginal farmers, landless agricultural labourers, those engaged in animal husbandry, beedi rolling, labelling and packing, building and construction workers, weavers, artisans, salt workers, workers in brick kilns and stone quarries. Attached agricultural labourers, bonded labourers, migrant workers, contract and casual labourers are categorized under terms of nature of employment. The third category of especially distressed are toddy tappers, scavengers, carriers of head loads, loaders and unloaders. Midwives, domestic workers, washermen and women, barbers, vegetable and fruit vendors, etc are a separate category under terms of service.

The report of the Committee on Unorganized Sector Statistics, National Statistical Commission, 2012 states that the unorganized or the informal sector account for more than 90 per cent of the workforce in the country and almost 50 per cent of the national income evolves from this sector.[10] It may be noted that this report considers all agricultural activities undertaken on agricultural holdings either individually or in partnership as being in the unorganized sector. The size of the unorganized sector is relatively large in India and is likely to continue so, as limited employment opportunities are created in the organized sector and also because of outsourcing of a number of activities. In the unorganized sector, a relatively greater concentration of women workers is seen from available statistics. Over the years the share of employment in the organized sector has declined and the share in the unorganized sector has increased both for male and female workers, the increase being more prominent in case of women workers. All the casual workers and unpaid family workers in all enterprises, irrespective of the sector, are considered as unorganized workers. In India, this sector accounts for 60% of Net Domestic Product, 68% of income, 60% of savings, 31% of agricultural exports, and 41% of manufactured exports (Dutta, 2009).

Women occupy a large presence in this unorganized sector. In 2011-12, 92.3% of the women workers were in the unorganized sector where there are no legislative safeguards even to claim either minimum or equal wages along with their male counterparts. Thus, the unorganized sector in India is the women's sector (Singh Mor, 2001). According to an estimate of the National Commission of Self Employment of Women, 94% of the total female workforce operates in the unorganized sector. They do arduous work as wage earners, piece rate workers, casual labour and paid family labour. The coverage of labour laws has not benefited these women workers in many areas of wages, working conditions, maternity benefits and social security. The NSSO employment-unemployment survey of 2011-12 reveal the huge gender disparity. There is no presence of women whether rural or urban in informal employment sectors like wholesale trade, manufacturing, financial services etc. On the other hand, women have been informally employed almost cent per cent in sectors like construction, manufacturing of tobacco products, manufacturing of textiles (Shrija and Shirke, 2014).

Similar is the scenario in the state of Odisha. The employment of women in the organized sector in the State is less than one per cent.[11] It is evident from the data from Census 2011 that more of women are either marginal workers or non-workers in comparison to men in Odisha.

The State ranked 20th amongst all states in the country with regard to the female work participation rate in 2001 moving up to the 16th position in the 2011 Census[12] as there was an increase from 24.7% to 27.2%. Nationally it has decreased from 25.6% to 25.5% during the same period 2001-2011. However, the gender gap remains. In the case of men, the work participation rate in the country has been increased from 51.7% to 53.3% during this decade while that of Odisha it had increased from 52.5 to 56.1. The female workforce across the total, main, marginal and other workers category as a percentage of the total female population of the state shows that women are mostly marginal and non workers (66.1%). About one in two males and two in three females are engaged in agricultural activities i.e. either as a cultivator or agricultural labourer. In fact, the highest presence as agriculture labourers is that of the women (57.78%). (Table 1)

Construction Sector

The construction sector is among the fastest growing sectors in India today, recording a growth of 156 per cent from 2000 to 2007 while providing employment to 18 million people directly. It has been steadily contributing about 8 per cent to

Table 1: Women Workers in Odisha: 2001 and 2011

Sl. No	*Item*	*Unit*	*2001*	*2011*
1	Total population	Million	36.805	41.974
2	Total female workers	Million	44.744	56.389
4	Total marginal workers	Million	4.687	6.834
5	Proportion of total workers to total population	Per cent	38.79	41.79
6	Main workers to total workers	Per cent	67.17	61.00
7	Male main workers to male population	Per cent	52.5	56.11
8	Female main workers to female population	Per cent	24.7	27.16
9	Female cultivators to total female workers	Per cent	20.11	12.92
10	Female agriculture Labourers to total female workers	Per cent	53.90	57.78
11	Female workers engaged in house hold Industry to total female workers	Per cent	8.53	6.10
12	Other female workers to total female workers	Per cent	17.46	23.20
13	Work participation rate	Per cent	38.8	41.8
14	Male work participation rate	Per cent	52.6	56.1
15	Female work participation rate	Per cent	24.7	27.2

Source: *Statistical Profile of Women Labour, 2001* and *Statistical Profile of Women Labour, 2011*, Labour Department, Government of India

the national GDP over the last 5 years. The current size of the construction industry in India is estimated at US$ 70.8 billion (Khanna, Nagrath and Mangrulkar, 2011) Climate and Construction-An Impact Assessment Project Report).[13] The construction industry is supported by the government's plan to transform urban India. Under the 100 Smart Cities Mission[14], the government aims to provide a more sustainable and clean environment by 2020. In total, Rs 480 billion has been allocated.

Research conducted by International Labour Organization reveals that the share of employment of construction industry in rural areas of India has increased from 14.4 per cent in 1999-00) to 30.1 per cent in 2011-12 (ILO, 2016). In the urban areas, this industry absorbs the migrant labour from rural areas. Overall, 56.1% of the workers in the unorganized sector work in the construction industry (NCEUS, 2007). The construction industry provides direct employment to at least 30 million workers in India but recent expansions have resulted in a higher number: trade unions estimate that there were roughly 40 million migrant construction workers in India in 2008 (Sarde, 2008)[15]. The NSSO report of 2011-12, however, states that 50 million workers are employed in the construction sector. Construction attracts both skilled workers (masons, carpenters) and unskilled workers. In the last two decades, massive construction activities in cities has led to an increase in the number of construction workers in India and some estimates say that more than 40 million people are employed in this sector, Delhi alone is housing more than 1 million workers, out of which nearly one fourth are women.[16]

Social Security of Unorganized Workers

Both men and women workers in the unorganized sector across the globe and particularly in India have been experiencing social exclusion, deprivation and poverty. Economists and sociologists are of the opinion that globalization, market economy and withdrawal of the State from many areas of public service have multiplied the magnitude and dimensions of deprivation. The unorganized workers are in a poverty trap, which development economics literature explains as 'vicious circle of poverty'. For example, the ill-being of a poor woman makes her further poor as she is being deprived of the basic needs of life that facilitate the fullest development of human potentials. Welfare economists and human right advocates argue that if the vicious circle of poverty is not transformed into 'virtuous circle of development' social cohesion and social development with inclusive growth will be a distant dream.[17] The 'virtuous circle of development' points out that intervention by the State by creating strong social security framework for the deprived and socially excluded will be able to break the 'vicious circle of poverty' and gradually the virtuous circle of development will make inroads into the social fabric. The nuances of this intellectual debate are grounded on the concept of 'social security' in social science research.

Since the beginning of organized societies, members of communities had recognized that there is a need for protection against unforeseen life circumstances. 'Friendly societies' in different countries served a critical role in provisioning 'social protection' to the needy cohabitants. The presence of social actions like 'mutuality 'and 'voluntarism' in Indian villages had developed a strong social security informal network in the pre-independent period. The development and establishment of formal social security systems came quite late in the late 19th century. Social security was understood in a very narrow way in medieval or early industrial society. Either it was in the form of the benevolence of the monarch or termed as 'poor relief' by a liberal democratic modern state of the 19th century which many marginalized groups boycotted as it demeaned their dignity and self-respect. The poor construed this 'relief for disadvantaged' as the ideological foundation of a 'property-owning democracy'. They preferred death for want to declaring themselves as 'poor' before the State. In the 1880s, Germany was the first nation to adopt a statutory social insurance system, thereby establishing the notion of benefits as a right and making it applicable to the industrial workforce as a whole. Some years later, similar schemes were introduced in Latin America (Argentina, Brazil, Chile and Uruguay). Existing insurance models were widened, new risks such as unemployment benefits were included, and the groups of persons covered were enlarged. In the early 20thcentury, Great

Britain adopted National Assistance Act in 1911 to insure the lives of workers. Wealthy industrialized nations followed the suit and extended social security to their workers. In the Nordic countries, not only the workers but also all the inhabitants had access to a universal social security safety net.[18]

The concepts of social security and social protection have evolved over time, and are used in various ways throughout the world. In addition, new terms have been added to the classical terminology, such as social protection, social transfers, conditional and unconditional cash transfers and the social protection floor. Due to the multiple forms that the concept of social security takes nowadays, achieving definitional clarity is a formidable challenge. The varied terminologies have emerged from different institutional framework of World Bank, Asian Development Bank, World Social Science Forum and ILO. However, the concept 'formal social security' has been used to describe the 'public social security system' which includes social assistance given by the State and non-state actors such as registered voluntary organizations and private sector enterprises, while informal includes occasional individual and collective arrangements made by some non-state actors like the private sector or civil society organizations.[19] In this paper, we are discussing the nature of the formal social security system particularly by the state for the unorganized workers.

The foundational understanding of 'social security' is that the poor often constituting the majority in less developed economies live so close to the subsistence threshold that even a small shock will push them into survival crisis. The vulnerability varies with the social positioning of the poor in a social hierarchy. Therefore, social security safety net has been developed by nations with an objective to reduce inequality and ensure social justice to the disadvantaged, deprived and socially excluded. The architects of the welfare state considered the essentiality of social security from 'cradle to grave' to protect every citizen during the lifetime. The social liberals like Hobson,[20] Hobhouse[21] and J.S. Mill[22] envisioned a just society in which none are denied the basic necessities of education, health care, food security, work and decent housing; it would be a society where everyone will develop their personality without fear and want. This idea was well explained in the Beveridge Report 1942[23] brought out by the British Government and implemented from 1945 onwards and later on followed by European nations and the post-colonial Third World States in their public policies.

The universal need for social security has been recognized by the world community as a human right. The right to social security is recognized as a human right in fundamental human rights international documents, namely the Universal Declaration of Human Rights, and the International Covenant on Economic, Social and Cultural Rights (ICESCR) and enshrined as such in other international and regional legal instruments. Universal Declaration of Human Rights passed by UN General Assembly in 1948 emphatically declares in its Article 22, "Everyone, as a member of society, has the right to social security and is entitled to realization, through national effort and international co-operation and in accordance with the organization and resources of each State, of the economic, social and cultural rights indispensable for his dignity and the free development of his personality". Its Article 25 also states, "Everyone has the right to a standard of living adequate for the health and well-being of himself and of his family, including food, clothing, housing and medical care and necessary social services, and the right to security in the event of unemployment, sickness, disability, widowhood, old age or other lack of livelihood in circumstances beyond his control". Article 9 of ICESCR states that the States Parties recognize the right of everyone to social security, including social insurance.

ILO, set up in 1919, defines social security as 'the security that society furnishes through appropriate organizations against certain risks to which its members are exposed. These risks are essentially contingencies against which the individual of small means cannot effectively provide for by his own ability or foresight alone or even in private combination with fellows, these risks being sickness, maternity, invalidity, old age and death'[24]. ILO in its Report published in International Labour Conference, 100th Session, 2011, recommended social security as a pivotal tool for social justice and a fair globalization, facilitating economic development and structural change, and managing crises. Social security plays a pivotal role in fostering decent work and economic development. Thus social security are all measures providing benefits, whether in cash or in kind, to secure protection, inter alia, from lack of work-related income (or insufficient income) caused by sickness, disability, maternity, employment injury, unemployment, old age, or death of a family member; lack of access or unaffordable access to health care; insufficient family support, particularly for children and adult dependents; general poverty and social exclusion. ILO considers social protection as a broader concept than social security (including, in particular, the protection provided between members of the family or members of a local community) to mean protection provided by social security systems in the case of social risks and needs.

There are three core pillars of Convention on Elimination of all forms of Discrimination Against Women (CEDAW): gender equality, non-discrimination, and State obligation, which are the bases for strengthening the gender dimensions in social protection systems. These provisions are the backbone for ensuring social security for the women workers, which are not discriminatory and protect their rights. India being a signatory to CEDAW is trying to implement the provisions. Article 11 outlines the right to work for women as "an unalienable right of all human beings". It stipulates equal pay for equal work, the right to social security, paid leave and maternity leave "with pay or with comparable social benefits without loss of former employment, seniority or social allowances". Dismissal on the grounds of maternity, pregnancy or status of marriage shall be prohibited with sanction.

Jean Dreze and Amartya Sen[25] however distinguish between two aspects of social security: 'protection' and 'promotion'. The former is concerned with preventing a decline in living standards in general and in the basic conditions of living in particular. The latter has the objective of enhancing normal living conditions and helping people overcome regular and persistent deprivation. The larger ambit of a number of promotional social security programmes is to be juxtaposed with the protective social security schemes.[26]

Therefore, the public social security system for women in India aims at the following : (i) a higher and more secure consumption base for women in terms of food, house and clothing; (ii) an increase in the capabilities of the economically poorer, excluded and marginalized groups by augmenting their capability for productivity; and (iii) a rise in productivity of the social security recipient with ownership and management of productive assets.[27]

The Legal Framework of Social Security of Unorganized Workers and Welfare Boards

In our study, we prefer the concept 'social security' to 'social protection' as the efforts of the Indian states is to make the workers, both men and women feel secure and empowered in the process of their struggle for survival. This is quite evident in the justifiable and non-justifiable rights of Indian citizens enshrined in the provisions under Fundamental Rights and Directive Principles of State Policy in the Constitution.

The Indian Constitution in its Part IV, Directive Principles of State Policy spells out the concept of social security. Article 38; Article 39(a), (b) and (c); Article 41; Article 42; Article 43; Article 47, Union List and the Concurrent List in the 7th Schedule of the Constitution of India specifically lists the unorganized women's work and labour laws.

There is a whole range of laws which directly and indirectly relate to the issues of unorganized women workers. There are those statutory enactments which are exclusively for women workers, and the laws include the Maternity Benefit Act 1961, the Equal Remuneration Act 1976 and the Sexual Harassment of Women at Workplace (Prevention, Prohibition and Redressal) Act 2013. Another set comprises those labour statutes which are to provide measures for workers at large and contain special provisions for women workers—some of these are Workmen Compensation Act 1923, the Payment of Wages Act 1936, the Factories Act 1948, the Minimum Wages Act 1948, the Employees' State Insurance Act 1948, the Contract Labour (Regulation and Abolition) Act 1970, the Payment of Gratuity Act 1972, the Inter-state Migrant Workmen (Regulation of Employment and Conditions of Service) Act 1979, Inter-State Migrant Workmen (Regulation of Employment and Conditions of Service) Central (Amendment) Rules 2015, the Employees Provident Funds and Miscellaneous Provisions Act 1952 and the Dangerous Machines (Regulation) Act 1983.

Overall, the important components of these laws are measures with regard to the health, safety and welfare of women; social security measures for women; and wage protection for women.

The work, employers and conditions of work are to be regulated and guided by these laws, which are to ensure the protection of women from exploitative working conditions, besides the protection of wages and health. The broader goal is to ensure that the rights and entitlements of women workers are guaranteed. These laws are to be implemented by institutional structures of the police and the labour and social welfare departments. However, in general, abusive working conditions can occur even under legal circumstances.[28] Too often, even when rights exist on paper, enforcement of these standards is weak and as patriarchal norms are deeply embedded in society there is frequent exclusion of women from decision-making structures, within the household, community and/or institutional level.

In the mid-90s, after a decade of civil society and union struggles, two very progressive pieces of legislation came forth —The Building and Other Construction Workers (Regulation of Employment and Conditions of Service) Act, 1996 and the Building and Other Construction Workers Cess Act, 1996. The first protected the interest of workers by ensuring the formation of a tripartite Welfare Board which they later provided for levy and collection of cess on the cost of construction incurred by an employer and the funds collected were mandated to be used for the benefit of workers. Interestingly, although the Act came into being in the year 1996, it took several years for states to formulate rules and initiate its implementation on the ground. The role of this Board was to protect interests of the workers and to monitor that various social security provisions for the workers including entitlements such as maternity benefit, pension, education loan, marriage allowance, death benefit etc were being provided.

The concept of welfare boards has been articulated in many of the laws and in India, the approach presently is to cover a wide gamut of unorganized workers under its net. Welfare Boards and Funds have been set up by special Acts of Parliament. For example, *beedi* workers are covered by the Beedi Workers Welfare Fund Act of 1976, Mine workers by the Iron Ore, Manganese Ore and Chrome Mines Labour Welfare Fund Act, 1976; and building workers by the Building and Other Construction Workers (Regulation of Employment and Conditions of Service) Act of 1996 and Building and Other Construction workers welfare Cess Act 1996. The Building and Other Construction Workers (Regulation of Employment and Conditions of Service) Act, 1996, is applicable to the establishments engaging ten or more building and other constructions workers. It seeks to regulate the employment and conditions of work for building and other construction workers and provides for their safety, health and other welfare measures. There exist broadly two types of welfare funds—contributory and tax-based. The Government of India has set up tax-based welfare funds for mine workers, beedi rollers, cine workers, and workers in the building industry; these funds are financed by cess levied on the production or export of specified goods. They are to provide mainly medical care, assistance for the education of children, housing and water supply, and recreational facilities.

In the country, welfare boards have been set up in the various states for the unorganized workers in different sectors.

In Kerala, there are nearly 20 welfare funds constituted by Government for different target groups such as agricultural workers, head-load workers, construction workers, coir workers, cashew workers, motor transport workers, auto rickshaw workers, toddy workers, and artisans. Toddy Tappers Welfare Fund, Provident Fund, and Old-Age Pension Schemes for Agricultural Workers, Motor Workers Welfare Fund, and Head Load Workers Welfare Fund, Anganwadi Workers and Helpers Welfare Fund, are some of the schemes being implemented. The Government of Assam has set up a statutory fund under Assam Plantation Employees Welfare Fund Act, 1959 for financing welfare measures of the plantation workers. Maharashtra Domestic Workers Welfare Board Act, 2008 has been enacted wherein there is a provision of a fund for providing various benefits to the registered domestic workers. There are 34 Mathadi[29] Boards in the state. Various other schemes framed for various workers in the sectors such as Grocery, Metal, Paper, Iron and Steel, Cotton, Cloth, Vegetables, Transport and Railway, and Clearing and Forwarding. There are welfare schemes for the Building and Other Construction Workers too. Around 14 welfare fund boards are constituted in Tamil Nadu till now. In 1994, the Government of Tamil Nadu constituted a Welfare Fund Board under Section 6 of the Tamil Nadu Manual Workers (Regulation of Employment and Conditions of Work) Act, 1982 (Tamil Nadu Act 33 of 1982), for the benefit of workers' in the construction sector namely 'The Tamil Nadu Construction Workers Welfare Board'. The Government of Tamil Nadu is implementing Tamil Nadu Social Security and Welfare Scheme, 2001, which covers manual workers, auto rickshaw, taxi drivers, washermen, hairdressers, tailoring workers, handicraft workers, palm tree workers, etc.

In the state of Odisha, the Building and Other Construction Workers' Welfare Board is one of the largest boards in terms of enrolment of workers. The Board was constituted in 2004 and re-constituted in 2008 under the Building and Other Construction Workers (Regulation of Employment &

Conditions of Service) Act, 1996. Cess is collected @ 1% from all construction works going on in the State and deposited in the said Fund. This fund is utilized in extending different welfare measures to the registered beneficiaries both men and women engaged in building and other construction work. The benefits given to the registered workers can be divided into the following categories: meant only for women workers (e.g. maternity assistance); meant for both men and women workers (e.g. bicycle, working tools, safety equipments); meant for the girl child of the men and women workers (e.g. educational assistance and marriage assistance) and meant for the children (girls and boys) of the workers (e.g. educational assistance). A cumulative total amount of Rs 1121 crores has been collected.[30] There are more than 14 lakh workers registered out of which women are approximately 28 per cent. The 6 labour districts which have the highest registered labourers are Jajpur (1,28,710), Khurdha (1,16,042), Cuttack (1,12,234), Keonjhar (98,202), Chhatrapur (85,573) and Ganjam (70,006). The highest number of women construction workers is in the Chhatrapur labour district followed by Ganjam and Rourkela. (Table 2)

Table 2: Registered District wise male and female construction workers in Odisha (2017)

	LABOUR DISTRICT	*Male*	*Female*	*TOTAL*	*% of female to total*
1	Angul	10533	2767	13,308	20.79
2	Balasore	34824	8496	43,323	19.61
3	Banai (DLO Rourkela)	0	0	0	-
4	Baragarh	32936	9816	44,086	22.27
5	Bhadrak	39726	7417	47,200	15.71
6	Bolangir	12306	1829	14,136	12.94
7	Boudh	16545	6464	23,023	28.08
8	Chhatrapur	40065	45492	85,573	53.16
9	Cuttack	96220	15966	112,234	14.23

10	Deogarh	12903	7902	20,805	37.98
11	Dhenkanal	45295	8259	53,558	15.42
12	Gajapati	9888	4282	14,357	29.83
13	Ganjam (Berhampur)	38199	31760	70,006	45.37
14	Jagatsinghpur	23203	3316	26,520	12.50
15	Jajpur	98446	30252	128,710	23.50
16	Jharsuguda	16779	5995	22,907	26.17
17	Kalahandi (Bhawanipatana)	34470	8385	42,856	19.57
18	Kandhamal	7626	4986	19,505	25.56
19	Kendrapara	34408	12444	46,955	26.50
20	Keonjhar	59228	38961	98,202	39.67
21	Khordha	78925	37110	116,042	31.98
22	Koraput (Jeypore)	27541	7175	34,730	20.66
23	Malkangiri	6674	3720	10,396	35.78
24	Mayurbhanj (Baripada)	37503	25003	62,511	40.00
25	Nabarangpur	3958	3149	10,509	29.96
26	Nayagarh	39286	5389	44,678	12.06
27	Nuapada	10510	3218	13,729	23.44
28	Puri	39877	6233	46,112	13.52
29	Rayagada	15033	9272	24,842	37.32
30	Sambalpur	18939	12553	31,604	39.72
31	Subarnapur	25035	5949	30,986	19.20
32	Sundergarh (Rourkela)	35900	25404	62,834	40.43
33	Talcher	7196	4597	11,794	38.98
	TOTAL	1,009,977	403,561	1,428,032	28.26

Source: Odisha Building and Other Construction Workers Board

Conditions of Work of the Unorganised Sector Women Workers

Globalization of economy and its new trends have created new opportunities for employment of women in India. In many regions women's participation in remunerative work in the formal and non-formal labour market has increased significantly. Globalization backed by rapid technological progress brings in its trail multi-skilling, alteration of the formal employer-employee relations by new relations which are characterized as contractualization, casualization and informalization. Low skill attainment among women and their consequence relegation to jobs which are labour intensive, time consuming and arduous in nature have been perpetuated by their unequal access to technology.[31] The transformation in production systems and growing competition had a major impact on employment, skill formation and on gender roles leading to the shrinkage of jobs in the organized sector resulting in more people entering the unorganized sector particularly, women who find easier to find jobs in the informal sector as it requires less skill.[32]

"Although the migrant workforce in construction is male-dominated, the share of migrants in overall female construction workforce is higher. NSS data shows that about 87% of the migrant women working in construction are not the head of their households, indicating that they have not moved alone and are not living on their own. Most migrant construction workers are working adults of both genders whose children move with them, in both rural and urban areas. Along with adults without children, they constitute nearly 70% of the migrant construction workforce in both rural and urban areas."[33]

Employment is obtained in the unorganized sector mainly through three modes, the importance of these three modes vary from activity to activity and industry to industry. First, is by 'standing at the factory gate', second is through a family, caste and community-based network and third is through labour contractors or 'Jamadars'. (NCRL,1991) In this context it has been observed in the National Perspective Plan for Women that the exploitation of workers might begin with the recruitment by the contractors who mobilize labour for construction work, particularly by age old method of recruiting by 'credit tying' and loan bondage method that are in routine used to mobilize migrant labour from the seasonal harvesting operation in high growth areas. These workers including female folks work as migrant labour moving from one place to the other depending on the discretion of the contractors by whom they have been recruited on the basis of loan bondage. This process enables the contractors to keep their margins of profit high as mentioned in the Core Group on National Perspective Plan for women 1988.[34]

The National Commission for Rural Labour in its Report mentioned that a major drawback of the contract labour system is that neither the contractor nor the principal employer takes responsibility for the working conditions and the workers' welfare (NCRL, 1991; Suryanarayanan, 2004). A part of workers' wages is paid as informal commissions to the middlemen (Srivastava, 2005). It is a feature of the unorganized sector that work goes on for 7 days a week.

The Maternity Benefits Act, 1961 provides for a minimum maternity leave of six weeks to a pregnant woman immediately following her delivery or miscarriage. The provision of paid maternity leave seems to be very rare in the unorganized sector, though the Labour Bureau surveys and some other researchers have found limited instances of women being given maternity leave without pay. In such instances, the women workers were assured of a job when they returned from maternity leave.

In the brick-kiln industry, workers work for the full season of about 6 months. Only the male workers are registered as workers in the muster roll of the employer and the rest of the family remains invisible to statistics, policy and social protection provisions. Working hours for all workers are about 12-14 hours, including for the women who are not on the muster rolls (Gupta, 2003).

Gender discrimination is well entrenched and women workers are paid much less than the men for similar work. Studies have observed that the benefits of most of the provisions of laws relating to wages and provident fund do not reach the construction workers and contract labour. While it is true that workers, irrespective of sex, are exploited in the unorganized sector, women suffer more by the fact of being a woman. Critical questions have been raised concerning their well-being in the construction industry, brick-kiln industry and domestic work (Sansristi, 2007)[35]. Women work in industries like tanning, tobacco, cashew, coir, textiles, garment, fish processing and canning, construction and domestic work, etc. In all these industries, they toil long hours as low paid, skilled or unskilled workers. As a result, they face serious health problems related to workplace hazards of pollutants on reproductive health including pregnancy.

Workers in the construction industry are worst affected by the exploitation meted out to them in the unorganized sector, particularly the women. Despite all this,the construction industry mainly attracts women workers. Women workers' skills are almost at the same level as that of male workers but they are not considered equal as such and asked to help their male co-workers. At present, the number of women in the construction industry has increased very rapidly. But, equal pay for equal work policy is not yet practised. Dr. B.D. Karhad in his study of 'Women Construction Workers in Pune City' published in 2014, states that though the women construction workers are relatively better off in Pune city, they get fewer wages than male workers in the industry. Surveys in the construction industry have found that crèche facilities are not available on worksites for young mothers with infants. (Labour Bureau 1979; Vaid 1997; Suryanarayanan 2004). An all-India study and many state-level studies have noted the lack of welfare measures such as crèches for children, rest-rooms for workers, separate toilets for women and potable drinking water. If housing is provided it is generally unfit for human living. Further, it was observed that there were no complaints from the labour administrators (Suryanarayanan 2004). One of the consequences of not having adequate crèche facility was that the children were often engaged in helping the mothers in their work. These women are mostly migrant workers who migrate from rural to urban areas to work in the construction industry or as domestic workers in individual households. Some women migrate from rural areas to work in the brick-kiln industry along with their children.

Vaid in a study conducted in 1997 had noted that an estimated 10.7 million construction workers, accounting for 83 per cent of all construction workers in India in that year, were employed through contractors and did not receive minimum employment protection and benefits whatsoever (Vaid, 1997). In the activities where contract labour is predominant, the contract system forces migrant workers to be available 'on call' through jamadar, mistri, muqaddam, dalal or another regional expression through a system of advances and loans (Suryanarayanan 2004, Srivastava 2005; Ghosh 2004, Sansristi, 2007).

Kalpana Devi and U.V. Kiran (2013) in their research paper titled 'Status of Female Workers in Construction Industry in India' observed that women work as unskilled labour and face several other difficulties in comparison to males. Sexual harassment, gender biases, wage discrimination are the major problems due to which the working environment becomes difficult for them in the industry. Even after years of work in the industry, women work as unskilled labourers. Dileep Kumar M. (2012) in his study titled 'Inimitable Issues of Construction Workers: Case Study' has exposed the deplorable condition of workers in the construction industry. Construction workers have reported a day off from work per week without wages. (Suryanarayanan 2004, Labour Bureau 1979, Labour Bureau 1995).

The percentage of workers with no job contract and ineligible for paid leave is increasing since the past decade simultaneously increasing the number of workers with no social security benefits. There is a sharp increase in the numbers of workers with 'flexible employment'. It also indicates that these workers with 'flexible employment' are highly vulnerable regarding job and social security. (Mishra, 2017)

However, women are mostly unskilled labourers. They are confined to menial roles of cleaning building sites, carrying gravel, mortar and water and accordingly, lowly compensated. They face serious problems related to their work, i.e. wage discrimination, gender and sexual harassment, unhealthy job relationship and low wages exposure to harsh environmental conditions like sun, rain which result in accidents and adverse health conditions (Thayyil Jayakrishnan et al, 2013). Women migrant construction workers are unskilled and illiterate which makes them vulnerable to exploitation (Keertigha and Selvam, 2017). These women experience severe back injury by carrying heavy loads on their head. (Banu and Kumar, 2018)

A closer look at the beneficiaries, and one realizes that women in construction work are most deprived when it comes to accessing entitlements. Ironically, the promulgation of legislation and welfare schemes which was seen to be more in the interest of women construction workers failed to reach out to them. A female worker needs to be a registered member of a construction workers' union to avail the benefits collected under the Building and Other Construction Welfare Trust. A recent data released by the Delhi Board (as on December 31, 2017) states that only Rs 1,414 crore has so far been spent on the welfare of workers.[36] And out of 5,18,184 registered workers, only 2,16,210 workers (41%) have received some kind of benefit (Scenario in Delhi)[37]. Clearly, these figures explain that while the State didn't fail its citizens in providing legislative protection, it is those manning the posts of implementation who have failed to do their due. And that is why we will continue to see images of children of construction workers tied to poles and not inside schools or crèches, and women in construction work will continue to have unsafe deliveries by the roadside.[38]

Women in the unorganized sector require social security addressing issues of leave, wages, working conditions, pension, housing, child care, health and maternity benefits, safety and occupational health. This can only be ensured by extending labour protection to those sectors in a manner that pays special attention to needs of women workers.[39]

Women Construction Workers: Odisha Scenario[40]

The focus group discussions done[41] with the women working in the construction sites across the state revealed the prevailing situation. The methodology of capturing the lived experiences of women construction workers was adopted to get a deep insights into their life.

The women work as unskilled labour in the construction sector such as the brick kilns, stone crusher units, road construction, building construction etc. The working conditions imply the duration of working hours, nature of work, terms and conditions of payment and overtime payment etc. The building and other construction workers survive in poor working conditions. All the workers particularly the women, work in conditions which violate of the norms which are laid down by law. The registered workers under the Board are to be provided with standard hours of work, welfare measures and other conditions of service such as crèches, urinals, drinking water etc. In none of the interactions across the 6 districts, did the workers mention being provided these facilities. Women who work on the construction sites have no toilet or drinking water facilities and are vulnerable to sexual exploitation. There are no sanitation facilities and crèches at the workplace. For the women workers, such services are a part and parcel of safe and dignified working environment.

Generally, the women are employed on a casual basis. Unstable employment/earnings and shifting of workplaces are the characteristics of work for construction workers. In most cases, safety norms are violated. The spouses of the women are in most cases engaged as labourers as skilled or semi-skilled workers in the sites.

The major source of income of the workers is wages. The gender disparity in wage rates is very much a reality. Across all the districts under study, the wage rates is different for the women and men for the same work. The wage rates for men, as quoted, ranges from Rs 350 to Rs 550; while for the women it ranges from Rs 200 to Rs 300.

Women workers are often not given paid maternity leave.

However maternity financial benefit as a registered board worker is available @ Rs 10,000 per child, only if the registration is more than one year. Additionally, the cash benefits scheme of Government of Odisha, MAMATA has been available on the fulfilment of the conditionalities as stipulated.

The educational status of women workers is very low. The middle-aged women and those of higher age groups are generally illiterate. However, there are exceptions where some women have learnt to maintain accounts, do bank transactions and also do household budgeting. This has been possible due to the involvement of women in Self Help Groups, Labour Unions etc.

Sexual exploitation of construction women workers by masons, contractors, and others is routine but unreported by women, for fear of the consequences (loss of employment, more violence). It is reported that some of them leave the job due to the exploitative behaviour of the employers. The Sexual Harassment of Women at Workplace (prevention, prohibition and Redressal) Act 2013 has provisions to protect the women workers but the implementation of the law has not yet reached the women workers in unorganized sectors of the State.

The women workers registered under the Board do possess cards under the Mahatma Gandhi National Rural Employment Guarantee Scheme (MGNREGS). The availability of work (100 days per household) as stipulated is very scarce. None of the participants in any of the focus group discussions had got more than two months (60 days) work under the MGNREGS in their village.

Most of the women are migrants. Women and children mostly migrate as associated migrants when the main decision to migrate is taken by the males of the household. The movement of people within the State for livelihood is well captured in the study. All across the 6 districts where fieldwork was conducted, the inter-district migration is the pattern. The permanent type of migration is generally observed in Bhubaneswar and Cuttack and Chhatrapur areas. In some instances, families have migrated a generation earlier.

Seasonal migration is observed in destinations of Ganjam and Jajpur particularly in the brick kilns and stone crusher units. For the migrants, many of their entitlements are available in the original/ domicile village. Main reasons for migration include small land holding or landlessness; no regular work in the local area, low wages paid at local worksites; limited resources and therefore unable to acquire advanced skills for employment; the lure and attraction of cities for higher income. However, migration has led to livelihood security. The nature of labour migration is such that the source area is wanting in terms of employment and income. In destinations they have poor living and working conditions yet the women manage to save as there is some steady source of income.

The Construction Board is yet to make its implementing mechanism robust at the district and block level due to which the benefits elude the women workers. The issues related to the benefits from the Board are—accessibility, availability and timely disbursement. The benefits are well-meaning but in the context of non-existent implementation and monitoring structures and mechanisms, at the district and block level, even the registered women workers are denied their dues. The problems begin with delayed enrolment and at times non-enrolment too and thus applications for benefits such as educational assistance for children are available after a long wait. For women workers, distance from the trade union office/labour office and non-accessibility to correct information puts them in an exploitative situation. They easily fall prey to unscrupulous agents.

Pension schemes for widows, old, and unmarried women are protective programmes that are available, but obviously, the coverage is not universal. Many instances have been identified where unmarried women who should have availed the Madhubabu Pension have been left out. The socio-economic condition of the unorganized women workers, irrespective of the sector in which they work, should not be seen in isolation. They are a part of the larger system of marginalization where they have limited access to resources, entitlements and livelihoods. In such a scenario, the social security net is to ensure that the women do not fall down to a lower level but are rather propelled to the next higher level of social and economic upliftment through coverage in social security schemes.

A quantitative analysis done by the card information of 135 registered women workers of Bhubaneswar reveals that most of the women are in the age group of 30 years and above and 92.3% of them are married. The registered women workers belong to the district of Ganjam (54.1%). As the sample was drawn from Bhubaneswar, the next highest proportion of women workers were from the district of Khurdha (20.7%). 80% of the women workers belong to OBC followed by SC (13%).

Conclusion

Our study has observed that women workers in the unorganized sector experience multiple vulnerabilities. Low earnings, poor working conditions, and limited access to social security protection are some of the problems. Promotional measures by welfare boards, old age pension, and maternity benefit schemes have been created but the major challenge is that all women workers are yet to be covered.

The condition of women workers in the construction sector leaves much to be desired. Constituting mostly of migrants, the women are in the lowest levels of survival. The ever-expanding construction sector, increasing the employment opportunities has drawn the labour force from rural areas to urban sites, but the employment is informal in nature. The presence of women in the informal labour force in the construction sector has its inherent vulnerabilities, for e.g., childcare facilities are not available in any worksites, legal statutes with regard to redressal of sexual harassments at workplace is not implemented. The women workers are vulnerable to exploitation due to illiteracy and have no effective bargaining power. A safe working environment still eludes women.

But alongside there is in existence a broad framework of welfare policies within which the Government has attempted to improve the livelihoods of the unorganized workers. The Construction Workers Welfare Board is one such robust initiative. But issues and problems relating to registration, disbursement of benefits persist. In the absence of a comprehensive and holistic implementation mechanism which percolates till the grassroots, the policy initiatives towards the benefits for women workers remains a distant dream.

Some of the recommendations related to policy are honest implementation of legislative measures related to labour wages, protection of women and rights of women along with administrative and monitoring structures of welfare boards at state, district and block level. Gender-responsive budgeting and ensuring women's participation in decision-making bodies will go a long way in ensuring substantive social security for the women workers. Adequacy of wages without any gender disparity, livelihood and employment guarantee and women's wage compensation due to pregnancy including child care such as crèches/mini/mobile anganwadi centres at construction sites are some of the suggestions with regard to the work and worksites of the women construction workers. Creating awareness among women workers as well as the employers about the institutional support available to them to protect their rights and grievance redressal mechanisms at the grassroots level has to be mainstreamed. Skill building of the women construction workers, so that women get upward mobility opportunities, need to be undertaken in a holistic manner. Social security measures in terms of land, house building assistance, health insurance, pension, food, need to be percolated to the women beneficiary level. Overall there is work to be done at policy, administration, legal and schematic levels. While coming together of administrative departments is of utmost importance, it is equally pertinent that the main vision of the welfare boards ought to be to empower the women workers in the construction sector through appropriate social security measures.

NOTES

1. *Global Employment Trends 2013*, ILO, https://www.ilo.org/wcmsp5/groups/public/---dgreports/---dcomm/---publ/documents/publication/wcms_202326.pdf
2. *India Labour Market Update*, July 2016, https://www.ilo.org/wcmsp5/groups/public/---asia/---ro-bangkok/---sro-new_delhi/documents/publication/wcms_496510.pdf
3. Government of India, *Report of the Working Group on Empowerment of Women*, (2006), p. 35.
4. Government of India, *Report of the Working Group on Social Security for the Twelfth Five Year Plan, (2012-17)*, p.169.
5. https://www.ilo.org/wcmsp5/groups/public/---dgreports/---dcomm/---publ/documents/publication/wcms_615594.pdf
6. http://shodhganga.inflibnet.ac.in/bitstream/10603/3800/11/11_chapter%204.pdf
7. http://shodhganga.inflibnet.ac.in/bitstream/10603/111432/2/11_chapter3.pdf
8. *Report on Condition of Work and Livelihood Issues of Unorganized Workers*, (2007), National Commission for Enterprises in Unorganized Sector, Government of India.
9. *"Unorganized Labour", 2009, Report of 2008* published by Ministry of Labour, Government of India. https://labour.nic.in/
10. https://www.lmis.gov.in/sites/default/files/NSC-report-unorg-sector-statistics.pdf
11. *Odisha Economic Survey*, (2016-17), Department of Planning and Coordination, Government of Odisha, p. 54, Women constituted only 0.98 percent of total organized sector employment in Odisha
12. *Statistical Profile of Women Labour, 2011*, Labour Department, Government of India.
13. https://www.researchgate.net/publication/312626681_Climate_and_Construction_An_Impact_Assessment
14. Scheme of Ministry of Housing and Urban Affairs, Government of India
15. www.migrant_workers_in_India.pdf
16. Khanijow, Smita, 28 April 2018, Why Women Construction Workers Will Continue to Deliver by the Roadside, https://thewire.in/women/women-construction-workers
17. ILO, 2011, Social Security for Social Justice and a Fair Globalization, Occasional Paper for 100th Session of ILO, p. 92.

In this the authors have mentioned that investment in social security will result in a virtuous cycle of social development.

18. Ibid.
19. Ibid., p. 15. It states, the development and establishment of formal social security systems for the provision of income support and medical care constituted a major step in the development of human societies. The emergence of different forms of formal social protection mechanisms, ranging from voluntary group-based social protection mechanisms to mandatory contributory or non-contributory public social security schemes throughout the world, bears witness to the universal human need for social security and the importance of clear rights and entitlements.
20. Hobson, J.A., (1938), *Confessions of an Economic Heretic*, London. bargaining power was unequal between buyers and sellers, in a competitive market. Therefore, markets are intrinsically unfair modes of distribution'. Distribution by needs is not even approximately achieved by the ordinary haggling in a so-called competitive market. Everywhere, inequality of bargaining conditions, based on differences of needs, is represented in different amounts of gain. Therefore, Hobson advocated for redistributive taxation, welfare spending and nationalization of industry to deal with the problem. He articulated an organic view of states in which free and fully realized individuals are essential for a healthy social organism.
21. Hobhouse, L.T., (1911), *Liberalism*, Oxford University Press, New York. Hobhouse has argued that the basis of property is social. The true function of taxation is to secure in society the element in wealth that is of social origin. This is no case of robbing Peter to pay Paul.
22. Mill, J.S., (1902), *Principles of Political Economy*, Unwin Books, London. Mill argued that right to property is not absolute. The additional riches should properly be diverted to those who lack basic needs of life by establishing a welfare state.
23. Beveridge, Sir William, Social Insurance and Allied Services, presented to Parliament by Command of His Majesty, November 1942 (H.M. Stationery Office, United Kingdom, 1969. Report pronounced the objective of the State to tackle five great evils in society- want, disease, ignorance, squalor and idleness.
24. International Labour Organization, 1942, Approach as to Social Security, p. 82.
25. Dev, S. Mahendra, 2005, September 26, Social security for

unorganized workers, *The Hindu*, Online Edition

26. The promotional programmes could include the Integrated Child Development Scheme (ICDS), the Public Distribution System (PDS) under the NFSA, the Mid-Day Meal Scheme for children in primary schools, housing schemes such as the PM Awas Yojana and the Biju Pucca Ghara Yojana, Vasundhara (land), old age, widow and disability pension and so on. The Mahatma Gandhi National Rural Employment Guarantee programme is also a part of the larger landscape of the social security measures provided.
27. Mehta, Anupma, 2013, *Women's Social Security and Protection in India*, Report of National Conference held on 6-7th May, Programme on Women's Economic, Social and Cultural Rights (PWESCR), New Delhi.
28. ILO Policy Brief on Anti-Trafficking Laws, Policies and Practices (http://www.ilo.org/newdelhi/whatwedo/publications/WCMS_545580/lang--en/index.htm).
29. Mathadi means a person carrying a load of material either on his head (matha) or on his back to stack at the appropriate place. These operations include loading unloading stacking, carrying, weighing, measuring or such other works including preparatory work or incidental to such operations.
30. The data given as in March 2017.
31. Bagchi, Kanak Kanthi and Nirupam Gobi, 2012, Social Security for Unorganized Workers in India, Madhav Books, Gurgaon, p. 144.
32. Giri, Ramadhar, 2007, *Industrial Relations*, Adhyayan Publishers and Distributors, New Delhi, p. 76.
33. Roy, Shamindra Nath and Manish Mukta Naik, June 2017, *Migrants in Construction Work: Evaluating Their Welfare Framework*, Centre for Policy Research, p. 5, Retrieved from file:///C:/Users/SWARNA%20TRIPATHY/Documents/Evaluating%20the%20welfare%20framework%20for%20building%20and%20other%20construction%20workers%20in%20india%201109%20(1).pdf
34. Report of the Core Group on National Perspective Plan for Women, 1988.
35. http://ncw.nic.in/pdfReports/NCWMigrationReportOrissa.pdf
36. https://thewire.in/women/women-construction-workers,

Also see for reference National Commission for Women, *Report on the Status of Women Workers in the Construction Industry*, 2005, p. 1.

37. Ibid.
38. Ibid.
39. Government of India, *Report of the Working Group on Social Security for the Twelfth Five Year Plan, 2012-17*, p. 169.
40. The article is based on a study conducted by Odisha State Commission for Women and Sansristi.
41. The field work was done in January–May 2017 in six labour districts of Odisha such as Jajpur, Khurdha, Ganjam, Chhatrapur, Keonjhar, Cuttack and Ganjam.

REFERENCES

Banu, S. Rasheedha and S. Sampath Kumar. 2018. Working Conditions and Issues of Women Workers in an Unorganized Sector - Special Reference to Construction Sector of Thuraiyur Taluk, Tiruchirappalli. *International Journal of Trend in Scientific Research and Development*, Vol. 2, Issue 3, April 2018, pp. 1369-1374, (https://www.ijtsrd.com/papers/ijtsrd11320.pdf).

Census of India. 2011. *Population Enumeration*. Details (http//censusof india.gov.in) Delhi.

Dutta, Indira. 2009. Women in the Labour Market of Gujarat. 51st Annual Conference of *Indian Journal of Labour Economics* held in Karnataka.

Ghosh, R. 2004. "Brick Kiln Workers: A Study of Migration, Labour process and Employment", NLI Research Studies Series No. 57/2004, V.V. Giri National Labour Institute.

Government of Odisha. 2005. *Gender Profile.*

Government of Odisha. 2017. *Economic Survey 2016-17.*

Government of India. 2006. *Report of the Working Group on Empowerment of Women.*

Government of India. 2012. *Report of the Working Group on Social Security for the Twelfth Five Year Plan 2012-17.*

Government of India. 2008. *Social Security Initiatives in the Unorganized Sector.* Ministry of Labour and Employment, New Delhi.

Government of India. 2009. *Statistical Profile of Women Labour 2007-08*, Ministry of Labour & Employment.

Government of India. 2014. *Statistical Profile of Women Labour, 2012-13.*

Ministry of Labour & Employment.

Gupta, J. 2003. "Informal Labour in Brick Kilns: Need for Regulation", *Economic and Political Weekly*, August 2.

Hobhouse, L.T. 1911. *Liberalism*, Oxford University Press, New York.

Hobson, J.A. 1938. *Confessions of an Economic Heretic*, Routledge, London.

ILO. 2002. *Women and Men in the Informal Economy, A Statistical Picture.*

ILO. 2013. Global Employment Trends 2013, (https://www.ilo.org/wcmsp5/groups/public/---dgreports/---dcomm/---publ/documents/publication/wcms_202326.pdf)

ILO. 2016. Indian Labour Market Update, *Journal of Social Sciences*, 53:2, 73-80.

ILO. 2018. *World Employment Social Outlook Trends 2018.*

Khanna, P., K. Nagrath and A. Mangrulkar, 2011. *Climate and Construction—An Impact Assessment*. Project report to CDKN, 2011. Development Alternatives Group, New India Labour Market Update, July 2016, https://www.ilo.org/wcmsp5/groups/public/---asia/---ro-bangkok/---sro-new_delhi/documents/publication/wcms_496510.pdf

Kalpana Devi and U.V. Kiran. 2013. *Status of Female Workers in Construction Industry in India: A Review* (https://www.researchgate.net/publication/264534904_Status_of_female_workers_in_construction_industry_A_review)

Karhad, B.D. 2014. Study on Problems of Women Workers in the Construction Industry, *Journal of International Academic Research for Multidisciplinary*, Vol. 2, issue 4, May 2014.

Keerthiga, V. Dhivya and K. Arul Selvam. 2017. A Study on Health Problems Among Women Migrant Construction Workers. *International Journal for Innovative Research in Multidisciplinary Field*, 3(8), 163-167 (https://www.ijirmf.com/wp-content/uploads/2017/09/201708030.pdf)

Labour Bureau 1979, Report Survey of Working and Living Conditions of Workers in the Unorganized Sector of Industries-Building and Construction Industry in Delhi, Ministry of Labour, Government of India, Chandigarh/Shimla.

Labour Bureau 1992. Report on the Working and Living Conditions of Workers in Handloom Industry in India, Ministry of Labour, Government of India, Chandigarh/Shimla.

Labour Bureau 1995. Report on the Working and Living Conditions of Workers in the Unorganised Sector, Beedi Industry in India, Ministry of Labour, Government of India, Shimla/Chandigarh.

Mill, J.S. 1902. *Principles of Political Economy*, Unwin Books, London.

Mishra, Satyam. 2017. Social Security for Unorganized Workers in India, *Journal of Social Sciences*, 53: 2, 73-80, DOI: 10.1080/09718923.2017.1340114.

National Commission for Enterprises in the Unorganized Sector (NCEUS). 2007. *Report on Conditions of Work and Promotion of Livelihoods in the Unorganized Sector.*

National Commission for Enterprises in the Unorganized Sector (NCEUS). 2009. *Report on Challenges in employment in India–An Informal Economy Perspective.*

National Commission for Women. 2005. *Report on the Status of Women Workers in the Construction Industry.*

National Commission on Rural Labour (NCRL). 1991. Vol. 1, Part II, *Reports of the Study Group on Migrant Labour*, Government of India, Ministry of Labour, New Delhi.

National Commission on Self-employed Women and Women in the Informal Sector, (1988), *Shrama Shakti*, New Delhi.

NSSO 61st Round Employment and Unemployment Survey 2004-05.

NSSO 68th Round Employment and Unemployment Survey 2011-12.

Choudhury, Ruchika and Sher Verick, Female Labour Force Participation in India and Beyond, Asia Pacific Working Paper Series, ILO, October 2014.

Sansristi, 2007, *Impact of Increasing Migration on Women of Odisha*, National Commission for Women, http://ncw.nic.in/pdfReports/NCWMigrationReportOrissa.pdf

Sarde, Sudarshan Rao. *Migration in India—Trade Union Perspective in the Context of Neo-Liberal.*

Second National Commission on Labour (SNCL), (2002), *Report of the National Commission on Labour*, Volume I (Part-I), Ministry of Labour, Government of India.

Shrija, A. and S. Shirke, 2014, An Analysis of the Informal Labour Market in India, https://ideas.repec.org/p/ess/wpaper/id6353.html

Singh Mor, D.P, 2001. 'Women and Unorganized Sector', *Social Welfare*, Vol. 48, No. 9, Mumbai.

Srivastava, Ravi and Rajab Sutradhar, (nd), *Migrating Out of Poverty? A Study of Migrant Construction Sector Workers in India*, Institute for Human Development, New Delhi.

Statistical Profile of Women Labour, 2001 and *Statistical Profile of Women Labour, 2011*, Labour Department, Government of India.

Suryanarayanan, S.S. 2004. "Labour Laws, Contractual Parameters and Conditions of Construction Workers: A Study in Chennai", NLI Research Studies Series No. 50/2004, V.V. Giri National Labour Institute, Noida.

Thayyil, Jayakrishnan et al, (2013), Occupational Health Problems of Construction Workers in India, *International Journal of Medicine and Public Health*, 3(5), 225-229.

Vaid, 1997. "Contract Labour in the Construction Industry in India", NICMAR Publication Bureau, National Institute of Construction Management and Research.